Reopening Watergate

Reopening Watergate

AN INSIDER'S ACCOUNT OF
WHY NIXON LOST

David M. Dorsen

University Press of Kansas

© 2025 by the University Press of Kansas
All rights reserved

Published by the University Press of Kansas (Lawrence, Kansas 66045), which was organized by the Kansas Board of Regents and is operated and funded by Emporia State University, Fort Hays State University, Kansas State University, Pittsburg State University, the University of Kansas, and Wichita State University.

Library of Congress Cataloging-in-Publication Data

Names: Dorsen, David M., 1935- author
Title: Reopening Watergate: an insider's account of why Nixon lost / David M. Dorsen.
Description: Lawrence: University Press of Kansas, 2025. | Includes index.
Identifiers: LCCN 2025003779 (print) | LCCN 2025003780 (ebook)
  ISBN 9780700639977 cloth
  ISBN 9780700639984 ebook
Subjects: LCSH: Nixon, Richard M. (Richard Milhous), 1913–1994—Impeachment | Nixon, Richard M. (Richard Milhous), 1913–1994—Resignation from office | Watergate Affair, 1972–1974 | BISAC: POLITICAL SCIENCE / Corruption & Misconduct | BIOGRAPHY & AUTOBIOGRAPHY / Presidents & Heads of State
Classification: LCC E860 .D67 2025 (print) | LCC E860 (ebook) | DDC
  973.924092—dc23/eng/20250722
LC record available at https://lccn.loc.gov/2025003779.
LC ebook record available at https://lccn.loc.gov/2025003780.

British Library Cataloguing-in-Publication Data is available.

Printed in the United States of America

10 9 8 7 6 5 4 3 2 1

The paper used in this publication is acid free and meets the minimum requirements of the American National Standard for Permanence of Paper for Printed Library Materials Z39.48-1992.

For Kenna

CONTENTS

Foreword by John W. Dean, ix

List of Abbreviations, xv

Introduction, 1

Part I: 1972—The First Year of Watergate

1 Before the Scandal, 9
2 Burglars Arrested, Cover-up Starts, 14
3 The "Smoking Gun" Conversations, 27
4 Simmering Below the Surface, 44

Part II: 1973—From Back Burner to Headlines

5 Watergate Burglars Convicted, Judge Sirica Stirs the Pot, 51
6 Senate Watergate Committee Hearings, 61
7 The Watergate Special Prosecutor and the Fight for Nixon's Tapes, 74

Part III: 1974—Days of Reckoning

8 The House Impeachment Committee Gears Up, 83
9 Cover-up Indictment and Transmission of a "Road Map," 98
10 Impeachment Proceedings Begin, 113
11 The Supreme Court Rules and Nixon Resigns, 128
12 A Missed Opportunity: Representing Nixon, 143
13 The Cover-up Trial, 156

Part IV: The Aftermath

14 Thoughts on Prosecuting Nixon, 171
15 Fifty Years of Misunderstanding, 180

Conclusion, 187

Acknowledgments, 195

Appendix A. List of Participants, 197

Appendix B. Reconstructed Transcript of Dean-Haldeman Conversation, June 23, 1972, 201

Appendix C. Haldeman's Notes of Conversation with Dean, 204

Appendix D. Transcript of Three Nixon-Haldeman Conversations, June 23, 1972, 205

Appendix E. Jaworski's Letter to Sirica, December 27, 1973, 211

Appendix F. Jaworski's Memorandum to Confidential Watergate File Regarding Meeting with Sirica, February 12, 1974, 213

Appendix G. Jaworski's Memorandum to Confidential Watergate File Regarding Events on or about March 1, 1974, 215

Appendix H. Jaworski's Letter to Rodino, June 28, 1974, 219

Notes, 221

Index, 259

FOREWORD

John W. Dean

I write this foreword because no living person knows more about this history than I do, which is not a boast but a statement of fact. I have both lived and studied this history. More importantly, I am responsible for David Dorsen undertaking this project.

At thirty-one years of age I became counsel to the president of the United States, Richard M. Nixon, in July 1970—about two years before the Watergate scandal started. In taking the White House job, I understood that my predecessor was moving up to become an assistant to the president with oversight of all domestic policy matters, and I knew he would remain Nixon's principal legal adviser. I was given the title, but I was hired to do the grunt work, not to advise the president. Still, who could turn down such a prestigious title just six years out of law school?

As a middle-level White House staffer, I saw what became the Watergate scandal coming and then experienced the whirlwind of it all: the good, the bad, and the ugly. I have written three books about the scandal, the most recent being *The Nixon Defense: What He Knew and When He Knew It* (2014). For this work, it took me five years to catalog and transcribe a thousand secretly recorded conversations on the subject. (I had thirty-seven conversations with Nixon, and I suspected that he was recording me, to which I later testified under oath. I have no doubt of Nixon's complicity, for when I tried to warn him to end the cover-up, he rejected my advice.)

David Dorsen's *Reopening Watergate: An Insider's Account of Why Nixon Lost* is not a rehashing of the scandal and its aftermath. This work began as a response to my provocations to reexamine this history because I knew it needed to be fixed. David was the deputy chief counsel to the Senate Watergate Committee and, decades later, my personal attorney in a civil lawsuit involving bogus Watergate revisionism, so I trusted his scholarship and intellectual honesty. I am also familiar with David's skill as a dogged researcher and careful writer, as evidenced by his remarkable judicial biographies: *Henry Friendly, Greatest Judge of His Era* (2012) and *The Unexpected Scalia: A Conservative Justice's Liberal Opinions* (2017). It was while David was finishing up his work on Judge Friendly and starting his biography of Justice Scalia that I told him about a memorandum I had written for which I had been gathering information over several decades. He was intrigued, so I sent him a copy.

I compiled the memorandum not as a Nixon defender or apologist but because I had been surprised when the U.S. Supreme Court forced Nixon to surrender sixty-four secretly recorded conversations. I had been amazed that no one in Nixon's circle ever tried to contact me to get my take on the events of June 23, 1972, about which I had testified before the Senate Watergate Committee. Needless to say, when the tape of Nixon's actions surfaced in the fall of 1974, it triggered more memories, and those memories were confirmed by H. R. Haldeman's contemporaneously prepared notes, which he buried in Nixon's records to prevent prosecutors from gaining access to them but later surfaced in *The Haldeman Diaries* (1994).

Notwithstanding the fact that I was cooperating with the Watergate Special Prosecution Force's investigation of Watergate, I remained friendly with several former White House colleagues, including Leonard Garment, a former Nixon law partner who became a temporary White House counsel with an undefined role in Nixon's defense. Garment and I were friends for decades after Watergate, until his passing. When press accounts of White House reactions to the tape appeared, I was astonished because it was clear that none of Nixon's team understood what had in fact transpired. Fred Buzhardt was the White House counsel in charge of Nixon's defense; he was operating out of my old office with my longtime secretary while coordinating with Nixon's outside criminal and impeachment defense attorney James St. Clair. When the "smoking gun" conversations were made public in early August 1974, neither made any effort to contact me or my attorney. Nor did they bother to check Haldeman's notes, to which they had access. Garment once explained this silence as "client fatigue." Nixon was telling them nothing, which left them scrambling whenever new information surfaced.

It was not until my October 1974 testimony in *United States v. Mitchell, Haldeman, Ehrlichman, et al.* that my knowledge of these events surfaced. In fact, because my testimony hurt the government's case, the prosecutors asked me for few details, other than broadly framing Haldeman's conversation with Nixon on June 23, 1972, as being related to donors who had been promised anonymity if they made their campaign contributions before the April 7, 1972, cutoff date when the law changed and all donors had to be identified (explained in chapters 1 to 3). What I knew was that Haldeman and Nixon were acting to protect anonymous donors to Nixon's reelection campaign when the FBI investigation discovered that certain donation checks had passed through the bank account of one of the burglars arrested at the Watergate office complex on June 17, 1972. These donors had nothing whatsoever to do with the bungled burglary of the Democratic National Committee (DNC) offices. Rather, these donations had everything to do with a major media brouhaha calling for Nixon to name his anonymous donors; they were not part of any investigation.

Suffice it to say, Haldeman recalled precisely what had occurred by the time he testified in his own defense during *United States v. Mitchell et al.* He had listened attentively as his lawyer cross-examined me, which surely refreshed his recollection. Because federal trials are not televised, and because only a few news organizations purchase the trial transcripts, Haldeman's accurate explanation of what occurred on June 23 went unnoticed. Nixon had already resigned, so no one cared, and historians have spent decades ignoring the actual events. With the thought of someday correcting the record, decades ago I began gathering mental notes and then collecting documents at the National Archives as they became available. Finally, in late 2010 and early 2011, I was conducting some serious research and assembling the information into a memorandum for my files. That is the memorandum I later sent to David, suggesting that it could be the basis of a book (I briefly discuss this incorrect history in *The Nixon Defense*, but not in the detail provided in this work).

Under the subject line "Nixon's Bad Rap on the 'Smoking Gun' Conversations," I wrote a thirty-five page, sixteen thousand–word document and gathered countless pages of exhibits explaining how history got the June 23, 1972, conversation wrong, notwithstanding the fact that it led to Nixon's resignation. My memo begins:

President Richard Nixon was forced to resign his presidency on August 9, 1974, after the U.S. Supreme Court ordered him to turn over some sixty-four secretly recorded conversations to the Watergate Special Prosecutor, and the conversations that had taken place on June 23, 1972, revealed the president approving a plan for his chief of staff H. R. "Bob" Haldeman to have the CIA tell the FBI to halt what appeared to be their Watergate investigation. At the time, these secretly recorded conversations were labeled "smoking gun" evidence because they purportedly were an indisputable confirmation that the president had engaged in obstruction of justice. That conclusion, however, was wrong.

The memo explains that, at the time of the tape's release, Nixon's supporters, not to mention his detractors, completely misunderstood the subject of the conversations between Nixon and his chief of staff six days after the Watergate burglars' arrests. For example, Charles Wiggins, leader of the conservative Republicans on the House Judiciary Committee opposed to Nixon's impeachment and de facto leader of the president's defenders in the House, was asked to visit the White House days before the conversation was made public to gauge his reaction. Wiggins, an able attorney later appointed to the U.S. Court of Appeals for the Ninth Circuit, misread the transcripts, believing they revealed the start of a conspiracy to obstruct the Watergate investigation. Accordingly, he advised the White House that he would have to vote for impeachment, which he did, along with all the other Republicans on the Judiciary Committee—resulting in a unanimous article of impeachment for Nixon's obstruction of justice. A similar reading in the Senate convinced Nixon that he would be removed from office.

Next, my memo distills the uncontested facts that were totally ignored at the time the information was first revealed in late July 1974. Clearly, Nixon had forgotten the actual context of the conversation six days after the arrests at DNC headquarters, and I found no evidence that he or his staff reached out to Haldeman or anyone else. The memo then reviews the law at the time to show that Nixon did not obstruct justice, and it notes that if Nixon had been charged in 1974, as some suggested, other presidents were probably guilty of criminal behavior as well. (Not until 2024, in *Trump v. United States*, did the U.S. Supreme Court grant a president immunity from federal criminal laws for the president's official actions. Nixon's actions on June 23, 1972—having the CIA approach the FBI regarding its investigation—appear to be official actions under the high court's ruling.)

David Dorsen's book goes well beyond my memorandum in correcting the historical record. My memo merely provoked his research into matters that needed to be reexamined. Indeed, he has gathered important new information regarding many events about which I had no knowledge. This is not a work of historical revisionism, however, for the core story of Watergate remains very much intact. Rather, this book is an example of what I would call significant historical tuckpointing. Tuckpointing, for those unfamiliar with the term, is a masonry procedure employed by bricklayers to repair or enhance the strength and integrity (if not the appearance) of a brick structure. The process involves examining the brickwork, identifying the need for repair, removing old or damaged bricks and mortar, and inserting new bricks and mortar (usually using a tuckpoint bag filled with cement—an industrial-strength version of the bag used to squeeze icing on a cake). When done well, tuckpointing results in greater structural integrity, and the whole work is better for the undertaking. Metaphorically speaking, this is what David Dorsen has done with the historical record of Watergate: he has strengthened the record assembled over the past half century. Although this account does not alter the basic history, it certainly adds to our understanding.

ABBREVIATIONS

CRP	Committee to Re-elect the President (Nixon)
DNC	Democratic National Committee
DOJ	Department of Justice
EOB	Executive Office Building
FCRP	Finance Committee to Re-elect the President (Nixon)
HRC-W&B	Notes of Bob Woodward and Carl Bernstein, Harry Ransom Center, University of Texas at Austin
LOC	Library of Congress
NARA	National Archives and Records Administration, College Park, MD
SSC Hearings	Senate Select Committee Hearings on Presidential Campaign Activities
WSPF	Watergate Special Prosecution Force

Introduction

Two years, one month, and twenty-two days after the initial arrests of the five burglars at the headquarters of the Democratic National Committee (DNC) in the Watergate Office Building on the early morning of Saturday, June 17, 1972, Richard M. Nixon became the first and only American president to resign. On August 9, 1974, Nixon left the White House and retreated to his estate in San Clemente, California, and Vice President Gerald R. Ford Jr. ascended to the presidency.

Accounts of these and related events have been the subject of hundreds of books and thousands of magazine articles and newspaper stories. The conventional wisdom has identified the precipitating event as the public disclosure on August 5, 1974, of transcripts of tape recordings of three conversations between President Nixon and Chief of Staff H. R. (Bob) Haldeman on June 23, 1972. That is largely correct.

The tapes purportedly revealed that Nixon directed Haldeman to have the CIA stop the FBI investigation of the Watergate break-in to prevent disclosure of the perpetrators' role in Nixon's reelection campaign. That has been the conventional interpretation of events for the past fifty years. However, that is incorrect, and that is what this book is about. The events that led up to Nixon's resignation are far more complex (and interesting) than was previously thought. It is time to set the record straight. The story of what led to Nixon's resignation on August 9, 1974, has never been properly told.

This book sheds new light on one of the most important events in American history. Although it does not contend that Nixon was innocent of wrongdoing—he was unquestionably guilty—it proposes a more nuanced and more accurate interpretation of key events, including release of the June 23, 1972, recordings, which arguably makes these "smoking gun" tapes far less damaging than they were initially perceived to be—an analysis first presented by John Dean.

This new account is largely the result of information that was unavailable or, in some cases, did not exist when older versions of the Watergate saga were written. Much of what transpired has been buried in archives, repositories, or little-read accounts, including interviews conducted by the Nixon Presidential Library in Yorba Linda, California; records of Leon Jaworski's Watergate Special Prosecution Force at the National Archives in College Park, Maryland; and the interview notes of Bob Woodward and Carl Bernstein, housed in the Harry Ransom Collection of the University of Texas at Austin. In fact, new material continues to be released. Although some of this material has appeared in print, most of these records remain unmined. Some of this information has been reported in books by Geoff Shepard and on his website; Shepard was an aide to J. Fred Buzhardt, one of Nixon's principal lawyers in late 1973 and 1974. What has been published has received little notice, however, and perceptions are essentially the same as they were half a century ago. Despite the death of most of the major players, there is sufficient evidence to reconstruct Nixon's downfall with reasonable accuracy.

Many of the recent disclosures can be traced back to the three most prominent institutions and individuals involved in Watergate in 1974: the U.S. District Court for the District of Columbia, represented by Chief Judge John J. Sirica; Special Watergate Prosecutor Leon Jaworski and his deputy Henry S. Ruth Jr.; and House Judiciary Committee Chairman Peter W. Rodino Jr. and his chief impeachment counsel John Doar. These bodies and individuals behaved unethically if not unlawfully, contributing substantially to President Nixon's resignation and to the conviction on January 1, 1975, of his top aides—former Attorney General John N. Mitchell, former Chief of Staff H. R. Haldeman, and former chief domestic adviser John Ehrlichman—for conspiracy, obstruction of justice, and perjury.[1] This book shows that even after the devastating Saturday Night Massacre and the disclosure of the June 23, 1972, conversations between Nixon and Haldeman, Nixon could have survived the scandal and completed his term as president.

There is another little-known dimension to the events of 1974. After the departure of Haldeman, Ehrlichman, and counsel John Dean from the White House in April 1973, Nixon received terrible legal support and advice from those who had not been involved in the Watergate cover-up. Ten months after the illegal break-in occurred and the pervasive cover-up began, Nixon's top aides who were familiar with the events departed. A new team took over, consisting primarily of Chief of Staff Alexander M. Haig Jr. and attorneys James D. St. Clair and J. Fred Buzhardt.

Criticism of Nixon's aides must be qualified by the fact that the president was a client from hell (by 1974 standards). He insisted on making erroneous decisions—both legal and political decisions—related to Watergate, such as concealing from his lawyers and senior staff the content of his conversations with Chief of Staff Haldeman on June 23, 1972. This has persistently and wrongly been interpreted as an effort by Nixon and Haldeman to stop the FBI's investigation into the Watergate break-in. That Nixon had obstructed justice made the task of his representatives more difficult but not impossible.

In general, Watergate-related events of 1972 and 1973 have been presented accurately (other than the events of June 23, 1972), including the Watergate break-in; the cover-up by Haldeman, Ehrlichman, Dean, and others and the payment of "hush money" to those indicted; the trial of the seven burglars (including G. Gordon Liddy and E. Howard Hunt) in January 1973; the hearings of the Senate Watergate Committee that spring and summer; the discovery of the White House taping system and the eighteen-and-a-half-minute gap in a conversation Nixon had on June 20, 1972; the Saturday Night Massacre in October; and the appointment of Leon Jaworski to replace Archibald Cox as special Watergate prosecutor. Despite all these events, however, a highly competent team might have preserved the Nixon presidency in 1974, however undeserved.

After the smoke of Watergate cleared, the reaction of many was that "the system worked." But this attitude disregards the failings on the part of those involved in pursuing wrongful conduct (along with some serendipitous events, such as Dean's decision in April 1973 to abandon the conspiracy). The salutary resignation of President Nixon was achieved by shortcuts and unethical and perhaps even unlawful actions by those empowered to protect the country, although it cannot be claimed that these same people did not perform a valuable service. People may not feel the same way about the conclusion of Watergate after reading this book.

Finally, it must be emphasized that this book is about "Watergate"—the two burglaries of DNC headquarters in the Watergate Office Building in Washington, DC, in the late spring of 1972 and the cover-up or cover-ups that followed. Thus, many of the other deficiencies and dubious if not criminal activity of the Nixon administration are not discussed. Nor is the work, most of it unheralded, of the Senate Watergate Committee examined in detail. One area that received considerable attention during the committee's public hearings in mid-1973 was the "Enemies List," a compendium of names of people the administration considered hostile.

Two other areas of the investigation are mentioned briefly. First, there were no public hearings on the Milk Fund—the payment by milk producers of hundreds of thousands of dollars to the Nixon reelection campaign in exchange for maintaining high milk prices. Instead, relevant material was quietly turned over to the House of Representatives Impeachment Committee and the Watergate Special Prosecution Force. It resulted in one proposed article of impeachment that the Impeachment Committee did not adopt and several criminal prosecutions. Most of these prosecutions were successful, but former Texas Governor John Connally was acquitted of bribery.

Second, there was the Nixon administration's Responsiveness Program, pursuant to which the administration pressed most agencies and departments to mobilize their power in favor of administration supporters. Committee staff searched the National Archives, where the Nixon administration had deposited hundreds of incriminating documents. Public hearings were held in late 1973 and early 1974, but they received little attention from the press or the public, despite their importance. Other congressional committees used this material and conducted their own investigations, as a result of which the Civil Service Commission was abolished and was essentially replaced by the Federal Office of Personnel Management. There were other important consequences as well, although none of them received much publicity.

Also missing from this book are the many major accomplishments of the Nixon administration both domestically and internationally, such as creating the Environmental Protection Agency, recognizing the rights of the disabled, and establishing diplomatic relations with China. As noted, this is a book about Watergate.

Finally, the book does not take into account recent changes in the law, particularly those effected by the Supreme Court's decision in *Trump v. U.S.*[2] That decision substantially narrowed a president's vulnerability to criminal charges, making evidence that would have been crucial to a prosecution of Richard Nixon unavailable and altering any future analysis of a president's conduct. Obviously, it would not retroactively affect Nixon's exposure to criminal charges.

PART I
1972—The First Year of Watergate

Before the Scandal

Shortly after John W. Dean became White House counsel in July 1970, others in the White House started to send him inquiries about demonstrations, leaks, and intelligence. Some inquiries came by way of memoranda from the president's chief of staff, H. R. (Bob) Haldeman, or his chief domestic adviser, John Ehrlichman. Dean once received a telephone call from the president himself about a demonstration in front of the Capitol. Most inquiries, however, came from a lower level. For example, Lawrence Higby, Haldeman's top aide, sent Dean requests for intelligence reports. Dean learned that it was paramount to prevent the president's exposure to any demonstrations; in particular, the possibility of the Democrats organizing a demonstration agitated the president and had to be dealt with quickly.[1]

Dean learned there was a similar concern in the White House about leaks to the media, so covert wiretaps of members of the White House national security team and reporters had to be arranged to discover their contacts and sources. Sometimes the concern seemed to reach crazy heights. Charles W. Colson, a lawyer and senior aide to Nixon, was actually taking steps to firebomb the Brookings Institution, a liberal Washington, DC, think tank, because he thought it had a copy of the Pentagon Papers, the top-secret study of the country's role in Vietnam between 1945 and 1967 that had been leaked to the press. Dean flew overnight from Washington to California to convince Ehrlichman to veto that plan, which he succeeded in doing.[2] Dean had discovered that sometimes it was best to ignore the ideas of Nixon and others and hope they would just go away, but Colson's plan was different.³ Dean was learning.

The "Do-It-Yourself" White House

When the Nixon administration took over in 1969, like previous administrations, it relied on established government agencies, most notably the FBI, to conduct domestic investigations. The Pentagon Papers, published in the *New York Times* on June 13, 1971, changed that. When the leaker was identified as former Defense Department analyst Daniel Ellsberg, Nixon expected the FBI to vigorously investigate him and his associates. But Nixon came to believe that FBI Director J. Edgar Hoover was not pursuing the investigation diligently because of his friendship with Ellsberg's father-in-law.

As a result, the insecure and do-it-yourself White House created its own investigative force, which it kept secret from most White House insiders as well as from the public. David R. Young and Egil (Bud) Krogh Jr. were given the assignment and an office in the basement of the Old Executive Office Building.[4] Their main operatives were former FBI agent G. Gordon Liddy, who was a lawyer with an intelligence background, and former CIA operative E. Howard Hunt, who had ties to Latin America. Because the unit was created primarily to stem leaks, it became known as the Plumbers. Although it did other work for the White House, its principal operation in 1971 was to find dirt on Ellsberg.

The White House Plumbers were separate from the operation of the reelection campaign and the so-called dirty tricks performed by Donald Segretti and others. Perhaps the most notorious of these dirty tricks was a forged letter that purported to come from Democratic presidential candidate and senator from Maine Edmund Muskie that used the derogatory term "Canucks" to refer to French Canadians. This letter was instrumental in causing the collapse of Muskie's competitive presidential campaign.

Tasked to find documents that discredited Daniel Ellsberg, the Plumbers devised a plan to burglarize the office of Ellsberg's psychiatrist, Dr. Lewis J. Fielding, in California. Three Cuban nationalists, acting under Hunt and Liddy, conducted the break-in in September 1971.[5] The hope of a surreptitious operation was dashed when the Cubans found the outside doors and file cabinets locked and had to forcibly break in. Finding nothing of interest, they trashed the office to make it look like the work of a drug addict. Although a police report was filed, the involvement of the White House was unknown until April 1973.

The debacle was promptly reported to Ehrlichman, who had authorized the operation.[6] However, it appears that he said little or nothing about it to Nixon or Haldeman at the time, probably because of his embarrassment over what had transpired.[7] As a result, Nixon and Haldeman, who knew about the creation of the Plumbers and some of Hunt's activities, were apparently ignorant in 1971 of the essential facts related to the Fielding burglary. No one else in the White House was aware of the caper.

Liddy Gets His Mandate

Political intelligence was another passion in the White House. Starting in late 1971 the White House worked to develop intelligence on Nixon's anticipated Democratic opponent in the 1972 race for the presidency. John Dean was asked to give up his deputy, Fred Fielding, so that he could become counsel to the Committee to Re-elect the President (CRP) and do intelligence work.[8] Dean balked and suggested another White House aide, David Young, for the job. Ehrlichman and Krogh, however, picked G. Gordon Liddy.[9] Soon, the White House pressed Liddy for information on the Democrats.

Liddy proceeded to draw up an elaborate plan that involved a series of remarkable operations, which he code-named Gemstone. These operations included renting a houseboat during the Democratic National Convention, populating it with prostitutes, and luring vulnerable Democratic convention delegates on board, where an electronic listening system would record their conversations with the prostitutes. Another operation required the use of an airplane to intercept aircraft belonging to the Democrats. Also, the team intended to bug the offices of Democrats to obtain information. Liddy gave each operation the code name of a jewel, such as Ruby, Diamond, and Emerald. He claimed there were so many that he had to name one Coal.

Liddy presented his plan to Attorney General John N. Mitchell on January 27, 1972, in his office at the Department of Justice. Also attending the meeting were Dean and Jeb Stuart Magruder, a former Haldeman aide who was temporarily heading Nixon's reelection campaign. (Mitchell would take charge of the campaign shortly.) Dean's presence was an afterthought.

Because Magruder did not get along with Liddy (Liddy once threatened to kill Magruder) and he did not know Mitchell, Magruder asked Dean to attend.[10] Liddy's plan, which would cost $1 million (equivalent to nearly $10 million today), shocked Mitchell and Dean, who stared at each other in disbelief. At the end of Liddy's presentation, the mild-mannered Mitchell told him the plan was not what he had in mind and instructed Liddy to come back with something more modest and suitable.

Liddy returned on February 4 with a scaled-down version that cost $500,000 and no longer employed airplanes. Dean arrived late to the meeting but immediately saw that the new plan was just as outrageous as the first. Interrupting Liddy, he announced that no one should discuss such activities in the office of the attorney general of the United States. The meeting disbanded.

Dean briefed Haldeman on what had occurred.[11] Both thought Gemstone was dead, but without their knowledge, Liddy submitted a similar but smaller plan to Magruder, with a budget of $250,000. When Liddy heard nothing, he complained to Colson through Hunt. Colson called Magruder and told him that the Plumbers were unhappy and wanted a decision on whether the plan would proceed. On March 30, 1972, in Key Biscayne, Florida, Magruder presented the revised intelligence plan to Mitchell, along with other items that required his approval. Also present was Mitchell's close aide, Frederick C. LaRue. Mitchell approved the plan, and news of his approval was forwarded to Liddy.[12] No one notified Dean or Haldeman, and they had essentially nothing to do with Gemstone until five people were arrested on June 17 in the Watergate Office Building.

Last Chance for Anonymous Contributors

One other relevant development preceded the arrests at the Watergate. On February 7, 1972, Congress passed a law that, as of April 7, 1972, abolished a person's right to make anonymous contributions to federal political campaigns and required candidates for federal office to identify their contributors. It also placed a ceiling on a contribution to any one entity.

The White House's goal was to collect as much money as possible during the two-month period between the law's passage and its effective date. Campaign finance chairman (and former secretary of commerce) Maurice H. Stans, campaign treasurer and former White House aide Hugh W. Sloan Jr., and regional finance chairmen spread out across the country to collect substantial sums. People were flying all over the nation to collect money and deliver it to the Finance Committee to Re-elect the President before the April 7 deadline. Nixon, Haldeman, Ehrlichman, and Dean, among others, were aware of and involved in this effort to various degrees. The endeavor was frantic and chaotic but extraordinarily profitable. The campaign supposedly ignored contributions of less than $50,000—too many contributors and not enough time.

Knowing that his fund-raising prowess did not equal that of his Democratic opponents or President Nixon, South Dakota senator and aspirant for the Democratic nomination George McGovern announced that he would voluntarily comply with the new law's disclosure provisions for contributions made before April 7 and would identify all his contributors. McGovern's announcement made other candidates seeking the presidency appear to be abusing a loophole in the law.

The *New York Times* lauded McGovern and called on all other candidates to follow suit. Georgia Governor George Wallace, former Vice President Hubert Humphrey, and Maine Senator Edmund Muskie released the names of their early donors. Public-interest groups such as Common Cause were openly critical of the Nixon campaign's refusal to report its pre–April 7 contributors. The controversy escalated on June 11 when the *Washington Post* reported that the Nixon campaign had collected some $10 million—an enormous sum in 1972—in anonymous contributions before the April 7 cutoff date.

John Mitchell, head of the Nixon reelection effort, had claimed that "releasing the names of all contributors would be unfair to those who had contributed money with the idea that they would remain anonymous." When asked about this statement, Lawrence F. O'Brien, chairman of the Democratic National Committee, said this was not a legitimate reason and, in fact, the Nixon campaign had "a moral obligation to release them." Discussions over whether to disclose the names of the anonymous contributors went to the highest levels. Nixon himself pondered options, including returning contributions from those who wanted their identities protected. The names were finally released many months after the statute went into effect.

The events of June 17, 1972, put all these matters in a new light.

2

Burglars Arrested, Cover-up Starts

In the early-morning hours of Saturday, June 17, 1972, four plainclothes Washington Metropolitan police officers arrested five middle-aged men dressed in business suits and in possession of latex gloves, cameras, and bugging equipment at Democratic National Committee (DNC) headquarters in the Watergate Office Building on Virginia Avenue, which is separate from but adjacent to the better-known Watergate Hotel.[1] The arrests attracted limited media attention. At the arraignment that same afternoon, one of the men, James W. McCord Jr., uncomfortably acknowledged that he had worked for the CIA, and it was quickly revealed that McCord was in charge of security for the Committee to Re-elect the President (CRP). The other four men arrested were Cuban Americans with a history of anti-Castro activity and with connections to conservative organizations.

Watergate Makes the News

Within a few days, the *Washington Post* disclosed that address books belonging to two of the burglars had been found in their rooms at the Watergate Hotel. They contained the name Howard Hunt with the notation "W.H." or "W. House" and a telephone number that accessed the White House. In the days after the arrests, the *Post* learned from a White House operator that Hunt worked for Charles Colson. In the hotel rooms, the police also found a check from Hunt made out to his country club. The *Post* revealed that "cash, totaling $2300 in $100 bills, was seized during the arrests [at the DNC], and police reported finding another $3,556 in the suspects' hotel rooms." The second cache of money included four packages of $100 bills "that were in the same serial sequence, which experts said it would be easy to trace."[2] The *Post* seemed to be doing most of the investigating, but reporters at a few other media outlets, including the *Los Angeles Times*, *Time* magazine, and WNBC, followed the same path.[3] On October 4, 1972, the *Los Angeles Times* ran an exclusive interview of Alfred Baldwin, a former FBI agent and the lookout at the Howard Johnson Motel across the street from the Watergate Office Building.[4]

On June 20, 1972, DNC Chairman Lawrence O'Brien directly linked the Watergate break-in at party headquarters to the White House and Nixon's reelection effort. The same day the DNC filed a lawsuit against the CRP, seeking $1 million in damages.[5]

On June 22, 1972, the front page of Washington's *Star*, the city's most prominent newspaper at the time, reported that "$90,000 drawn from a Mexico bank was deposited in the Miami account of Bernard Barker, one of the four Cuban nationalists arrested on June 17." This raised the question of who orchestrated the burglary. Was it the work of anti-Castro Cubans trying to find out whether George McGovern and the Democrats were planning to reestablish relations with the Castro government, or was it the handiwork of the White House or other Republicans?

The CIA, which had a limited mandate that prohibited U.S. operations, was notoriously secretive. In the first few days after the arrests, FBI agents investigating the Watergate break-in thought that, in view of the burglars' numerous contacts with the agency, the break-in was a CIA operation. These facts, which were slowing becoming public knowledge, included McCord's and Hunt's longtime employment by the CIA and connections between the arrested Cubans and efforts to liberate Cuba from Fidel Castro. One of the Cubans was still on the CIA's payroll. Of course, at first, no one outside the CIA knew whether an FBI investigation might uncover the CIA's involvement.[6]

"What the FBI Almost Found"

The FBI touted the scope and intensity of its investigation. However, deficiencies were rampant from the start, although they were not the subject of much discussion either at the time or in the years that followed. In particular, the FBI was delinquent in promptly following up leads on James McCord, E. Howard Hunt, G. Gordon Liddy, and Alfred Baldwin. Baldwin, who transcribed the telephone calls intercepted from the DNC offices, turned the essentially worthless transcripts over to Haldeman aide Gordon Strachan to give to his boss. Baldwin could have immediately identified Hunt and Liddy as being involved in the break-in, but the FBI did not speak to him until after he approached the U.S. attorney's office and secured immunity from prosecution.

While there might be some plausible excuse for not immediately interviewing or getting search warrants with respect to Hunt and Liddy (although evidence of Hunt's participation was immediately available to law enforcement), the failure to follow up on the arrested McCord was indefensible. The FBI obtained a search warrant and searched McCord's hotel room at the Watergate Hotel, which was highly productive, but agents did not search his home in Rockville, Maryland, or his vehicle, which was parked at his home from June 17 on. In a book he wrote, then Acting FBI Director L. Patrick Gray III acknowledged, "We always knew that McCord had some of the keys," and he described early discussions about contacting McCord. Despite its transparent flaws, Gray praised the FBI's investigation.[7]

After his arrest, McCord was able to telephone his wife, who disposed of some incriminating material. The FBI did not visit McCord's office in downtown Washington until Monday, June 19. A few days later, after he posted bail and was freed from jail, he disposed of other evidence at his home and in his vehicle. McCord's book details what the FBI would have found in his vehicle had they searched it on the day of his arrest: "In my vehicle returned by Alfred Baldwin to my home, on June 17, 1972, they would have found tape recorders, 2 electric typewriters belonging to White House consultant E. Howard Hunt, and other electronic equipment removed from the Howard Johnson Motel by Alfred Baldwin, all rapidly traceable to their original source of purchase." Similarly, if the FBI had searched McCord's home:

In my residence, they would have found additional electronic equipment related to the overall Watergate operation: $18,000 in $100 bills left over from the operation, subsequently used for lawyers fees; some carbon copies of recent wiretap logs, which I later destroyed; a copy of a letter signed by John Mitchell authorizing me to go to the Internal Security Division of the Department of Justice and obtain information regarding violence allegedly planned for the Republican National Convention, and some penciled notes from January and February 1972 mentioning not only John Mitchell's name but the names of John Dean and Jeb Magruder as meeting with Mitchell during those early 1972 months to discuss the Watergate break-in.

McCord destroyed everything except for the typewriters, which he returned to Hunt. He continued: "Thus, the search that senior FBI personnel sought of my residence would have led immediately to John Mitchell, Jeb Magruder, John Dean, my equipment suppliers, the Internal Security Division of the Department of Justice, and to the White House consultant E. Howard Hunt."[8]

If that material had come to light, it could have radically changed the course of events. McCord also claimed he would have told the whole story if he had been approached at the time by an FBI agent he trusted. His primary loyalty was to the CIA, not Nixon.[9] In varying degrees, similar conclusions can be reached about Hunt, Liddy, and Baldwin, all of whom avoided early searches and destroyed incriminating evidence.

At first glance, the FBI's fumbles aided the burglars, the immediate cover-up, the White House, and the president but magnified some of their later problems. The FBI's missteps occurred in the first few days after the arrests, before Nixon became directly involved. Arguably, delays in discovering and processing incriminating evidence against Hunt, Liddy, Magruder, and Mitchell allowed the cover-up to continue until April 1973, with devastating results for Nixon and his top aides.

It is impossible to know what would have happened if the FBI had searched McCord's vehicle and home and had pursued other investigations promptly. But a good case can be made that the entire history of Watergate would have been different. Although some illegal actions occurred in the first day or two after the burglars' arrests, it is doubtful that President Nixon or his senior staff would have had a chance to engage in illegal or improper conduct. In other words, John Mitchell and Jeb Magruder probably would have become the subjects of a criminal investigation, but it is unlikely that Nixon, Haldeman, Ehrlichman, or Dean would have been implicated for their conduct immediately after the arrests. But that is not what happened.

The White House Gets Involved

While the press grappled to uncover the story behind the Watergate break-in, the White House was moving secretly on a faster track. One of the first discussions among Nixon's aides occurred at the Beverly Hills Hotel in Los Angeles on the morning of June 17, who were there for a campaign fundraiser after Liddy telephoned Magruder with the news that McCord had been arrested. Magruder immediately spoke to John Mitchell and his top aides Fred LaRue and Robert Mardian. According to Magruder's 1973 testimony and later book, the subject was how to get McCord "out of jail before they find out who he is. . . . Then maybe he could just disappear." Magruder continued: "Around 3:30 that afternoon I called my office [at the CRP in Washington] and talked to Bob Reisner and Bob Odle about removing the Gemstone file and other political files from my office."[10]

Upon learning of the arrests, junior White House staff and campaign officials, including Magruder, Strachan, and Liddy, immediately and spontaneously (as well as pursuant to directions from Mitchell and Haldeman) began the wholesale shredding and burning of documents that could tie the White House or the CRP to the Plumbers, the burglary at the Watergate Office Building, or other improper activities.[11] Liddy was a major participant in the destruction of evidence, including the shredding of left-over and incriminating $100 bills.[12] None of this was public knowledge until the spring of 1973.

On Saturday and Sunday, June 17 and 18, Haldeman and Ehrlichman were engaged in a frantic effort to find out what had happened, but there was considerable confusion and suspicion. Haldeman received a report from Magruder early on June 17. After speaking with Haldeman, Mitchell, and Mardian, Magruder flew back to Washington on Sunday, June 18. On Monday, Magruder learned from Liddy that all the records related to Gemstone had already been shredded. Strachan agreed to dispose of additional incriminating documents.[13] Events were proceeding rapidly, and the White House struggled to keep ahead of the police.

Apparently with Mitchell's blessing, Liddy sought out Attorney General Richard Kleindienst at the Burning Tree Country Club in the Washington suburbs and partially filled him in on recent events at around noon on June 17. (Kleindienst dismissed Liddy and refused to help get the burglars out of jail but did not report the approach.) Haldeman and then Ehrlichman were informed.

On Monday morning, June 19, Dean, who had returned from a speaking engagement in Manila the day before, was instructed by Ehrlichman to learn what had led to the break-in. Dean was familiar with the pre–April 7 fund-raising events, and he soon learned about the Plumbers. He spoke initially to Liddy, Strachan, and Hugh Sloan, treasurer of the Finance Committee to Re-elect the President (FCRP). All of them were candid, including Liddy, who revealed that the first break-in at the Watergate had taken place at the end of May, when bugging equipment was installed in DNC offices. When Dean and Liddy took a walk outside the White House gates, Dean learned the facts with respect to the Watergate burglary and the initial unsuccessful wiretap of a telephone there, three weeks earlier. Liddy also informed Dean of Dr. Lewis Fielding's office. Liddy was contrite and readily took the blame for the failure of the DNC operation and said if anyone wanted to shoot him on the street, he was ready. Dean replied they were not at that point yet, and they separated.

The Watergate burglary was a disaster. The four arrested Cuban Americans, who had worked for Hunt during the 1961 invasion of the Bay of Pigs (the CIA's unsuccessful attempt to liberate Cuba from Fidel Castro), found nothing of value in the DNC offices on June 17, their second intrusion. Liddy had organized the second break-in to fix a wiretap on a telephone that was not working and to photograph documents that could be useful to Nixon's re-election campaign. No effort was made to sanitize the burglars or their hotel rooms after either intrusion. Liddy made other serious mistakes.

Liddy also briefed Dean on the burglary at the office of Daniel Ellsberg's psychiatrist, revealing that two of the arrested Cubans had been involved in that break-in as well. Nixon and Haldeman spoke Monday evening, but there is no record of that conversation. By that time, Hunt, but not Liddy, had been implicated. Many in the press, as well as Gray at the FBI, still suspected that this was a Cuban operation and that the CIA was involved. Meanwhile, except for McCord, the arrested burglars remained in jail.

Liddy had made a commitment to the Cuban American burglars that they and their families would receive financial support if they were apprehended. Apparently, Liddy informed Dean of that commitment and Haldeman, Ehrlichman, and Mitchell agreed to honor it.

Dean quickly learned more about the money in the burglars' possession, receiving unwelcome news about certain financial transactions from Mitchell, Magruder, and Sloan. Mostly through Sloan, Dean learned that the FCRP had given a total of $199,000 in $100 bills to Liddy in the spring of 1972 to use in his intelligence activities. Mitchell and Maurice Stans had authorized those payments to Liddy, but Sloan could tell Dean little more. Meanwhile, the FBI was tracing the money through the FCRP and back to pre–April 7 donors to the Nixon campaign.

To deal with concerns about the scope of the investigation, Dean was dispatched on June 20 to meet with Attorney General Kleindienst, for whom Dean had worked before joining the White House staff. Kleindienst referred Dean to Henry E. Petersen, the assistant attorney general in charge of the Criminal Division and a respected career official in the Department of Justice (DOJ). Petersen told Dean that the DOJ would thoroughly investigate the burglary but would not engage in a fishing expedition to investigate the Nixon campaign.[15] In other words, in Petersen's opinion, the DOJ had no facts or allegations that warranted an investigation of campaign financing.

The White House learned that someone had laundered $25,000 through a Miami bank where burglar Bernard Barker had an account. That money was originally a campaign contribution from Dwayne Andreas, a Democrat and close friend of Senator Hubert Humphrey. Andreas had given money to Kenneth Dahlberg, a regional chairman of Nixon's FCRP. Dahlberg gave the check to Sloan. Because there was a question about whether it was pre- or post–April 7, Sloan then gave it to Liddy, who was general counsel to the FCRP. Liddy gave it to Barker to cash. After he cashed the check and received new $100 bills, Barker gave the cash to Liddy, who then gave the money back to Sloan (minus a commission).

Apparently, people involved in the Nixon campaign received Andreas's check before April 7, but the FCRP in Washington did not receive it until after that date. The use of intermediaries raised the question of when the contribution became effective. Because of the uncertainty over whether the money qualified as a pre–April 7 donation, it could not be treated as part of those funds. But because the donor expected anonymity, the contribution could not be treated as a post–April 7 donation, which would have required publishing the donor's name. So the money was placed in the FCRP's safe and commingled with a $350,000 slush fund that consisted mostly of money left over from Nixon's 1968 presidential campaign. Another $89,000 from Texas oilman Robert Allen and his friends had been laundered with the help of Mexico City lawyer Manuel Ogarrio through a bank there. That money was also converted by Liddy to $100 bills and delivered to Sloan, who added it to the cash in the safe.

Later, Sloan took money from the safe and gave it to Liddy for his operation. The burglars possessed some of the $100 bills laundered through Barker and Ogarrio when they were arrested. Significantly, not only the FBI but also members of the media were aware of most of these facts, and by June 22, the full picture of how the DNC burglaries were funded began to emerge.[16]

The FBI interviewed White House and campaign staff in the days following the arrests. Senior aide Charles Colson was interviewed on June 22, and speculation about him thundered at Ehrlichman's instruction. Dean sat in on Colson's interview as well as those involving other White House personnel, even though the FBI did not ordinarily allow lawyers to be present for such interviews. It turned out that although Colson had been involved in some other intelligence matters, including ITT, he was not involved in the Watergate break-in, and the FBI learned nothing of importance.

At the time of the break-in, Hunt was still on the White House payroll and had an office and a safe in the Old Executive Office Building. Dean promptly commandeered the contents of the safe, which included a variety of documents. There were classified State Department documents, papers relating to Daniel Ellsberg, some involving Hunt and his wife, and several unusual documents that were extremely sensitive and potentially explosive, including a fabricated cable that falsely implicated President John F. Kennedy in the assassination of South Vietnam's President Ngo Dinh Diem on November 2, 1963.

Dean met with Ehrlichman to discuss the sensitive documents. Ehrlichman suggested that Dean shred the documents and "deep-six" the briefcase that had contained the evidence, by which he meant toss it into the Potomac River while driving across a bridge. But neither Ehrlichman nor Dean wanted to be responsible for destroying documents, so they gave them to recently appointed Acting FBI Director L. Patrick Gray III, with instructions that they should never see the light of day. Gray, who had been appointed to the position following the death of J. Edgar Hoover on May 2, 1972, was conspicuously not part of the Hoover entourage. Haldeman and Dean were pleased that they could say they gave the documents to the FBI. The amiable Gray had taken one problem off their hands, at least temporarily.[17] Dean continued to keep Haldeman and Ehrlichman fully informed.

Nixon Is Briefed on Watergate

Unbeknownst to Dean and almost everybody in the White House and beyond, a dozen or so meetings and telephone conversations occurred between June 20 and June 22 that related to Watergate and involved Nixon and Haldeman, Ehrlichman, Colson, or Press Secretary Ronald L. Ziegler, usually one at a time. Their principal concern was keeping the Watergate scandal away from the White House (as opposed to Nixon's reelection campaign, which was headed by Mitchell). They speculated whether Liddy would accept full responsibility for the break-in, given the fact that he was "nuts."

These conversations, which took place in the Oval Office or in Nixon's office in the Old Executive Office Building, were secretly tape-recorded by the president. There was a voice-activated system that recorded the great majority of presidential conversations, the existence of which was not publicly disclosed until July 1973 at a Senate committee hearing. (The product of the elaborate recording system was released in dribs and drabs starting in the late fall of 1973 and continuing for a year, but some of the tapes were just recently transcribed.[18])

Nixon, who had been in Florida, knew virtually nothing about the break-in until Sunday, June 18. He was most concerned about the possibility that it was an operation by Charles Colson, and he apparently spoke to Colson by telephone twice that day. Colson denied any involvement. Nixon also spoke to Haldeman for eighteen minutes on Sunday in a recorded telephone conversation, after Haldeman had been briefed by Magruder and was told that Liddy and Hunt were involved. But the facts were difficult to come by. On Monday, June 20, Nixon flew back to Washington.

Many significant events occurred before Nixon became aware of the details of the Watergate fiasco and in the days before he and Haldeman had their historic conversations on Friday, June 23, 1972. Conventional wisdom, including beliefs held by prominent and knowledgeable people, concluded, wrongly, that Nixon originated the cover-up. For instance, in his memoir *Inner Circle*, Alexander M. Haig Jr., who became Nixon's chief of staff in May 1973, wrote about the tape of the June 23 Nixon-Haldeman conversation, which Nixon listened to for the first and only time in May 1974: "Nixon ... heard this tape ... and realized that it contained the key to proving his guilt as the author of the Watergate conspiracy."[19] Haig was not alone in asserting that

Nixon originated the cover-up, a false allegation that magnified Nixon's role in the public's mind.

For more than two years, no one outside a small group of Nixon's senior aides knew the contents of his discussions about Watergate. As discussed later, a tape of a June 20, 1972, conversation between Nixon and Haldeman was disclosed in the late fall of 1973, but it contained nothing about Watergate because eighteen-and-a-half minutes of that tape had been intentionally (and clumsily) erased. Tapes of the three conversations between Nixon and Haldeman on June 23, 1972, were disclosed on August 5, 1974.

About fifteen years ago, John Dean and other people he hired transcribed about one thousand tapes of conversations between Nixon and his senior aides, providing a clearer picture of what Nixon knew and did in the days immediately after the burglars' arrests. But Dean did not publish these transcripts, and some are revealed here for the first time. They show that shortly after June 17, Nixon was informed about some aspects of the Watergate break-in. What seems clear is that Haldeman, who was the most knowledgeable of Nixon's aides and the main person providing him with information, did not give him many details. In part, the reason is that Haldeman was receiving conflicting stories. Dean was in the early process of interviewing the participants; then, on the evening of June 19, he started to meet with Haldeman, Ehrlichman, and Mitchell. It took several days for the White House to understand what had happened. Everyone was being wary, and there was considerable suspicion.

There is no evidence that Nixon had advance knowledge of any *specific* operations, as opposed to knowing that the aides were doing something covert and possibly shady. On June 20 Haldeman told Nixon that there were "other things . . . fringe bits and pieces that you, that you don't want to know about." Haldeman's notes for this meeting with Nixon read: "Colson stay away from press, don't give P [the president] details."[20] No one mentioned Daniel Ellsberg or his psychiatrist, Dr. Lewis Fielding, in any of the recorded talks with the president in the days after the arrests. This is somewhat strange, especially considering the importance of the break-in at Fielding's office. Ehrlichman, who approved of that break-in, probably concealed major aspects of it from Nixon and Haldeman out of embarrassment. In any event, it is unlikely that the erased June 20 conversation was as incriminating or as detailed as the June 23 Nixon-Haldeman conversation, discussed shortly.

Nixon, who never testified in court or at a congressional hearing, wrote a letter to a federal judge on April 29, 1974, stating that no one informed him of the Fielding break-in until March 17, 1973.[21] Nixon's memoirs, published in 1978, said the same thing.[22] The accuracy of these statements cannot be either confirmed or refuted, as specific evidence is lacking. Nixon testified before a grand jury in 1975, but he was not questioned about the June 23 conversations with Haldeman or related events because those issues were no longer relevant to any proceeding (Nixon had been pardoned and most of the perpetrators had been convicted).

At a meeting on the afternoon of June 21, Nixon and Haldeman discussed Stans's concerns, which included the fact that many anonymous contributors to Nixon's campaign were Democrats who did not want their identities revealed. Haldeman reminded Nixon that Mitchell and Stans wanted to honor their promise of anonymity to those contributors, and Nixon agreed to help. Moreover, in the days after the arrests, the issue of pre–April 7 anonymous contributions was getting more attention on most media outlets than the break-in at the Watergate.[23]

Nixon Moves out Front on Watergate

On the morning of June 22 Haldeman brought Nixon up to date about the money seized from the Watergate burglars, including how difficult it would be for investigators to trace it back to the original donors, even though they had traced it to a Miami bank.[24] At that point, the White House believed the donors had used money orders drawn on a South American bank and had given the money directly to the burglars. Haldeman told Nixon the money could not be traced further back, and even if it could be, "it wouldn't be a very great problem, unless it can go two more steps."[25]

"Well, that's good," Nixon interrupted. "But if they get past it, then they might be able to get to the South American country and find out where the money order [sic] came from, and that isn't good. . . . But, but up to that point we're all right, and they can't even go to the next place. So we're okay on that." Thus, on June 22 Nixon and Haldeman were focused on the contributors to his campaign but did not appear worried.

In an effort to get ahead of the news reports of the Watergate break-in and to deal with the persistent stories about the anonymous contributors to his presidential campaign, Nixon scheduled a press conference for the afternoon of June 22. He held it in the Oval Office with a small group of reporters, rather than in the East Room with the full White House press corps. The first question was whether "any sort of investigation [had been] made to determine whether" stories about the break-in were true. Nixon disposed of the question briskly:

Mr. Ziegler [White House Press Secretary Ronald Ziegler] and also Mr. Mitchell, speaking for the campaign committee, have responded to questions on this in great detail. They have stated my position and have also stated the facts accurately. This kind of activity, as Mr. Ziegler has indicated, has no place whatever in our electoral process, or in our governmental process. And, as Mr. Ziegler has stated, the White House has had no involvement whatever in this particular incident. As far as the matter now is concerned, it is under investigation, as it should be, by the proper legal authorities, by the District of Columbia police, and by the FBI. I will not comment on those matters, particularly since possible criminal charges are involved.

The press asked no further questions about Watergate. Later, a reporter from *Time* magazine asked Nixon about disclosing the identities of anonymous donors to his reelection campaign. She noted, "Mr. Mitchell has declined to make public the source of about $10 million of contributions to your reelection fund. I know that this is in the letter of the law, but I wonder in the spirit of the law, of more openness, what you think about that and might you make them public?" The president replied:

Mr. Ziegler has, I think, responded to that, and Mr. Mitchell and Mr. Stans. I think it is Mr. Stans who has declined to do that. I support the position that Mr. Stans has taken. When we talk about the spirit of the law and the letter of the law, my evaluation is that it is the responsibility of all individuals, a high moral responsibility to obey the law and to obey it totally. Now, if the Congress wanted this law to apply to contributions before the date in April that it said the law should take effect, it could have made it apply. The Congress did not apply it before that date and under the circumstances Mr. Stans has said we will comply with the law as the Congress has written it, and I support his decision.

Enlisting the CIA and FBI

On the evening of June 22 Dean spoke to Mitchell by telephone. He told Mitchell that Gray thought the CIA was involved in the activities at the

Watergate, and Mitchell said he was not surprised. Mitchell had just been briefed about Hunt's and Liddy's activities at the White House, and he was aware that the CIA had assisted Hunt earlier, including in the burglary at Dr. Fielding's office. Mitchell suggested that Dean recommend that Haldeman call in General Vernon Walters, the newly appointed deputy director of the CIA and a longtime friend of the president (Walters, acting as an interpreter, had accompanied Nixon on several international trips when he was vice president), and have Walters tell Gray that the FBI should stay out of CIA activities in Mexico.

Nixon believed the CIA was too independent—for example, it had refused to provide him with its files on the Bay of Pigs invasion to CIA Director Richard Helms—and this rankled Nixon. This was an unusual event detailed in both Nixon's memoirs and a biography on CIA Director Richard Helms.[26] Nixon wanted to control the CIA, which was one reason he made an outsider, army General Walters, deputy director rather than promote someone internally, a move he made at the FBI as well.

3

The "Smoking Gun" Conversations

The events of June 23, 1972, played an outsized role in Watergate and in the fate of Richard Nixon. Most important were the three conversations between President Nixon and H. R. Haldeman, but there were two other important conversations that day—one between John Dean and Haldeman, and one that involved Haldeman and John Ehrlichman from the White House and CIA Director Richard Helms and his deputy Vernon Walters. All these conversations were kept under wraps for nearly a year. The content of the ones between Nixon and Haldeman took another year to become public.

John Dean Presents Mitchell's Plan

The first significant event of June 23 was Dean's telephone call to Haldeman, designed to catch him in his White House office before his usual morning meeting with President Nixon. This conversation was not recorded (only conversations that took place in Nixon's offices were recorded) and has received little attention. Indeed, it is rarely mentioned, even though it served as the backdrop to the three crucial conversations between Nixon and Haldeman later that day.

By far the most thorough account of the unrecorded Dean-Haldeman conversation is Dean's reconstruction of it, which is published here for the first time.[1] Previously, only Haldeman's cryptic notes of this conversation, which he brought to his meeting with Nixon, were available.[2] The conversation explains what prompted Dean to telephone Haldeman—namely, concerns over the disclosure of anonymous campaign contributors. This was the prelude to the historic conversations between Haldeman and Nixon in the Oval Office, the first of which followed immediately.

"Well, the FBI is following every lead," Dean began his call to Haldeman. "Liddy and Hunt left tracks everywhere they went, and most everything they did. As I told you they have traced the numbers on the new $100 bills they found on the burglars and in their hotel room, to banks in Philadelphia and Miami."

Haldeman was interested: "This sounds like they are investigating campaign law violations, which Gray was not going to pursue."

"Bob, the investigation is out of control. . . . All these people [pre–April 7 contributors to the Nixon campaign] were promised anonymity. Mitchell says the FBI is barking up the wrong tree. He's concerned they're looking for ways to embarrass the president, not to mention his supporters."

"So is the FBI investigating campaign activities?"

"That's not supposed to be the focus of their investigation," Dean explained. "But they are running out leads way beyond what is necessary and getting into political stuff. Petersen agreed that they would not go on a fishing expedition, and campaign law violations were not going to be pursued. . . . Gray has no control of the investigation, or the leaks that are coming out of it. . . . Mitchell thinks with the FBI going every which way, that this investigation is at the brink right now, and it can go one of two ways: Either it's going to open up everything, and that will be an even worse disaster, or it can be closed down, contained, and not get into unrelated matters like the source of the Mexican money." Dean added that no one was providing any guidance to the FBI on the scope of its inquiry.[3]

"It doesn't seem anyone knows how to do that," Haldeman said to Dean.

"Mitchell and I talked about that," Dean continued. "Another real possibility, given the people involved, is that it was a CIA operation. Frankly, I am not sure that any of those theories are totally wrong, or mutually exclusive. . . . Gray called Helms, who told him there was no CIA involvement, but Gray still thinks they've run into a CIA operation, and given the bad blood between the agencies, the CIA is not talking."

"The president just buzzed me," Haldeman said. "What's the bottom line?"

"Mitchell's most worried about the Mexican money. They don't know what it involves. He thinks you should call Walters . . . and tell him you don't know where this FBI investigation is going, but the White House needs some help, and the CIA may need some help as well. I agree that the investigation is out of control, and the Hoover legacies at the FBI have their own agenda."

Haldeman hung up and walked over to the Oval Office.

There can be no doubt that Dean's call to Haldeman was primarily about campaign financing and, in particular, about the pre–April 7 contributors' desire for anonymity. That was how Dean began and ended his remarks. Likewise, there is no doubt that Haldeman understood this. Dean certainly was not talking about stopping the entire investigation into the Watergate break-in. There was never any question of doing that, and the president had just publicly blessed that investigation.

Dean's statement that "the Hoover legacies at the FBI have their own agenda" referred to the fact that senior people at the FBI were unhappy with Nixon's appointment of outsider Gray as acting director rather than one of their own. Apparently, someone in the FBI was leaking information, spreading rumors, and otherwise engaging in an effort to harm Gray and possibly get Nixon to remove him.

Mark Felt, later labeled "Deep Throat" by the *Washington Post*, was Bob Woodward's secret source glorified in *All the President's Men*. Felt was leaking information to Woodward, to Pulitzer Prize winner and *New York Times* reporter John M. Crewdson, and perhaps to others, even though he solemnly denied doing so to Gray, among others.[4] Some accounts attribute to Felt the commendable motive of trying to curb the excesses of the Nixon administration, but he was largely motivated by his personal disappointment over not being chosen to succeed Hoover as director of the FBI. Felt was a protégé of Hoover's, whose penchant for dubious conduct was well known. One of the ways Felt pursued his goal (whether hoping for a future appointment or hoping to get revenge) was by undermining Acting FBI Director Gray, an outsider resented by the FBI hierarchy.[5]

The First "Smoking Gun" Conversation

Virtually nothing was known about the three conversations between Nixon and Haldeman until Nixon, facing enormous pressure, released transcripts to the public on August 5, 1974, just days before he resigned.

Haldeman began this conversation by saying: "Now, on the investigation, you know, the Democratic break-in thing, we're back . . . in the, the problem area because the FBI is not under control. Because Gray doesn't exactly know how to control them, and ... their investigation is now leading into some productive areas, because they've been able to trace the money, not through the money itself, but through the bank, you know, sources the banker himself. And, and it goes in some directions we don't want it to go."[6]

The Watergate break-in itself was not a "problem area"; rather, campaign financing was the problem area. The $100 bills into which the contributions had been converted had been traced to burglar Barker. Nixon and Haldeman were concerned about the FBI's attempts to trace the initial source of that money—namely, to contributors who did not want to be publicly identified. When Haldeman said they were "back in the problem area," he was speaking of something narrower than Watergate. Moreover, the pre–April 7 donations were front-page news from time to time.[7]

There is no doubt that Haldeman was not referring to Howard Hunt, the Plumbers, or the break-in at Dr. Fielding's office. This was not a subject that Haldeman and Nixon spoke about; for that matter, it was not something Nixon was familiar with. It was a closely guarded secret overseen by Ehrlichman. Haldeman, moreover, would not refer to the Fielding break-in as something that put them back in the "problem area" or something they did not want the FBI to pursue. The FBI was ignorant of the Fielding matter, and nothing about it had been made public.

Haldeman suggested having "Walters call Pat Gray and just say, 'Stay the hell out of this, this is, ah, business here we don't want you to go any further on it.' ... It's [the money is] directly traceable and there's some more through some Texas people in, that went to the Mexican bank which they can also trace to the Mexican bank, they'll get their names today." The White House was concerned about disclosure of the source of the money laundered through a Mexican bank and a Miami bank. Haldeman was addressing the subject Dean had raised.

Haldeman continued: "Mitchell came up yesterday, and John Dean analyzed carefully last night and concludes, concurs now with Mitchell's recommendation that the only way to solve this—." But then Haldeman interrupted himself and turned to media coverage. He tried to sell his position to his boss. "We're set up beautifully to do this," he said, "in that the only network that paid any attention to the Watergate story last night was NBC," which did "a massive story on the Cuban thing, and all that." Nixon agreed. The two did not seem concerned about the Watergate break-in.

Haldeman then pivoted back. "The way to handle this now is for us to have CIA Deputy Director Vernon Walters call Pat Gray and say, stay the hell out of our business here, we don't want you to go any further on it." He added that that would not be "an unusual development," to which the president replied, "Right." Then Haldeman concluded, "And that would take care of it."

"Our business here" could not refer to the entire Watergate scandal; no one had discussed stopping the investigation into the Watergate break-in. And it could not refer to the Fielding burglary because the FBI was unaware of it and thus had done nothing about it. That becomes even clearer with the next exchange.

"What about Pat Gray, you mean he doesn't want to?" asked Nixon.

"Pat does want to. He doesn't know how to, and he doesn't have any basis for doing it. Given this [a request by the CIA], he will then have a basis. He'll call Mark Felt in, and Felt wants to cooperate because he's ambitious, and say, 'we've got the signal from across the river to put the hold on this.' And that will fit rather well, because the FBI agents who are working the case, at this point, feel that it is the CIA."[8] Haldeman thought they could use the FBI's restriction to domestic matters and the CIA's to international ones to limit the investigation. The CIA had no basis for closing down the Watergate investigation, but it could warn the FBI off one of its foreign operations.

"But they've traced the money to whom?" Nixon asked, referring to the campaign contributions. By "traced the money," he meant finding the original source of the money donated to the Nixon campaign and given to Liddy. It was common knowledge that the Finance Committee to Re-elect the President had given the burglars the $100 bills seized from them after their arrest.

"Ken Dahlberg," Haldeman said, understanding Nixon's reference.

"Who the hell is Ken Dahlberg?"

Haldeman erroneously explained that Dahlberg had contributed $25,000 to Nixon's campaign in Minnesota (actually, Dwayne Andreas had given cash to Dahlberg), which had then been converted into cashier's checks and delivered to the FCRP and then to Barker, who converted them to cash. Nixon picked up what Haldeman was saying. Referring to Dahlberg, Nixon correctly said about the fund-raiser, "His base is Stans."

"Yes, it is," Haldeman agreed. "It's directly traceable and there's some more through the Texas people [Robert Allen and friends] that went to the Mexican bank which they [the FBI] can also trace to the Mexican bank, they'll get their names [Allen and friends] today."

"I'm just thinking," Nixon said, "if they [the donors] don't cooperate, what do they say? They were approached by the Cubans. That's what Dahlberg has to say, the Texans, too. Is that the idea?"

Nixon was testing how things could play out—which might include perjury by the campaign contributors (whom he thought were in direct contact with Barker or one of his colleagues), who needed protection. The discussion was about the path the money took.

Haldeman was more cautious. "Well, if they will. But then we're relying on more and more people all the time. That's the problem. And the FBI will stop if we could take this other step." Haldeman was again trying to sell his approach to Nixon, which would avoid involving the contributors.

"All right, fine. Right," Nixon agreed.

"And they seem to feel the thing to do is to get them [the FBI] to stop."

"Right, fine," Nixon repeated.

"They say the only way to do that is a White House instruction. And it's got to be Helms and, ah, what's his name Walters. . . . And the proposal would be that that Ehrlichman and I call them in—."

By including Helms and Ehrlichman, Haldeman attributed a grander plan to Mitchell and Dean than Dean had mentioned to him. Mitchell and Dean wanted to give Gray a push, something that would get him to confront his out-of-control agents and force them to comply with FBI practice and not embark on the fishing expedition into campaign financing that Petersen had excluded. Because Dean had discussed campaign financing with Gray and Petersen, Nixon's personal involvement was neither contemplated by Mitchell and Dean nor needed. Nor did they think Ehrlichman's involvement was necessary. Haldeman and Nixon were taking a simple comment by a presidential aide that Gray's FBI subordinates were exceeding their mandate and escalating it into a presidential directive that the recipients would likely interpret as unusual and significant. It was becoming, in Haldeman's words, an "unusual development."

Nixon was thinking of bigger issues than contributors to his reelection campaign. "Of course, you will uncover a lot of, see, you open that scab, there's a hell of a lot of things that we just feel it would be very detrimental to have this thing go any further. This involves these Cubans, Hunt, and a lot of hanky-panky that we have nothing to do with ourselves," Nixon added vaguely. Nixon was focusing on his leverage with the CIA, perhaps sensing that the CIA would be reluctant to get involved with the FBI, as the two agencies were not close. He seemed to be distracted from the issue of providing cover to the anonymous donors and more concerned with international intrigue. Nixon concluded from Haldeman's remarks that Hunt, a former CIA operative linked to the Watergate burglary, could be used to embarrass the CIA.

But Nixon pivoted again, this time to a new topic: "One thing I want to know, did Mitchell know about this thing to any much of a degree?"

"I think so."

"Shit."

"I don't . . . think he knew the details, but I think he knew," Haldeman said, evidently referring to the Watergate burglary and Liddy's briefing of Mitchell about Gemstone.

But Nixon was thinking about Mitchell's connection to campaign financing: "He didn't know how it was going to be handled, though, with Dahlberg and the Texans and so forth, did he? Well, who was the asshole that did this thing? Is it Liddy? Is that the fellow? He must be a little nuts." Nixon had suddenly switched back to the details of the break-in. And he knew about Liddy, as the newly transcribed early White House tapes show.

"He is," Haldeman said in response to Nixon's comment about Liddy's mental state.

"I mean he just isn't well screwed on, is he? Isn't that the problem?"

"No, but he was under pressure, apparently, to get more information, and as he got more pressure, he pushed the people harder to move harder on," Haldeman said, referring to Gemstone.

"Pressure from Mitchell?"

"Apparently." Haldeman incorrectly named Mitchell as the person pressing for a decision on Gemstone, rather than Colson.

"All right, fine, I understand it all. We won't second-guess Mitchell," Nixon said. Then he exclaimed, "Thank God it wasn't Colson."

Haldeman took Nixon's exclamation about Colson as a sign he wanted to know where Colson stood. "The FBI interviewed Colson yesterday. . . . An interrogation, which he did, and . . . the FBI guys working on the case had concluded that there were one of two possibilities, one, that this was a White House—they don't think that there is anything at the Election Committee—they think it was either a White House operation and they had some obscure reasons for it, non-political . . . or it was," and here Nixon completed the sentence, "a Cuban thing," to which Haldeman added, "and the CIA." Haldeman continued, "Yesterday, they concluded it was not the White House, but are now convinced it is a CIA thing, so the CIA turnoff would—."

"Well, [I'm] not sure of their analysis, I must say that," Nixon interrupted. "I'm not going to get that involved," he added. He seemed skeptical about the CIA's involvement but could not be certain. He also seemed unconcerned that the FBI was speaking to his senior aides.

"No, sir. We don't want you to."

"You call them in."

"Good," Haldeman replied.

"Good deal. Play it tough. That's the way they play it and that's the way we are going to play it." Nixon was escalating the meeting with the CIA.

"O.K. We'll do it," Haldeman agreed. It seemed as though everything had been resolved, but Nixon wanted to keep talking about the CIA.

"Yeah, when I saw that the [daily White House Presidential] News Summary item, I, of course, knew it was a bunch of crap, but I thought, ah, well it's good to have them off on this wild hare thing because when they start bugging us, which they have, we'll know our little boys will not know how to handle it. I hope they will though. You never know. Maybe, you think about it. Good!"[9] Nixon seemed to be saying that tracking down suspicions about the CIA's involvement in the Watergate break-in was a wild goose chase. The reference to "our little boys" is unclear.

"When you get in these people, when you get these people [the leaders of the CIA] in," Nixon continued, "say, 'Look the problem is that this will open the whole, the whole Bay of Pigs thing, and the President just feels that,' I mean, without going into the details, don't, don't lie to them to the extent to say there is no involvement, but just say 'this is sort of a comedy of errors, bizarre,' without getting into it, 'the President believes that it is going to open the whole Bay of Pigs thing again.' And, ah, because these people are playing for, for keeps, and that they should call the FBI in and say, 'we wish for the country, don't go any further into this case.' Period. And that destroys the case."

Haldeman indicated that he agreed, and Nixon added, "That's the way to put it, do it straight now."

Nixon's reference to "this case" and "the case" must mean the laundering of campaign contributions, which was the primary focus of both the

Haldeman-Dean conversation and the Nixon-Haldeman conversations. It is unclear what "no involvement" Nixon was referring to.

The president injected both the CIA-led Bay of Pigs invasion and himself ("just say ... the President believes") into the conversation. The Bay of Pigs debacle may have been attractive to Nixon because it reflected badly on both John F. Kennedy, his opponent in the 1960 election, and the CIA, which he had difficulty bending to his will. Unquestionably, the CIA was uncomfortable talking about the disastrous Bay of Pigs invasion—an incident that gave the CIA a black eye.[10]

It is unlikely that Nixon had anything specific in mind when be brought the Bay of Pigs into the conversation, but he wanted the CIA to know that he would use whatever ammunition he had; he wanted to put the CIA on the defensive. He wrote in his memoirs, "I saw that Howard Hunt would give us a chance to turn Helms's extreme sensitivity about the Bay of Pigs to good advantage."[11] Nixon had managed to convert the Bay of Pigs invasion from a piece of background information that explained the Cubans' involvement in the Watergate break-in into an integral but unclear part of Haldeman's presentation to the CIA.

Nixon's reference to the Bay of Pig was confusing to Haldeman, who acknowledged in a later interview that he had no idea what Nixon was talking about when he referred to the Bay of Pigs. Nevertheless, he followed the president's order, as was his custom. On April 17, 1988, he said in a private interview:

Haldeman: See I met with Walters [on June 23, 1972] at the President's instruction. In that instruction, the President gave specific things I was supposed to raise with—it was Helms and Walters—about the CIA and the Bay of Pigs. . . . I remember thinking (. . . because it was so strange) that this was kind of bizarre. But he told me to do it and I was used to dealing with things that I didn't know what I was doing. . . .
Interviewer: You didn't understand?
Haldeman: About the Bay of Pigs?
Interviewer: Right.
Haldeman: Which I still don't understand.[12]

More than a half century later, the relation of the Bay of Pigs to Watergate is obscure, which adds confusion to understanding Nixon's intent and the meaning of the conversation.

Enlisting the CIA

Haldeman left the Oval Office but returned before meeting with Helms and Walters. Contrary to Nixon's memoirs (and the assertions of several authors), the president did not buzz Haldeman and ask him to come back to the Oval Office.[13] Haldeman, not Nixon, was the moving force on this matter. Haldeman wanted to make sure Nixon was on board and perhaps clarify his orders.

Haldeman's second conversation with Nixon started a few minutes after 1:00 p.m., when the president finished editing a public statement he planned to make on an unrelated matter. Nixon spoke first:

I'd say the primary reason you've got to cut it the hell off. I just don't think, ah, it would be very bad to have this fellow Hunt, ah, you know, he, he knows too damn much. And he was involved, we happen to know that. And if it gets out, the whole, this is all involved in the Cuban thing, it's a, it's a fiasco, and it's going to make the FBI, the CIA look bad, it's going to make Hunt look bad, and it's likely to blow the whole, ah, Bay of Pigs thing, which we think would be very unfortunate for the CIA, and for the country at this time, and for American foreign policy. And he's just got to [tell him], lay off.

Nixon was not being constructive—or coherent. He was babbling and not making sense; perhaps he was trying to show that he was in control of things. He had already suggested that he did not believe the CIA was involved, and Hunt had nothing to do with campaign financing. Impatient to get to his meeting with the CIA, Haldeman interrupted: "Yeah, that's, that is the basis I'm going to do it on. Just leave it at that." He wanted to narrow his approach to the CIA and depart for the meeting.

But Nixon was not finished. "I don't want them to get any idea that we're doing it because of our concern about the political, and, ah, . . . I wouldn't tell them it is not political. . . . I'd just say, look, it's because of the Hunt involvement, just say, yeah, Hunt got involved, is involved, ah, in this sort of thing, the whole cover is, ah, basically this. Going to be [unintelligible word]. That cover, it's a good move." Nixon was not concerned about the Bay of Pigs being a potential problem. It was a "cover" for something else. Presumably, mention of Hunt and the Bay of Pigs would get the CIA on board.

The second Nixon-Haldeman meeting was largely about Hunt, even though that was not what Haldeman (or Dean) had in mind. Hunt had nothing to do with campaign financing. Nixon's comment, "he knows too damn much" could not have been related to the Watergate break-in for the simple reason that there is nothing to suggest that Hunt knew more about that operation than any of the others did. Certainly, Nixon was not in a position to make that judgment.

Nixon later explained in his memoirs that he "was not sure whether the CIA actually had any bona fide reason to intervene with the FBI," but he believed there "was enough circumstantial evidence to suggest there might be. . . . If the CIA would deflect the FBI from Hunt, they would thereby protect us from the only White House vulnerability involving Watergate that I was worried about exposing—not the break-in, but the political activities Hunt had undertaken for Colson," especially the ITT matter, in which Colson was deeply involved.[14]

The White House Confronts the CIA

Haldeman went directly from the Oval Office to Ehrlichman's office, where CIA Director Richard Helms, Deputy CIA Director Vernon Walters, and Ehrlichman were waiting for him. The meeting, originally scheduled for 1:00 p.m., began about half an hour late. Unlike the two preceding Nixon-Haldeman meetings and the third that followed, this meeting was not recorded. A year later, in July and August 1973, all four participants testified before the Senate Watergate Committee (and later wrote or cooperated in the writing of books). To a large extent, their accounts were consistent.

Haldeman, who did almost all the talking on behalf of the White House, opened the meeting by referring to the flak taken by the White House and the Nixon campaign because of the break-in at the Watergate Office Building. It was a major political issue and the president had no alternative but to order an investigation by the FBI. There was concern, however, that such an investigation would stumble onto an unrelated and unknown CIA operation or reveal CIA assets, Haldeman explained. Moreover, he said the FBI investigation was running into some important people, according to a memorandum about the meeting prepared by Walters.[15]

Haldeman acknowledged the inevitability of the FBI's investigation into the Watergate break-in. The term "important people" could refer only to campaign contributors, not Committee to Re-elect the President (CRP) officers such as Mitchell and Stans. Haldeman would never suggest to Helms and Walters that the White House or the administration might be involved in the break-in. Helms then emphatically stated that the Watergate break-in was not a CIA operation. He had told Gray the same thing the day before and was unhappy with press reports to the contrary.

According to Haldeman, when he made a reference to the Bay of Pigs invasion, it elicited a strong reaction from Helms. He described Helms's "curious response [to a] question of whether there was a CIA problem with relation to the Bay of Pigs, saying Mr. Helms jumped very rapidly and very defensively to say, 'That is no concern at all. We don't want to get into this at all.'"[16] Helms described the exchange differently: When Haldeman made an "incoherent reference" to an investigation in Mexico or running into the Bay of Pigs, Helms assured Haldeman that the CIA had no interest in the Bay of Pigs.[17]

The discussion then turned to whether the FBI was running into CIA operations or assets in Mexico. Although it was doubtful that the FBI investigation was touching any of the CIA's covert projects, according to Walters's testimony, Haldeman insisted that this was a possibility: "Nevertheless, there is concern ... that this investigation in Mexico may expose some covert activity of the CIA, and it has been decided that General Walters will go to Gray and tell him that the further pursuit [of] this investigation in Mexico ... could jeopardize some assets of the Central Intelligence Agency."[18] Helms generally agreed with Walters but added that he did not remember certain events until Walters refreshed his memory.[19] Pushed by Haldeman, the CIA officials said they would check with others at the agency.[20] To White House aides, Haldeman's statement was a suggestion; to the CIA, it was an order. Walters agreed to meet with Gray.[21]

The major discrepancy between the accounts of the White House aides and the CIA officials was contained in a memorandum Walters wrote and dated five days after the meeting. The memorandum, which was made public at the Senate hearings held a year later, noted that the two White House aides had suggested that the investigation could be concluded because the five Watergate burglars had been arrested, which was a stronger statement than either Haldeman or Ehrlichman described.[22] The memorandum was probably inaccurate on this point. Officials at the White House knew it was only a matter of time before the FBI arrested Liddy and Hunt, who had already been publicly identified. Furthermore, Walters's memorandum contained another error. It incorrectly stated that he returned to CIA headquarters in Langley,

Virginia, between his meeting with Haldeman and Ehrlichman and his meeting with Gray that same afternoon.[23]

The timing of Walters's writing of the memorandum may also be significant. He wrote it five days after the June 23 meeting, and only when he believed that Dean's later suggestions to him might be inappropriate. At the Senate Watergate Committee hearings on August 3, 1973, Minority Counsel Fred Thompson asked Walters, "What caused you to start systematically writing memorandums of the events that were taking place?" Walters responded: "Mr. Dean's [later] exploration of whether the Agency could produce bail and pay the salaries of the defendants while they were in jail."[24]

Briefing Nixon

After the meeting with Helms, Walters, and Ehrlichman, Haldeman again met alone with Nixon at 2:20 p.m., this time in his office in the Old Executive Office Building. During this conversation, which was also recorded, he reported: "Well, it's no problem. Had the two of them in, and—."

"You scare Helms to death, did you?" Nixon interrupted, perhaps sensing that triumph over the CIA was the meeting's main accomplishment. Interestingly, Nixon's first question was not about whether the CIA had agreed to speak to the FBI but about the CIA director's emotional reaction to Haldeman's approach. The CIA's independence bothered Nixon and may have been uppermost in his mind at the time, suggesting that the president was not terribly concerned about the real purpose of the meeting. This indicates that the problem was the anonymous donors and not the Watergate investigation itself.

"Well it's kind of interesting," Haldeman continued. "Walters sat there. Made the point, I didn't mention Hunt at the opening of it, I just said that, that, ah, this thing would lead in the directions that were going to create some very major potential problems, that they were exploring leads that lead back into, to ah, areas that would be harmful to the CIA, harmful to the government, there were—."

An unrelated telephone call from Colson, which Nixon took, interrupted the discussion. After the call, Haldeman reported that, according to Helms, Gray had called to say that the FBI might have "run right into the middle of a CIA covert-operation here." Helms told Gray that the CIA had nothing going on, whereupon Gray said, "It sure looks to me like we did," and Helms replied, "Nothing that we've got going at all." And that was the end of the conversation.

"We said, well, 'the problem is that it tracks back to the Bay of Pigs,'" Haldeman continued. "'It ... gets to areas that are going to be raised. The whole problem of this, this fellow Hunt.' ... At that point Helms kind of got the picture, very clearly. He, he said, he said, 'we'll be very happy to be helpful to, ah, you know, and we'll handle everything you want. I would like to know the reason for being helpful.'" Haldeman did not explain this comment, but his statement to Nixon suggests that he wanted Helms to understand that something was going on that Haldeman was not explaining explicitly. It was the equivalent of a wink. Everyone understood it was a cover story.

"How would that work though?" Nixon asked. "How would, for example, if the judge ... asked for somebody from [the] Miami bank to be here, account for assets in the bank?" Nixon had suddenly leaped back to the issue of campaign contributions. But he was unclear, indeed, indecipherable. If Nixon was thinking about the burglars' break-in trial, it would take an extraordinary judge to be concerned about how the bank in Miami treated monetary transactions on its books. It was also a remarkable thing for Nixon to consider at this juncture, unless he was contemplating the laundering of campaign contributions.

Haldeman acknowledged that the FBI was creating a problem unnecessarily. "The point that John [Ehrlichman] made is ... the Bureau is going all in on this, because they don't know what they're uncovering. Because they think they need to pursue it, [but] they don't need to, because they've already got their case as far as the, ah charges against these men, or something, so they don't need anything further on that. And, ah, as they pursue it they're uncovering stuff that's none of their business."

Ehrlichman, who was a lawyer, was saying that the FBI had enough evidence for the trial of the Watergate burglars and was unnecessarily delving into issues that were beyond the scope of the investigation of the break-in. Ehrlichman's claim that the FBI agents "don't know what they're uncovering" cannot refer to involvement by the CRP or the FCRP; that was already known. Moreover, investigating who was behind the break-in was precisely what the FBI should have been doing. It would be ridiculously naïve of Haldeman or Ehrlichman to say that identifying the mastermind of the Watergate break-in was "none of their [the FBI's] business." Ehrlichman's statement that "they [the FBI and U.S. attorney] don't need anything further on that [the case]" made the valid point that the ultimate source of the $100 bills that were transferred from Sloan to Liddy to Barker was irrelevant to the prosecution of the burglars. (That information was not used at the trial.) Thus, Ehrlichman concluded, "they think they need to pursue it," but "they don't."

Nixon responded: "I'd just say, look, it's because of the Hunt involvement, just say, yeah, Hunt got involved, is involved, ah, in this sort of thing, the whole cover is, ah, basically this.. ... That cover, it's a good move." Once again, Nixon was thinking about Hunt and the CIA.[25] He seemed to be saying that he had developed a good "cover" for the White House's approach to the CIA, but again, his meaning is not clear.

The Situation Confronting the White House

There is an important question: If, as many believed, the White House was asking the CIA to convince the FBI to stop the investigation into the Watergate break-in, why were White House aides talking to the CIA about Mexico? Indeed, why was the White House talking to the CIA at all if it wanted to stop the entire FBI investigation?

It is important to understand that the White House could not have stopped the FBI's investigation of the Watergate break-in on June 23 even if it wanted to. Moreover, the investigation was concededly "out of control." FBI Assistant Deputy Director Mark Felt later said, "No one could have stopped the force of the investigation without an explosion in the Bureau—not even J. Edgar Hoover."[26] Angelo J. Lano, the FBI agent in charge of the investigation, later said that, within a week, twenty-four to twenty-seven agents had been assigned to the case. He said the investigation was "like a freight train rolling along at 100 miles an hour. ... We went everywhere."[27] It was not feasible for Gray to simply call off such a massive FBI investigation, even with the CIA's help. Petersen had made that clear to Dean on June 20.[28]

In fact, on June 23 there was no reason for the White House to stop the FBI investigation into the Watergate break-in. Nixon, Haldeman, and Ehrlichman had little to fear from such an investigation, and despite his meetings with Liddy, neither did Mitchell at that point. With Magruder involved in the cover-up and Liddy remaining mute, Mitchell seemed well protected.

In June 1972 there was no reason to believe that an investigation into the Watergate break-in would uncover the break-in at Dr. Fielding's office, even if that was on the mind of Ehrlichman. Even months later, they did not believe an investigation into the Watergate break-in would lead to the White House. For one thing, Liddy, Hunt, and the Cubans were "soldiers" and unlikely to talk, or at least that was the assumption. Depending on McCord's silence may have been questionable in retrospect, but he was not involved in the Fielding break-in and apparently did not know much about the Plumbers' operations. Moreover, he was loyal to the CIA and tight-lipped about activities, especially if they involved international matters. It would take a unique series of events for an investigation into the Watergate break-in to lead to the Ellsberg break-in.

Nixon, Haldeman, and Ehrlichman were talking about something much narrower than shutting down the FBI investigation into the Watergate break-in. What was the White House so concerned about that it would talk to the CIA and FBI? The anonymous contributions were a major embarrassment to the Nixon campaign at the time and were receiving considerable publicity. In the first few days after the burglars' arrests, there was some confusion over whether money received from campaign contributors had directly funded their activities, which could have been a public relations disaster. The issue of campaign contributions was not important to the CIA, however, which was a plus as far as the White House was concerned. The CIA had nothing to lose by approaching the FBI.

The June 23 conversations, viewed in context, show that Haldeman and Nixon had very different concerns. Haldeman was focused on the promise to maintain the anonymity of donors who would have been embarrassed if an FBI investigation resulted in the disclosure of their identities. This was a political problem. Nixon, in contrast, was concerned about the national security implications if the FBI uncovered Hunt's political activities, although it is unclear whether he saw that as a problem or as an inducement to obtain the CIA's cooperation. Rather than deal with *what* the White House was telling the CIA to do and why, Nixon spoke about *how* to get the CIA to do what he wanted and other collateral matters. He darted from one issue to another. His attention to the anonymous campaign contributors was sporadic but significant.

Implementing the Plan

The FBI investigation was not a threat to any CIA operation, but on June 23 and for a few days thereafter, the CIA did not reject Haldeman's assertion that the FBI might run into some CIA assets. Walters's June 28 memorandum, which he wrote for his personal use, claimed that he had told Gray, "If the investigation gets pushed further south of the border, it could trespass onto some of our covert projects. Since you've got these five men under arrest, it will be best to taper the matter off there."[29] Walters seemed ready to perpetuate the fiction of a vulnerable CIA operation. It is not clear what the CIA leaders thought about the White House's request, but they were prepared to go along with it, at least temporarily.

The person to whom Nixon and Haldeman directed the request to restrict the FBI investigation, Acting Director Gray, construed it as applying to only a narrow phase of it—namely, the scheduled interviews of Dahlberg and Ogarrio which, unknown to him, were links to the anonymous donors. This also suggests that the CIA was focused on campaign financing, a focus it could have received only from Haldeman. It is not clear whether any other consequences flowed directly from the meeting between the CIA and Gray, other than the postponement of the interviews of some CIA personnel, which had nothing to do with Watergate but concerned their earlier dealings with Hunt.

Gray later claimed that the CIA misled him. Walters neither informed him on June 23 that the message emanated from a meeting between CIA officials and top White House aides nor told him the truth about other matters. The CIA was distorting events to enhance its own reputation, he maintained, although it is not clear how this would have exonerated Gray or how he would have behaved differently if he had known the truth.[30] But Gray's understanding that his meeting with Walters was arranged through Haldeman and Ehrlichman rather than Nixon also suggests that the CIA's request was not a momentous one. Rather than stopping the entire investigation of the Watergate break-in, the FBI was asked not to pursue a tangent the Department of Justice had previously disclaimed any interest in.

Simmering Below the Surface

Meetings that involved Haldeman, Ehrlichman, Mitchell, Dean, Gray, Helms, and Walters in various combinations continued, as the participants discussed possible CIA activities that might be uncovered by an FBI investigation of the Watergate break-in. The CIA was not immediately willing to challenge the White House, especially in such a fluid and delicate situation, and agency officials probably recognized that bending to the wishes of the White House might be a good strategy, at least in the short run.

Cleaning up Loose Ends

With the arrested burglars' financial demands on everyone's mind, Ehrlichman asked Dean to approach Walters about getting the CIA to pay sustenance and attorneys' fees for them, as almost all the burglars had some connection to the CIA. Dean had three meetings with Walters on June 24, 25, and 26, 1972, but Walters was adamant that the CIA would not support the Watergate burglars, and the White House abandoned this idea.[1] The White House had no plan until Mitchell suggested using Herbert W. Kalmbach, Nixon's personal lawyer and a seasoned fund-raiser, to come up with the money for the burglars' silence. Haldeman and Ehrlichman approved and directed Dean to meet with Kalmbach. On June 29 Kalmbach reluctantly agreed to raise the funds and proceeded to do so.

On June 27 Helms finally told Gray the CIA had no interest in

Ogarrio or Dahlberg and the FBI was free to interview them. Dean then promptly asked Gray to postpone the interviews on national security grounds, which he did. The next day, Helms asked Gray to delay questioning CIA employees who had furnished Hunt with disguises and equipment in July 1971, but those interviews had nothing to do with the Watergate break-in.[2]

On June 30 Press Secretary Ronald Ziegler announced that the White House had no involvement in the Watergate burglary. When John Mitchell resigned as Nixon's campaign chairman on July 1, some reports tied it to the Watergate break-in, but others attributed it to personal issues with his wife. Soon thereafter, Gordon Liddy, counsel to the finance arm of Nixon's reelection campaign, was publicly implicated and arrested for his role in the burglary. So was Howard Hunt, a longtime CIA employee whose name had surfaced even before Liddy's. The list of those arrested for the break-in at the Watergate Office Building now numbered seven.

According to President Nixon's memoirs (and confirmed by Gray[3]), he called Gray on July 5, 1972, to congratulate him on the FBI's successful prevention of a hijacking. Gray took the opportunity to express his concern that people at the White House or on the campaign staff were trying to cover things up, and he could no longer delay the interviews of Dahlberg and Ogarrio. Nixon recalled, "I was suddenly confronted with something I most wanted to avoid: White House involvement in Watergate. I told Gray emphatically to go ahead with his full investigation."[4] In retrospect, it was an unusual conversation for the FBI director to have with the president, who ordinarily would not be involved in internal FBI matters. Moreover, the White House and Nixon's reelection campaign were already involved because of the evidence against Hunt, who had been identified as a White House consultant and Liddy as a former White House aide. In any case, media stories about Watergate focused almost entirely on the Nixon campaign rather than the White House.

Indictment of the Burglars

The White House pursued its goal of discouraging witnesses from disclosing damaging facts to prosecutors as well as from the few reporters who were pursuing the scandal. Dean received from Gray and Assistant Attorney

General Petersen FBI's reports of interviews of potential witnesses (known as 302s), which were not very enlightening, and permitted him to actually attend the FBI interviews of Colson.[5] This effort allowed Dean to follow the investigation closely.

Simultaneously, the White House worked to keep the FBI from interviewing other potential witnesses; if that failed, they tried to convince the witnesses to lie. Thus, the White House succeeded in preventing the FBI from interviewing senior staff, as well as other knowledgeable people whose identities were unknown to the FBI or the initial prosecution team.[6] This included CRP employee Robert Riesner, a campaign aide involved in coordinating the Mitchell meetings and destroying evidence after the initial arrests. The White House could not prevent the interviews of others, principally Jeb Magruder, FCRP treasurer Hugh Sloan, and CRP employee Herbert L. (Bart) Porter. The topics of these interviews included the two meetings in Mitchell's office, the amount of money paid to Liddy, and the involvement of anyone higher than Liddy and Hunt in the break-in. Thus, it was necessary for these three men to lie.

Magruder was ready and willing to lie, and he did so on his own initiative.[7] The party line, created at the CRP, was that the initial meeting scheduled in Mitchell's office had been canceled and the rescheduled meeting concerned campaign finance laws. (They could not simply deny that the meetings took place because Magruder had noted both in his diary.) The witnesses would claim to know nothing about Liddy's use of the money.[8] Magruder convinced Porter to lie, but Sloan rebelled and refused to lie. He told the FBI, the prosecutors, and the grand jury about the slush fund and how he had doled out $199,000 to Liddy in installments on the say-so of Mitchell and Stans, although he did not know what Liddy did with the cash. Sloan's independence worried the White House.

On September 15, 1972, a federal grand jury sitting in the District of Columbia indicted the seven directly involved in the Watergate break-in (Liddy, Hunt, McCord, and the four Cubans). To the disappointment of many but to the relief of those in the White House, no one senior to Liddy and Hunt was named.[9] The White House was relieved.

Nixon and Haldeman invited Dean to the Oval Office for an evening of stroking—a meeting that did not become public until nearly a year later. They discussed a variety of subjects, ranging from details of the Watergate break-in to the civil suit brought against the Committee to Re-elect the President (CRP) to wiretapping by other presidents.[10]

Washington Post stories alleged that Mitchell, Haldeman, and the latter's assistant Gordon C. Strachan were among those who controlled the secret slush fund, which the media now correctly reported was $350,000, and that Magruder had handled the fund as well. It also reported that the CRP had destroyed records soon after the arrests. Other *Post* stories tied Nixon's CRP to the Watergate break-in.

Behind the scenes, Kalmbach's efforts to provide payments to the seven defendants continued, a task that became increasingly difficult as the months passed. Another incentive to encourage the burglars' silence, and the subject of much comment later, was the possibility that President Nixon would grant them executive clemency. Rumors and stories involving improper Republican interference with the 1972 election persisted, including a series of so-called dirty tricks sponsored by the CRP. The White House maintained its innocence, and the stories did not gain traction. More important, Plumber and burglar E. Howard Hunt started threatening the White House that he would disclose the Dr. Fielding burglary and other unseemly acts if substantial funds were not given to him and the other burglars.

Nixon Wins in a Landslide

Nixon handily defeated Democrat George McGovern on November 7, 1972. It was a landslide by any definition. Nixon received more than 60 percent of the popular vote and lost only seventeen votes in the Electoral College. The White House had succeeded in winning the 1972 presidential election and seemed barely scratched by the bad publicity, which was limited to the area around Washington. However, Seymour Hersh of the *New York Times* was delving into the payments for the burglars.[11]

To the shock of many, the very next morning the White House ordered virtually all employees, including some in relatively senior positions, to submit their resignations, and it accepted many of them. Longtime aide Dwight Chapin later called it "a very dumb management move," and he was personally crushed.[12] Rather than savor his victory, it appeared that Nixon was becoming more partisan and more vindictive. While it is impossible to know what effect, if any, this action had on the last year of the Nixon administration, it rid the White House of some long-standing loyalists and caused anxiety and insecurity among those who remained.[13] Haldeman, Ehrlichman, and Dean remained secure.

On December 8, 1972, Dorothy Hunt, the wife of Howard Hunt and a former CIA employee herself, died in a domestic plane crash along with everyone else on the flight. There was no evidence of foul play. Investigators found media asserting that Mitchell had sanctioned the Watergate break-in, Howard Hunt had promised the burglars that their families would be supported if they were sent to prison, and the seven defendants were being paid for their silence. Hunt's principal lawyer, William O. Bittman, a former Department of Justice prosecutor and now a partner in a prestigious District of Columbia law firm, was identified as an important conduit for payments to both Howard and Dorothy Hunt.

There were various efforts to get all the defendants to plead guilty. McCord later recounted discussions with John J. (Jack) Caufield, who was an assistant to Ehrlichman, then Dean, then Mitchell at the CRP, and then at the Treasury Department (starting on April 28, 1972). The conversations were about everyone pleading guilty in exchange for monetary payments and clemency.[14] But McCord demanded immediate freedom and not clemency later. The most intense discussions took place during the first two weeks of 1973 but continued until January 25, two weeks after the burglars' trial started. Caulfield met secretly with McCord at an overlook on the George Washington Parkway outside of Washington and, according to McCord, claimed "that he was carrying the message of clemency to me 'from the Highest levels of the White House.'"[15] Caulfield, who later testified at the burglars' trial, explained that he had dealt only with Dean, although he assumed that Dean was in touch with Ehrlichman. Caulfield said he was a friend of McCord's and had never threatened him.[16] A distraught Hunt pleaded guilty (after being assured that clemency would be granted later). The Cuban Americans took Hunt's plea as a sign and pleaded guilty. Discussions about guilty pleas ended, and the trial continued against Liddy and McCord.

Meanwhile, Richard and Pat Nixon spent New Year's Eve at Camp David in Maryland. The president's inauguration on January 20, 1973, coincided with his highest approval ratings, which approached 70 percent.

PART II
1973—From Back Burner to Headlines

5

Watergate Burglars Convicted, Judge Sirica Stirs the Pot

The jury trial of the Watergate burglars began on January 8, 1973, before Chief Judge John J. Sirica, who had assigned the trial to himself. Sirica was notoriously pro-government and harsh on defendants. He was not known as a legal scholar or a profound thinker; rather, he was known as "Maximum John" for his lengthy sentences. Sirica's reputation as a judge was mixed at best, but much of the negative was forgotten or ignored in the telling of Watergate.[1]

As noted above, five of the defendants pleaded guilty, but Liddy and McCord pleaded not guilty and went to trial. Liddy apparently did so to avoid admitting any wrongdoing. When asked, he said his plan was to "keep my mouth shut and go to prison." He was prepared to do whatever was necessary to protect Nixon.[2] It seems that the White House should have been able to convince Liddy and McCord to plead guilty, although many of the relevant facts are unknown.

The prosecution's approach oddly mimicked the Committee to Re-elect the President's (CRP's) and Finance Committee to Re-elect the President's (FCRP's) position—that is, the Nixon campaign had paid Liddy for legitimate intelligence-gathering activities, but Liddy had diverted the money. That was why no one superior to Liddy had been charged, the prosecutors explained. Magruder denied any involvement in the break-in, and Hunt denied knowing about any other covert operations. The Cubans denied that they worked for the CIA, claiming they had participated in the break-in to protect Cuba from communism and no one was paying them. Liddy remained impenetrable.

Outside the presence of the jury, Judge Sirica stated his belief that senior officials in the administration or the campaign were involved. He did not believe burglar Bernard Barker's assertion that he did not know where the $100 bills came from, and he did not believe campaign treasurer Hugh Sloan's account that he had transferred $199,000 in cash to Liddy on the simple say-so of Stans and Mitchell, without any additional knowledge or documentation (although it turned out that Sloan was telling the truth).[3] The jury, which rendered its verdict on January 30, 1973, took less than ninety minutes to find Liddy and McCord guilty of all charges.

The trial of Liddy and McCord had serious consequences for the Nixon administration. It seems likely that without a trial, which led to Sirica's strong assertions that the break-in involved persons superior to Hunt and Liddy, there would not have been a Senate Watergate Committee. Without that committee, it is unclear whether Dean would have gone public with his allegations. Without public hearings, it is uncertain that the existence of the White House recording system would have been disclosed. It also seems likely that there would have been no special prosecutor, no Saturday Night Massacre, no indictment of Nixon's top aides, no impeachment investigation by the House of Representatives, and no resignation by Nixon. The Watergate burglars' demands for support would increase, and that may have led to the unraveling of the cover-up. But that is speculation.

Arguably, *Washington Post* reporters Woodward and Bernstein's most important role in Watergate was to maintain pressure on the White House and the Nixon reelection campaign and to keep the matter alive, which was a considerable achievement. Without them, Sirica probably would not have reached the conclusions he did. More allegations surfaced. On January 14, 1973, the *New York Times* reported that unnamed persons were paying money to most of the burglars arrested on June 17. On February 7 it reported that Haldeman's aide Strachan knew about the Liddy-Hunt intelligence operations as early as February 1972.

The Senate Opens an Investigation

In February 1973 the Senate, prompted largely by Sirica's comments at the burglars' trial, decided to conduct an investigation of Watergate. On February 12, by a vote of 77–0, the Senate Select Committee on Presidential

Campaign Activities was created to investigate irregularities in the 1972 presidential campaign. Its chairman was Sam J. Ervin Jr., a Democrat from North Carolina; its vice chairman was Howard H. Baker Jr., a Republican from Tennessee. In all, the committee would consist of four Democrats and three Republicans.[4] The Democratic majority in the Senate defeated amendments proposed by Republicans that would have required the committee to investigate earlier elections or otherwise broaden its inquiry.

The Select Committee almost immediately became known as the Senate Watergate Committee, elevating the Watergate break-in to unique heights in the public's mind and minimizing other wrongdoings by the Nixon administration and the reelection campaign. In a sense, every wrongful act became subsumed under the label "Watergate." If it was Watergate, the committee investigated it; if the committee investigated it, it was Watergate.

Nixon Nominates Gray as FBI Director

Surprising to many was Nixon's formal nomination on February 17, 1973, of Patrick Gray as FBI director, a position he had filled on an acting basis since May 1972. Nixon's memoirs blandly stated, "I decided to nominate Gray to be the FBI's permanent director.... I assured him that I was not worried about anything that might come out of his confirmation hearings about Watergate." Nixon's memoirs mentioned no input from anyone else.[5]

In his book, Haldeman wrote, "[Nixon] says he's inclining to go along with Gray at the FBI and to get [William C.] Sullivan under him."[6] (Hoover had fired Sullivan, his former assistant, in 1971.) Ehrlichman wrote succinctly: "he nominated Pat Gray to be permanent director of the FBI." A few pages later, however, Ehrlichman remarked, "On top of everything else, our Senate-watchers reported that Pat Gray's nomination was in serious trouble. Gray had been a poor witness."[7] It is unlikely that Nixon knew how vulnerable Gray was regarding both his receipt of the documents from Hunt's safe and the relationship with Dean, yet Ehrlichman, Nixon's domestic adviser, remained strangely silent. It was a fateful decision on his part.[8]

Nixon and Ehrlichman met with Gray on February 16 for thirty minutes, which Gray detailed in twenty-four pages of his 2008 book. There is also a recording of the conversation, much of it difficult to decipher, but no published transcript.[9] The meeting did not cover Gray's earlier dealings with

Ehrlichman and Dean but concerned leaks by the FBI (with Mark Felt being the principal suspect), bugging by J. Edgar Hoover and Lyndon Johnson, standing up to the Democrats during his confirmation hearings, exhibiting a firm leadership style, and a brief discussion of other Watergate matters. Nixon did most of the talking. Ehrlichman played a negligible role at the meeting, and he neither disclosed any problems nor asked Gray any pertinent questions about his actions. Gray said little and volunteered nothing.[10] The participants recognized that Gray would be subjected to hostile questioning by Democrats Edward Kennedy and John Tunny at his Senate confirmation hearings, but the prospect did not seem to disturb them. In retrospect, it was a strange meeting in view of earlier events.

Gray's confirmation hearings before the Senate Judiciary Committee began on February 28, 1973. *Washington Post* editor Barry Sussman later called the Gray nomination and Senate confirmation hearings "the beginning of the end for Nixon."[11] The first day of the hearings demonstrated that Gray would answer any question; in fact, he would provide explanations even when no question was asked. Gray delivered to members of the committee whatever documents they requested. He quickly involved Dean and Ehrlichman. He revealed that he was in constant contact with Dean and had supplied him with reports of interviews and allowed him to attend many of the interviews conducted by the FBI. The senators demanded to hear from Dean. But Nixon refused to let Dean testify. Gray admitted destroying documents Ehrlichman and Dean had given him from Hunt's safe; he told the senators he had burned them in his fireplace after Christmas, along with decorations and wrapping paper.

Gray also admitted that the Department of Justice set the parameters for the FBI's investigation. He confirmed that people in the CRP had destroyed documents immediately after the break-in. He also revealed that Mitchell had vetoed any FBI interview of his wife. He explained the interactions between Donald Segretti, the master of dirty tricks, and the White House and reelection campaign. His testimony was a disaster. The White House had no solution. In the words of Ehrlichman, they "let him twist slowly, slowly in the wind."[12] The hearings were adjourned for two weeks.

When the hearings resumed on March 21, Gray erroneously testified that Dean had "probably lied" when he told the FBI he did not know whether Hunt had an office in the White House. This caused another storm, and Dean vehemently disputed Gray. The key issue was the precise wording of the FBI's question: was Dean asked if Hunt had an office in the White House complex, or was he asked whether the committee could visit his office? Hope for confirmation disappeared. (On April 5 Gray asked the White House to withdraw his nomination as FBI director.)

The White House wondered how the situation could get worse. But it did, quickly.

McCord Writes to Sirica

March 23, 1973, was an important day in Watergate lore. On March 21 while Dean was telling Nixon there was a cancer on the presidency, McCord delivered a letter to Sirica, which the judge read in open court on March 23. The letter seconded Sirica's suspicions. McCord's revelations were apparently precipitated by fear of Sirica's lengthy sentences, along with the judge's indication that reduced sentences were possible if the defendants incriminated higher-ups. A former CIA agent, McCord sought to protect the CIA from the false accusations that it was involved in the Watergate break-in.

McCord lacked firsthand information about many of the events, but he named Mitchell, Dean, and Magruder as approving the break-in, based on what Liddy had told him. Liddy could not resist gossiping about his exploits. McCord revealed that political pressure had been applied to get the defendants to plead guilty, witnesses had perjured themselves, and other persons were involved. What McCord did not mention in his letter to Sirica was that he and the other burglars had been paid hundreds of thousands of dollars to keep quiet, which may have been Nixon's greatest vulnerability. In addition, McCord knew about discussions with the White House about granting clemency to the burglars. He asked to meet with Sirica without the FBI or the prosecutors, whom he did not trust. This was a classic failure by Liddy, the leader of a covert operation, to confine sensitive information to only those people who needed to know. That failure, one of many by Liddy, would have profound effects.[13]

To pressure the defendants to turn against the White House and the Nixon campaign, Sirica imposed Draconian provisional sentences (subject to his later review) on a number of the defendants, up to thirty-five years in prison in some cases, although he did not impose provisional sentences on Liddy or

McCord.[14] At the time, few complained about the questionable use of judicial power to coerce defendants to implicate higher-ups, particularly when the facts were contested. Few questioned whether this was the proper function of a judge.

Dean Breaks Ranks

Meanwhile, a critical event was quietly taking place behind the scenes: John Dean was breaking with the White House. Under the belief—or hope—that Haldeman and Ehrlichman were withholding information from Nixon, Dean had informed Nixon what was happening with respect to Watergate, expecting the president to end the cover-up. Nixon's reaction surprised and disappointed him. Dean suspected that the White House was setting him up to take the blame, but he was unsure of his criminal liability. Finally, accepting the fact he engaged in an obstruction of justice, he realized that he could no longer participate in the cover-up and had to terminate his involvement immediately.[15] He hired criminal lawyer Charles N. Schaffer and informed his superiors at the White House that he planned to contact the prosecutors. He hoped this disclosure would end the cover-up. It did not.

On April 3, 1973, Dean (through his lawyer) approached Assistant U.S. Attorneys Earl Silbert and Seymour Glanzer, the prosecutors who had tried the burglars.[16] At Shaffer's insistence, they obtained an agreement that nothing Dean told the prosecutors would be used against him and that they would not inform their superiors at the Department of Justice of his communications. When Shaffer and Dean learned that the prosecutors had broken the agreement and shared Dean's revelations with the Justice Department, negotiations ended.

But Dean was determined to end the cover-up and there was another show in town, and the Senate Watergate Committee was willing to accept Dean's conditions. The committee had no evidence that Dean was involved in the Watergate break-in or cover-up, and it was eager to learn more. Congress's role is not to prosecute criminals, so the committee had no reservations about granting Dean immunity to get the full story out.

Starting in late April, Dean met secretly with Senate Watergate Committee counsel Samuel Dash (with Senator Ervin's blessing) to prepare to tell his story publicly. The meetings were held at Dean's home in Alexandria,

Virginia, or Shaffer's office in Maryland to avoid detection. They spent days recovering Dean's account, which would remain off the record until he secured immunity from a judge.

When the Watergate Special Prosecution Force (WSPF) learned of the Senate committee's plans, it filed a motion with Judge Sirica to prevent Dean from obtaining immunity. The WSPF acted for two reasons. First, it wanted to prevent Dean from giving the White House and others a preview of his testimony. Second, it wanted to be on record as opposing public testimony that could prejudice a jury pool. Judge Sirica readily granted Dean "use" immunity, which meant that the prosecutors could not use anything Dean testified to. The Senate Watergate Committee readied itself for public hearings in mid-May.

Early Watergate Litigation

During 1973 the lawyer handling most Watergate-related disputes for Nixon was Charles Alan Wright, a University of Texas professor who was assisting Nixon part time. James Hamilton, assistant chief counsel for the Senate Watergate Committee, handled most of its litigation, while Philip Lacovara, counsel for the WSPF, was responsible for litigation in that office. I represented the Senate Watergate Committee in one piece of litigation that is worth noting.

On April 17, 1973, Nixon announced that on March 21 he had received new information and, as a result, he intended to personally investigate Watergate. He said that "no individual of major importance in the administration should be given immunity from prosecution" and agreed that his aides could testify under oath before the Senate Watergate Committee. That was a transparent attempt to prevent Dean, whom he believed was reluctant to speak without immunity, from testifying. Also on April 17, Nixon's press secretary announced that previous White House statements on Watergate were "inoperative."

In April 1973 Dean had in his possession some highly sensitive and potentially damaging documents related to domestic intelligence gathering that bore the label "Top Secret/Handle Via COMMINT Channels only" (a classification so high that the classification itself was classified). The documents pertained to Charles Thomas Huston, a White House aide who had been involved in gathering covert intelligence. Dean wanted to relieve himself of the documents, so he and his lawyer came up with the idea of putting the documents in a safe deposit box and giving the key to Judge Sirica—facts that Sirica promptly made public.[17]

I represented the Senate Watergate Committee at the hearing Sirica had scheduled to deal with the contents of the safe deposit box. The courtroom was packed, and shortly after the hearing began, I asked for permission to address the court, which Sirica granted. I informed the court that there was in fact no matter before Judge Sirica (no "case or controversy," in constitutional parlance), and the court had no jurisdictional basis for holding a hearing or taking possession of the key to the safe deposit box. I made this statement because I thought it was right and because, in a case as important as Watergate, the courts should follow the law or, at the very least, everyone should be aware of the law. There was a moment of silence. Sirica's response? "Does anybody have anything else?"

On April 27 federal prosecutors in California informed the judge presiding over the criminal trial of Daniel Ellsberg (charged with unlawfully disclosing the classified Pentagon Papers) that Hunt and Liddy had burglarized the office of Ellsberg's psychiatrist, Dr. Lewis Fielding. Nixon announced that he had recently learned about the burglary of Fielding's office. The judge dismissed the case on May 11. It was a major event that the administration was not adequately prepared for.

In fact, it was the Justice Department's decision to disclose the burglary to the judge in California, ensuring that the case against Ellsberg would be dismissed. To try to save the case, the White House could have made the revelation in Washington to the Senate Watergate Committee. After all, the burglary did not produce any evidence against Ellsberg. The Department of Justice could have argued that the purpose of the burglary was to learn whether any classified material had been given to other countries, in an effort to distance the break-in from Ellsberg's trial. But that did not happen. The dismissal of the Ellsberg case increased interest in the Senate committee's hearings.

Nixon Cleans House

In a nationally televised speech from the Oval Office on April 30, Nixon announced that Haldeman, Ehrlichman, Dean, and Kleindienst were no longer associated with the administration and that he had named Elliot Richardson as attorney general. Shortly thereafter, Nixon named U.S. Army General Alexander M. Haig Jr., foreign policy adviser Henry Kissinger's top military aide, as his new chief of staff and appointed his longtime law colleague Leonard Garment as White House counsel, although Garment was no longer close to Nixon. Haig, who started his new job on May 8, immediately arranged for J. Fred Buzhardt, counsel to the Department of Defense, to be assigned to the White House legal staff. Buzhardt was a well-connected southern conservative and had served as chief of staff to Senator Strom Thurmond of South Carolina in 1965 to 1966. Buzhardt was not versed in the criminal law. Nixon did not name anyone to replace Ehrlichman as chief domestic adviser.

Haig later said that Nixon had no lawyer when he and Buzhardt arrived in early May 1973.[18] Buzhardt became the White House lawyer most involved in Nixon's Watergate-related tapes. The lawyer's December 17, 1978, obituary in the *Washington Post* quoted him as saying his role was "'not that of investigator,' but rather one primarily involved in supplying information and documents to the Senate Committee and the special prosecutor's office." Apparently, no one was responsible for giving Nixon legal advice.

Although Nixon appointed experienced individuals to his senior staff, his two major additions—Haig and Buzhardt—were uninformed about Watergate. That may have been one of Nixon's criteria; it could have been part of his effort to control the situation and minimize his embarrassment in dealings with his staff. Indeed, Haig later said, "I didn't even know what the hell Watergate was," which was a bit of an overstatement.[19] As a result, no White House aide knew the facts of Watergate better than Nixon, whose knowledge was spotty.

A Special Prosecutor Is Named

Secretary of Defense Elliot Richardson (previously secretary of health, education, and welfare) became attorney general after he promised at his Senate confirmation hearing to appoint a special prosecutor that only he could remove, and then only for "extraordinary improprieties." He did this without consulting the White House, which, he later said, was an unwise and perhaps unconstitutional concession.[20]

After several candidates rejected the job of special prosecutor, Richardson named Archibald Cox, a liberal Harvard Law School professor, on May 18,

1973, the day before the Senate Watergate Committee's hearings began. Cox had served as solicitor general under President Kennedy and was a friend of the Kennedy family (many of whom unwisely attended his swearing in as special prosecutor). Nixon was unhappy with the choice of Cox, and for good reason. Cox, a Democrat, proceeded to build a staff of young, talented, aggressive lawyers, many of whom had gone to Harvard Law School or were alumni of the U.S. Attorney's Office in the Southern District of New York.[21] Cox's staff was overwhelmingly composed of Democrats, which concerned Nixon.[22]

On May 22, the third day of the Senate Watergate Committee hearings, Nixon announced seven "categorical" responses to the allegations against him, including that he had no prior knowledge of the Watergate break-in, was unaware of any cover-up or any violation of the campaign finance laws, did not try to implicate the CIA, and did not learn until March 21 about any effort to pay the burglars. Replying to allegations that he had misused the CIA following the arrests of the Watergate burglars, Nixon said:

I instructed Mr. Haldeman and Mr. Ehrlichman to ensure that the investigation of the break-in not expose either an unrelated covert operation of the CIA or the White House investigative unit, and to see that this was personally coordinated between General Walters, Deputy Director of the CIA [and] Mr. Gray of the FBI. It was certainly not my intent or my wish that the investigation of the Watergate break-in or related acts be impeded in any way.[23]

Nixon had elevated the cover story and made it a main purpose of the intervention. He had forgotten that he and Haldeman were discussing the protection of the anonymous donors to his reelection campaign.

6

Senate Watergate Committee Hearings

The Senate Watergate Committee's public hearings began on May 17, 1973, about three months after it was created. The first phase of the hearings, which covered the Watergate break-in and cover-up, ended on August 7, 1973.[1] Witnesses testified four days a week from 10:00 a.m. to approximately 5:00 p.m., with breaks for lunch and interruptions when the senators had to vote on pending bills. There were three one-week adjournments.

The hearings were held in the large, ornate Senate Caucus Room before a standing-room-only audience of hundreds of spectators and members of the media. The seven senators on the committee, along with its chief counsel, minority counsel, and occasionally assistant chief counsel, sat at a long table on a dais; the witnesses sat in front of and below them. The audience was largely anti-Nixon, and Chairman Sam Ervin occasionally had to tap his gavel to restrain applause or laughter. The hearings were broadcast live on network television and then repeated on public television in the evenings. The public watched ravenously.[2]

Testimony Begins

Little information about the Watergate cover-up was known to more than a handful of senior aides in the White House. But the day before a witness testified, the press obtained leaked information about the anticipated testimony based on summaries prepared for the senators.[3] The first weeks featured low-level witnesses from the White

House and Nixon reelection campaign, who described the operation of the campaign and the early days of the cover-up.

The committee was constructing its defense slowly.[4] The first witness who had any contact with the top echelon at the White House was Jeb Stuart Magruder, former assistant to Haldeman and later deputy to Mitchell at the CRP. Magruder, who testified in mid-June, wounded both John Mitchell (regarding the meetings with Dean and his approval of Gemstone) and H. R. Haldeman (regarding his control over the $350,000 slush fund) but had nothing to say about Nixon's involvement.[5] He produced no documentary corroboration.

At the request of the White House, the appearance of John Dean, which had generated massive anticipation, was deferred one week to accommodate the visit of Leonid Brezhnev, General Secretary of the Communist Party, with Nixon leaks and rumors about Dean's testimony multiplying. For the first time, the public would hear testimony about the role of the president in Watergate. All three networks broadcast Dean's testimony, and the public outside of Washington paid attention.

Between 10:00 a.m. and 6:00 p.m., with a break for lunch, he read his detailed statement in a monotone voice and virtually without interruption before a transfixed audience. Over the following four days, Chief Counsel Sam Dash and Minority Counsel Fred Thompson questioned Dean. His testimony ranged far beyond the break-in of the DNC at the Watergate Office Building. In addition to the cover-up Dean described other dubious conduct on the part of the campaign and White House.

Dean testified that although he joined the White House staff in July 1970, he did not speak to Nixon for more than two years; he reported to Haldeman and Ehrlichman.[6] Dean corroborated Magruder's testimony concerning the January 27 and February 4, 1972, meetings with Mitchell and Liddy, although produced little documentary evidence. He discussed the frantic first days after the burglars' arrests but barely mentioned his June 23, 1972, conversation with Haldeman that led to the latter's conversations with Nixon. In fact, the June 23 meetings received little attention.

It was Dean who first seriously implicated Haldeman, Ehrlichman, and Nixon in a criminal cover-up, but the president's involvement began only in March 1973. Indeed, before the Senate Watergate Committee hearings, the press and the public had focused on the Watergate break-in; there was no real conception of a cover-up.

Dean recounted the details of his September 15, 1972, meeting with Nixon and Haldeman but said he could not be certain how much Nixon knew about the Watergate break-in. Dean's testimony before the committee implied more knowledge on Nixon's part than the recording did.[7]

Dean then described a March 1973 conversation with Nixon about the burglars' demands for money. When Nixon asked how much was needed to pay them, Dean testified that he replied, "$1 million." According to Dean, Nixon's response was: "That should not be a problem; I know where that amount of money could be obtained."[8]

Dean described other meetings with Nixon, including one on April 15, his famous "cancer on the presidency" statement, at which Nixon said he had made a mistake in discussing clemency for Howard Hunt. Dean testified that Nixon had moved to the side of the room and spoke in a hushed tone, leading Dean to believe that the conversation was being recorded.[9] But Dean admitted that he had little corroboration; it was his word against the word of a number of others, including the president.[10] Nevertheless, it was shocking testimony. After five full days of testifying, Dean was permitted to retire. Gradually, the investigators, the media, and the public realized the limitations of the evidence presented.

It appeared that the Senate Watergate Committee hearings would titillate but had resolved little. Following Dean's testimony, Nixon's approval rating, which had reached a high point (nearly 70 percent) with his January 1973 inauguration, dipped. As the summer started, his approval-disapproval numbers were approximately equal. Around July 1 Nixon's approval rating began a rapid decline. The pro-Nixon forces had yet to testify.

The White House Recording System Is Revealed

John Mitchell testified before the committee after a one-week recess for the Fourth of July holiday. Basically agreeing with Dean, he described the two meetings with Liddy in his office as "a complete horror story that involved a mishmash of code names and lines of authority, electronic surveillance, the ability to intercept aircraft communications, the call girl bit and all the rest of it." However, he vehemently denied that he had approved Liddy's plan during his Key Biscayne, Florida, meeting with Magruder and LaRue on March 30, 1972, although he acknowledged he could have been firmer in his rejection of Liddy's espionage plan. He could not explain how his rejection of Liddy's plan had been misconstrued as approval or how the break-in at the Watergate Office Building had proceeded.[11]

After the arrests on June 17, 1972, there were a number of meetings involving White House aides at which they discussed, in Mitchell's words, various "White House horrors," including the break-in at the office of Daniel Ellsberg's psychiatrist. That was when Mitchell first learned about these events, he said.[12] On the cover-up, Mitchell's position was nearly 180 degrees from Dean's. Mitchell minimized his own involvement in questionable conduct and described himself as a moderating influence. He denied speaking with Nixon in 1972 about Gemstone and the Watergate break-in. Nixon, he said, would have been furious and would have shut down any cover-up, which would have destroyed his chance for reelection.

On July 10, 1973, shortly before he was scheduled to be interviewed by Senate Watergate Committee staff, Haldeman's top aide Lawrence Higby informed White House Counsel Leonard Garment that, at Alexander Haig's suggestion, he was prepared to reveal that the White House had recordings of conversations. Garment told Higby that he was not required to volunteer that information, but he should answer truthfully if asked a direct question. No one asked Higby about taping. Garment could not recall whether he spoke to former White House aide Alexander P. Butterfield before the latter's interview, but Garment noted that he would have given Butterfield the same advice.[13] Haldeman later recalled: "Higby had warned me that any of us might be asked about the tapes. And I told Haig that, if asked, we would have to answer truthfully. But I don't believe Nixon felt that the question would ever arise."[14]

Monday morning, July 16, 1973, Senator Ervin announced that a new (and mysterious) witness, Alexander P. Butterfield, administrator of the Federal Aviation Administration, would testify that afternoon. It turned out that Butterfield had been deputy assistant to the president and secretary to the cabinet from January 21, 1969, until March 14, 1973, with administrative and security duties that involved working directly with the president. His testimony was momentous.

Butterfield explained to a rapt audience that in early 1971 the Secret Service installed and thereafter maintained a comprehensive recording system that was geared to tape-record all the president's meetings and telephone conversations in the Oval Office, in the president's private office in the Old Executive Office Building, in the Lincoln Sitting Room in the White House, and in the president's office at Camp David. The system was voice-activated and no one, including Nixon, could turn it off. The recordings of telephone calls were far superior in audio quality to those of in-person meetings. The Secret Service changed the reels of tape and stored them in a locked room but did not listen to them.

Initially, only Nixon, Haldeman, Higby, Butterfield, a secretary, and the Secret Service knew about the recording system. Haig learned about it when he became chief of staff, and aide Stephen Bull was informed after he took over Butterfield's job. Thus, Mitchell, Dean, and Charles Colson were unaware that the system existed until Butterfield disclosed it.[15]

The reason it was installed, Butterfield and Haldeman later explained, was that Nixon wanted an accurate account of his presidency. With tape recordings, Nixon could be confident that history would not be distorted. Now, as a result of Butterfield's testimony, the public became aware of a possible means of corroborating—or refuting—Dean. The White House promptly stopped taping.

Nixon's memoirs state, "Early Monday morning Haig called to tell me that Haldeman's former aide Alex Butterfield had revealed the existence of the White House taping system to the Ervin Committee staff and that it would become public knowledge that day."[16] Haig's account differs:

On Monday, July 16, I drove to Bethesda and spent some time with the President. On my return to the White House in the early afternoon, my assistant, George Joulwan, greeted me with the news that Alexander P. Butterfield, a retired Air Force officer and former assistant to Haldeman, had revealed the existence of a White House taping [system] in testimony before the Ervin committee.... This was the first I had heard of the existence of an eavesdropping system that recorded every word uttered in the presence of Nixon, and it was a total surprise to me.[17]

That statement was false. In fact, Haig contradicts it six pages later in his memoirs, where he notes that Nixon told him sometime around May 1, 1973, that there was a taping system and that his conversations with Dean had been recorded. Haig wrote, "This came as no surprise to me." Moreover, Haig said that White House aide Stephen Bull delivered tapes to Nixon, who listened to them a few days after May 1, 1974.[18] As noted earlier, both Butterfield and Higby also contradicted Haig.

One other observation is relevant. Both Higby and Butterfield made rational and proper decisions not to lie. Garment gave them sound and ethical advice. What happened in 1973 should be contrasted with events of a year earlier, when Magruder and Bart Porter lied to prosecutors and the grand jury. Had the participants acted otherwise in mid-1973, it is entirely possible that the taping system would not have been discovered and the core of the cover-up would not have been compromised without the taping system. Nixon was very close to escaping judgment.

Nixon faced the question of what to do about the tapes—in particular, should they be destroyed? Legal, moral, and practical considerations influenced the decision. Destruction of the tapes might constitute obstruction of justice, and some, including Garment, counseled against taking this action.[19] Haig, Buzhardt, and senior aide Patrick Buchanan disagreed.[20] Garment described discussions about the fate of the tapes after Butterfield's disclosure on July 16 and said that Haldeman was against destroying the March 21, 1973, tape because he thought it would help Nixon, narrower grounds than Garment asserted. Many were confident that the tapes would remain the property of the president and that no court could possibly order their disclosure. In any event, destroying scores if not hundreds of reels of tape presented enormous tactical challenges. Nixon, who was hospitalized at Walter Reed with pneumonia on July 16, obviously could not destroy the tapes himself.

There was some sentiment that disclosure of the tapes' content would not severely damage Nixon and would probably be less harmful than their destruction. Indeed, Nixon believed that the recordings would improve his case. Haig wrote in his memoirs: "Richard Nixon's belief that the tape recordings of his conversations with the Watergate conspirators would prove his own innocence invested the controversy over the release of the tapes with a deep irony."[21] Defense attorney John J. Wilson told Woodward and Bernstein in late 1974 that Haldeman did not believe the tapes were damaging and favored their release, although it is unclear to whom, if anyone, Haldeman expressed his views at the time.[22] Haldeman was not a lawyer, and he may have been focusing on the issue of the lack of advance knowledge of the Watergate break-in, in the mistaken belief that the White House had not acted illegally afterward. Significantly, other than the president, no one in the White House was familiar with the content of the tapes, and Nixon was hardly in a position to make a reliable judgment, although he continued to maintain his innocence.

Initial Attempts to Acquire the Nixon Tapes

Both the Senate Watergate Committee and the special prosecutor subpoenaed the White House for tapes.[23] The special prosecutor's subpoena sought tapes of conversations between Nixon and Dean that the latter had described in his Senate testimony, for which there were relatively strong arguments for release. The special prosecutor also wanted tapes of a few other conversations, including the one between Haldeman and Nixon on Tuesday, June 20, 1972. This took place just after the president had returned to the White House from California and was his first known conversation with Haldeman after the arrests. The Senate committee's subpoena was broader. When the White House refused to comply with the subpoenas, both entities went to the district court to compel production of the tapes. Judge Sirica heard the motions. Meanwhile, the committee hearings continued with the testimony of Haldeman, Ehrlichman, and CIA officials.

A few questions arise. Why was approval and enforcement of the subpoenas entrusted to Sirica? The break-in case had ended months earlier, and it was not standard practice for subpoenas and other new matters to be brought to the chief judge; there is usually a motions judge whose obligations rotate among the judges. One answer is that the Watergate Special Prosecution Force and the Senate committee brought the subpoenas to Sirica to sign, which he promptly did for the WSPF but not the committee.[24] Signing a subpoena does not immediately lead to retaining the case it applies to, but retain the matter Sirica did.

To become effective, the subpoenas still had to be served on Nixon. What would have happened if the White House had simply closed its doors will never be known because White House attorney J. Fred Buzhardt accepted service of the subpoenas. It should be noted that Buzhardt was not a litigator, and accommodation was more his style than confrontation. It was a reasonable thing to do but not necessarily the smart thing for a lawyer representing Nixon to do. Some would consider Buzhardt's action weak if not self-destructive. Nixon had already declared that the White House would stonewall its opposition, and he was not in an accommodating mood.

Later, Archibald Cox, the original Watergate prosecutor, was critical of the White House's decision to accept service without a fight: "He should have simply stood on the fact that 'I am President. I have my independent responsibilities.'" Behind closed doors, Cox and his staff were pacing with worry. Cox's sources had told him that Nixon's lawyer, Professor Charles Alan Wright, was confident that he could prevail on the merits of the issue.[25] But there were no guarantees.

Too much should not be made, however, of Buzhardt's accepting service of the subpoenas. If he hadn't, Nixon would have been unable to physically leave the White House because of the risk that he would be served, which would have confined and embarrassed him both domestically and internationally. Also, the WSPF and Sirica might have found an alternative to personal service on the president. The most likely result would have been a delay of a month or two in the WSPF's obtaining the tapes. Apparently, that potential consequence was not considered at the time.

Hearing from the "Berlin Wall"

Ehrlichman and Haldeman—sometimes called the "Berlin Wall" for their diligence in protecting Nixon from others—testified separately between July 24 and August 1, 1973, and both dubiously denied having contemporary knowledge of the Plumbers' expeditions. Both specifically claimed that they knew nothing about the burglary at the office of Ellsberg's psychiatrist until April 1973, along with the rest of the public, which was obviously false.[26] They were both represented by the same attorney, John J. Wilson.

Ehrlichman, who testified first, explained that in September 1971 he had authorized an *investigation* of Dr. Fielding to learn more about Ellsberg but insisted that he had not authorized physical entry into the psychiatrist's office.[27] Ehrlichman stated that he had authorized a White House investigation because FBI Director Hoover was a close friend of Ellsberg's in-laws and refused to investigate the family.[28] Both Ehrlichman and Haldeman rejected any suggestion that the burglary was a crime under the circumstances (citing national security).[29] Their testimony about ignorance of the Fielding break-in was inconsistent with other evidence, including Dean's and portions of Mitchell's testimony (about White House meetings after the burglars' arrests), but they steadfastly maintained their positions.

Haldeman and Ehrlichman repeatedly insisted that they had no recollection of hearing about Liddy's intelligence plan prior to June 17, 1972, including any activities related to DNC headquarters. Haldeman specifically denied that Dean had briefed him about meetings held in Mitchell's office in early 1972. In addition, they both denied any knowledge of the improper shredding or other disposal of documents after the burglars' arrests. Both Haldeman and Ehrlichman also maintained that before March 1973—that is, before Dean briefed him—Nixon had only limited knowledge of the events that constituted a cover-up of the Watergate break-in and related illegalities.

In his testimony before the Senate Watergate Committee, Haldeman emphasized that his first conversation with Nixon on June 23, 1972, was hardly momentous (although he had every incentive to minimize the significance of what they discussed that day). Watergate was not dominating the White House, he maintained. Neither was the fate of anonymous campaign contributors, although that issue received considerable media attention. These were only two of countless matters Nixon and Haldeman were dealing with, and they were not the most important ones. Also, the words spoken were not pondered, filtered, or edited. Free association interrupted logical thought. "This was not a major official edict by the President of the United States signed on parchment paper," Haldeman said, implying that a few remarks should not be given exaggerated importance.[30] In any case, the meetings between Haldeman and Nixon on June 23, 1972, received little attention from the Senate committee; the press and the public largely ignored what little information they had.

Haldeman and Ehrlichman testified that they met with officials from the CIA and FBI on June 23, 1972, but the meeting's purpose was to find out what was happening and ensure that no CIA operation would be compromised; there was no attempt to subvert or restrain the FBI's investigation of the Watergate break-in. Haldeman said he never "ask[ed] the CIA to participate in any Watergate cover-up, nor did I ever suggest that the CIA take any responsibly for the Watergate break-in. . . . I believe that the action I took with the CIA was proper, according to the President's instructions, and clearly in the national interest."[31] Haldeman repeated that they were concerned the FBI investigation might "run into CIA operations in Mexico and that it was desirable that that not happen and the investigation, therefore, should be either tapered off or reduced or something, but there was no language saying stop, as far as I recall."[32] The senators also asked extensive questions about offers of presidential clemency to the seven burglars, particularly to Hunt. Haldeman and Ehrlichman denied that the White House made such offers.[33] No one asked Haldeman if the White House had ever been concerned about interfering with a CIA operation abroad before.

Haldeman and Ehrlichman acknowledged that Herbert Kalmbach collected substantial sums of money that were paid to those arrested in connection with the Watergate break-in. However, they maintained that the payments were charitable and legitimate and were not intended to buy the burglars' silence. Ehrlichman compared the payments with the defense funds set up for Angela Davis or Daniel Ellsberg. Chairman Sam Ervin wryly remarked that he did not realize the Committee to Re-elect the President was an "eleemosynary institution," which produced loud laughter from the spectators.[34] Neither Haldeman nor Ehrlichman mentioned campaign contributors in their testimony.

In fact, the White House and campaign had a plausible argument to assist the Cuban-American burglars. The Cuban-Americans, they could have argued, were super-patriots; they were anti-Castro and had risked their lives, including at the Bay of Pigs invasion to save democracy, which was a US operation. Through no fault of their own, they had gotten involved with G. Gordon Liddy, a campaign employee who had converted CRP's intelligence operation into a criminal enterprise. For these reasons, it was appropriate to assist their innocent families. While some of these statements were vulnerable, the position was not frivolous.

The committee also asked Haldeman to identify the tapes he had listened to. He admitted to listening to the conversations involving Nixon, Dean, and himself on September 15, 1972, and on March 21, 1973, including portions of the meetings he had not attended, but no others.[35] Nixon had waived executive privilege with respect to what White House personnel knew firsthand (a dubious move about which little is known), but he did not waive his privilege with respect to information Haldeman learned solely by listening to the tapes. Evidently, the president wanted to avoid jeopardizing his claim that the tapes were protected by executive privilege. Ervin, however, denied Nixon's claim of privilege in its entirety, which meant that the committee could ask Haldeman about those portions of the two meetings involving Dean and Nixon at which Haldeman was not present. Ervin's denial of privilege was not binding on a court.

Haldeman did not dispute that at the March 21, 1973, meeting in the Oval Office Dean identified the need to raise as much as $1 million for the burglars or that Nixon said there would be no problem doing so. Haldeman testified, however, that Nixon promptly added, "But it would be wrong."[36] Committee

Vice Chairman Howard Baker pressed Haldeman, but he stood his ground. Haldeman was lying, but it is not clear why he chose to do so or why he was so emphatic.

Minutes before Haldeman finished testifying, Minority Counsel Thompson focused on what the White House was asking the CIA to accomplish with the FBI on June 23, 1972:

Q. Were there any restraints placed on them [the FBI], so far as you know, in the Bureau with regard to this particular investigation [Watergate]?
A. None, except in the very limited sense that I have talked about and in a limited period of time with regard to national security considerations.
Q. At that particular time did the White House staff, so far as you know, the President—
A. Let me go back. I am sorry, Mr. Thompson, just a second. Those were no limitations to the Watergate investigation, they were limitations on going beyond that into other areas.[37]

Chairman Ervin then summarized the record as of August 1, 1973: "We haven't got a particle of testimony so far that the President himself personally took any active interest at any time between June 17, 1972, and March 1973, except through inquiries allegedly through Dean as to how this all happened." Haldeman responded that Nixon also learned facts through Ehrlichman and himself. Ervin asked what he and Ehrlichman did about it, and Haldeman said, "We referred them [inquiries about Watergate] to John Dean, who was the man responsible for dealing with them."[38]

Incredulous and with his jowls quivering, Ervin asked Haldeman, "Oh, so John Dean was the only man in the White House who was asked to take any concern of finding out how it was that these burglars were caught in the Watergate with the President's campaign funds in his [sic] pocket?" The audience awaited the response to the seemingly damning question. But Haldeman forcefully answered: "That is absolutely correct, Mr. Chairman; he was the only man in the White House asked to do that because there were hundreds of people outside of the White House in the executive branch doing precisely that."[39]

Haldeman explained that neither he nor Nixon was in Washington on June 17, 1972, and neither of them was immediately caught up in the aftermath of the Watergate arrests. Haldeman insisted that his role was to ensure that others were doing their jobs, not to conduct an investigation himself.

More generally, he denied that Nixon "withdrew from the political scene" following the Watergate arrests, as some had suggested; rather, he "withdrew from the mechanics of the operation of his political campaign. There is quite a difference."[40] Haldeman was emphasizing Nixon's distance from Watergate and his focus on more substantive matters, especially international ones.

The Final Witnesses

CIA Deputy Director Vernon Walters and Director Richard Helms were the next to testify at the Watergate hearings. They described their meeting with Haldeman and Ehrlichman (summarized in chapter 3), which remains the most detailed account of that meeting by far. Helms acknowledged that it was rather strange for Walters, rather than Helms, to be asked to talk to FBI Director Gray.[41] However, Walters was a longtime acquaintance of Nixon and considered more trustworthy. There was an important exchange during Walters's questioning by Minority Counsel Thompson, which followed introductory questioning by Chief Counsel Dash:

Q. General Walters, as I understand it, it was your feeling and is your feeling that on June 23 you were asked to deliver a message which would in effect limit the Watergate investigation with regard to the Mexican part of it because of the possibility of either compromising some covert CIA activities or CIA employees, is that correct?
A. Yes, it is.
Q. It seems to me that the crucial question is whether or not you were being told to limit the investigation in any other respect. Were you or were you not?
A. I was not, Mr. Thompson.[42]

Although the testimony did not involve Nixon, it provided further evidence that the focus on June 23, 1972, was campaign financing, not halting the Watergate investigation in general.

By the summer of 1973, the CIA, which had never been seriously implicated in the Watergate break-in and had no operation in Mexico that the FBI investigation might have disrupted, was probably attempting to downplay the scope of Haldeman's request (or direction) to Walters. The CIA wanted to emphasize its independence from the White House. Moreover, the CIA had to coexist with the White House, which was still in the hands of Nixon (though not Haldeman and Ehrlichman), and it wanted to avoid conflict.

The Republicans on the Senate Watergate Committee and staff revived the theory that the CIA had played a major role in Watergate. Later, Dean described their efforts: "Howard Baker had developed an interesting ploy to deflect the true responsibility of Watergate from the Nixon White House. Baker had cleverly raised the issue of the CIA's involvement in Watergate and had suggested, during the hearings, that it really was the CIA that was the culprit. This was hogwash, for I knew of no evidence to support it."[43]

The Republicans investigated whether the CIA had advance knowledge of the break-in and whether it had destroyed its own tape recordings and other evidence of its involvement, but they developed no significant evidence to support their theory. With inconsequential exceptions, the Senate Watergate Committee hearings were the only public discussion of the June 23, 1972, meetings until August 5 and 6, 1974. What emerged from the hearings was that the June 23 meeting among Haldeman, Ehrlichman, Helms, and Walters was concerned with the CIA, including the potential impact of the Watergate investigation on the CIA's operations. There was no mention of shutting down the massive investigation into the Watergate break-in.

On August 7, 1973, the Senate Watergate Committee recessed. It continued its work and held extensive public and nonpublic hearings during the next year, mostly on subjects other than the Watergate break-in and cover-up.[44] But it was evident that its days in the sun were over.

7

The Watergate Special Prosecutor and the Fight for Nixon's Tapes

From the beginning, Special Prosecutor Archibald Cox showed signs that he would conduct an aggressive and broad investigation into the Plumbers, the dirty tricks played on the Democrats, and even allegations related to Nixon's income tax returns, the last of which reportedly enraged the president. News of some of these investigations led several of Nixon's aides, including Alexander Haig, Fred Buzhardt, and Leonard Garment, to complain about Cox to Attorney General Elliot Richardson, but that was not publicly known and apparently had little effect. Cox quickly, but not surprisingly, became a problem for the White House.

The person in charge of transcribing the Nixon tapes in the fall of 1973 was Buzhardt. He was a workaholic (according to Haig, Buzhardt worked twenty hours a day), and he had a small team of perhaps four or five lawyers assisting him, along with a secretary or two, who often prepared first drafts of the transcripts. The lawyers were engaged in the job of identifying, collecting, scrutinizing, cataloging, transcribing, editing, and finally transferring copies of nine tapes to the Watergate Special Prosecution Force.

Judge Sirica ruled in favor of the WSPF but against the Senate Watergate Committee on their respective subpoenas for the Nixon tapes, an important and intelligent decision on his part.[1] By enforcing the WSPF's grand jury subpoena but not the committee's subpoena, he focused on the right of a president to withhold relevant evidence in a criminal case. Although Congress has an important power to conduct investigations, its focus is on informing the public, which the courts have concluded does not deserve the same respect as prosecutors' authority to try criminal defendants. It appears that Sirica never seriously considered giving the tapes to the Senate Watergate Committee, whose members were leaking material wholesale.[2] He ordered the White House to produce the subpoenaed tapes initially for his *in camera* review before he gave them to the special prosecutor. Nixon appealed to the U.S. Court of Appeals for the District of Columbia Circuit, which held Sirica's order in abeyance. Unusually, before rendering its decision the appeals court asked the WSPF and the White House to try to resolve the dispute, but they were unable to do.

Acting quickly, the court of appeals affirmed Sirica's order relating to the special prosecutor on October 12, 1973.[3] The court balanced a president's legitimate interest in preserving confidentiality with the powerful obligation by prosecutors and federal grand juries to fulfill their constitutional responsibilities in applying federal law to possible criminals. The court noted, however, that a president's communications are presumptively protected: "We end, as we began, by emphasizing the extraordinary nature of this case. We have attempted to decide no more than the problem before us—a problem that takes its unique shape from the grand jury's compelling showing of need." The decision was narrowly crafted to apply to criminal prosecutions alone.[4]

The question of Congress's right to receive grand jury minutes was not before the appeals court. However, it specifically noted: "That the Impeachment Clause may qualify the court's power to sanction non-compliance with judicial orders is immaterial."[5] Put differently, the court's opinion did not support any other litigant seeking documents from a president in any other context, including the House of Representatives considering impeachment of the president. Any such litigant had to overcome the president's presumptive privilege and other burdens. Indeed, courts might be powerless in an impeachment proceeding to order a president to deliver material to Congress.

To satisfy the WSPF's subpoena, Nixon offered to provide authenticated summaries of the conversations prepared by the White House, and he adopted Buzhardt's suggestion that Senator John Stennis (a conservative southern Democrat who was elderly, hard of hearing, and the victim of a recent mugging) should authenticate them.[6] The Senate Watergate Committee embraced the plan—otherwise, it would likely receive nothing—but Cox balked on the grounds that he needed the original tapes to use as evidence.

Haig, assisted by Nixon, Buzhardt, and Charles Alan Wright, tried to reach a compromise with Richardson and Cox.[7] But attempts to resolve the dispute, which seemed promising at first, collapsed.

Buzhardt told Woodward and Bernstein in a series of interviews after Nixon resigned that the White House believed Cox would resign rather than challenge Nixon. He also said the White House's offer to have Stennis verify the tape transcripts was made in good faith.[8] Although many ridiculed the idea of using Stennis, Cox did not seem concerned about the senator's qualifications. He rejected the Stennis plan on the grounds that selecting one man to verify the tapes was unsatisfactory and he needed the tapes themselves. Most importantly, Cox would not agree to forgo later attempts to obtain additional tapes. According to Haig, the White House was shocked and disappointed.[9]

Nixon loyalists claim that Richardson switched his position on Cox and doubled-crossed Nixon. "Elliot put a knife in the president's back," Haig said.[10] In any event, Nixon was making his decision in difficult circumstances. A major war was brewing in the Middle East. On October 10, 1973, Vice President Agnew resigned in disgrace. On October 12 the court of appeals ruled against Nixon on the tapes and gave him one week to comply with the subpoena or seek Supreme Court review. On October 19 and 20 he was negotiating with the Soviet Union to try to end the war in Vietnam. He was also receiving inconsistent reports, including that Richardson would accept a compromise and that Cox would resign rather than challenge the president.[11]

With the future uncertain, the WSPF moved quickly to accept a guilty plea from John Dean, a major and unexpected event that caught the public's attention. Dean's lawyer Charles Shaffer believed his client had a strong defense to any criminal charges because his (immunized) testimony before the Senate Watergate Committee was so well known but could not be legally used against him, and he advised Dean to stand trial. Dean nevertheless decided to plead guilty and did so the day before the so-called Saturday Night Massacre.

The Saturday Night Massacre

After Cox rejected the Stennis compromise, on Saturday, October 20, Nixon directed Attorney General Richardson to order Cox to refrain from seeking any other tapes of presidential conversations. Richardson refused and resigned, largely because of assurances he had made to the Senate Judiciary

Committee at his confirmation hearing. Nixon then directed Richardson's deputy, William Ruckelshaus, to fire Cox. He too refused and resigned. Solicitor General Robert H. Bork, the next in line at the Department of Justice, fired Cox.[12] Almost immediately, FBI agents secured the WSPF offices and refused to let anyone enter or remove anything. Some reports claimed the WSPF was abolished. The situation was explosive.

The country, or at least Washington, DC, erupted in what became known as the Saturday Night Massacre. Signs around the perimeter of the White House grounds urged drivers to honk their horns if they wanted Nixon impeached, and many did. Thousands of telegrams poured into the White House, and they overwhelmingly supported Cox. Some Republican lawmakers joined their Democratic colleagues in condemning Nixon's action. Democratic members of the House of Representatives filed bills to commence impeachment proceedings against Nixon. Haldeman later noted: "In this case, as in the past, Nixon did just enough—by firing Cox—to infuriate the nation, but not enough to save himself."[13]

Nixon had to decide what to do next. Although the president met with his lawyers hours before a scheduled hearing before Judge Sirica, the decision to surrender the tapes was a political decision that had already been made. None of his advisers—namely, Haig and lawyers Garment, Buzhardt, and Wright—argued against giving the tapes to the WSPF.[14]

At the hearing, Wright, a respected professor of constitutional law at the University of Texas, announced to Sirica that Nixon would surrender the subpoenaed tapes in accordance with the court order and would appoint a successor to Cox.

On November 1 Nixon named Leon Jaworski, a prominent Texas lawyer and Democrat, to the post of special prosecutor. Jaworski had participated in the prosecution of Nazi war criminals after World War II and was a former president of the American Bar Association, a position known more for its social than legal skills; little was known about his views. The Senate confirmed him on November 5. Jaworski started work the same day with the staff he inherited from Cox. The crisis was defused, at least partially and temporarily.

On November 15, 1973, the House voted 367–51 to authorize $1 million for its Judiciary Committee (later known as the Impeachment Committee) to initiate an impeachment inquiry against Nixon under the chairmanship of down-to-earth Democrat Peter W. Rodino. A product of the New Jersey political machine, Rodino had just become chairman in January following the defeat of longtime previous chairman Emanuel Celler by upstart Elizabeth Holtzman in a Democratic primary for his Brooklyn seat. Along with an inexperienced chairman, the senior democrats on the committee were long-time politicians. There was a shortage of former prosecutors.

Commentator Jimmy Breslin wrote: "The primary election between Holtzman and Celler could be considered one of the most meaningful elections the nation has had. If Celler had won, he would have dominated the impeachment process with the Judiciary Committee, as he dominated everything else about the Committee for his thirty years as Chairman. Brilliant but egotistical, he would have been quite abrasive in such a delicate process."[15] Celler would have appointed an aggressive counsel and would not have tolerated delay. As will be seen, Nixon had bad luck in the selection of both his own counsel and that of the House.

The Eighteen-and-a-Half-Minute Gap

The White House informed Sirica on November 21 that two of the subpoenaed conversations had not been recorded and that the tape of the conversation between Nixon and Haldeman on June 20, 1972, contained a buzzing sound lasting eighteen and a half minutes at the point where they turned to the subject of Watergate, making that portion of the tape unintelligible. The White House claimed that Rose Mary Woods, Nixon's longtime personal secretary, had inadvertently caused five minutes of the erasure. The media was all over this revelation.

Dissatisfied with the White House's explanations, Sirica ordered a public hearing. At the hearing on November 26, 1973, Woods attempted to re-create the erasure at a replica of her desk constructed in Sirica's courtroom, but that became a fiasco. It was physically impossible for her to have made the erasure the way she and the White House claimed.

A team of experts appointed jointly by the White House and the WSPF announced that the gap in the June 20, 1972, tape was intentional, caused by repeated efforts to obliterate that portion of the tape. Someone erased the original recording by manually recording over it at least five or six times. Apparently, aside from Secret Service personnel (who had nothing to do with the content of the tapes), only Nixon, Woods, and aide Stephen Bull had access to the tapes after Butterfield left. The erasure was a clumsy job that effectively eliminated Woods as the perpetrator. Many were betting that Nixon was the culprit, as he had access to the tapes, had the gumption to erase a recording of a presidential conversation, and was known to be notoriously unmechanical.[16] Although extraordinary efforts were made to discover the content of the June 20 meeting, they were all unsuccessful.

On December 21, 1973, in preparation for the impeachment hearing, House Judiciary Committee Chairman Peter Rodino replaced committee counsel Jerry Zeifman, who had a reputation as a hothead, with John Doar, a registered Republican, for the impeachment efforts. The chairman then built a large unified staff that was under his and Doar's control.[17] Doar had distinguished himself as a champion of the desegregation effort in the South. However, he had apparently prosecuted just one case and had recently served as president of the New York City Board of Education. Rodino, who insisted that he had the final say regarding who was on the committee's staff, allowed the Republicans to pick a part-time chief minority counsel, Albert E. Jenner Jr., a prominent lawyer and head of the large Chicago firm Jenner and Block. Jenner was not a major factor in the proceedings.[18]

According to Haig, Jenner had been a fund-raiser for Democratic presidential candidate Adlai E. Stevenson III and had publicly announced that the president should be legally responsible for the actions of his aides, even if he did not know about them in advance.[19] This was a rather radical position and certainly not in accord with Nixon's position. There is no suggestion that Haig even thought about becoming involved in selecting the Republican counsel for the Impeachment Committee.

Judges and Prosecutors Converse

One other relevant event occurred in December 1973. Chief Judge Sirica and Judge Gerhardt Gesell, the DC district court judge who presided over the case related to the burglary at Dr. Fielding's office, met with Jaworski, his deputy Henry S. Ruth Jr., his counsel Philip Lacovara, and Assistant Special Prosecutor Richard Ben-Veniste. That meeting, presumably arranged by Sirica, dealt with the anticipated filing of indictments by the special prosecutor. Unusually, Jaworski waited two weeks to confirm the content of the meeting, or at least a sanitized version of it, in a vague letter to Sirica dated December 27, 1973.[20] The meeting was divulged only decades later when the WSPF's files were released to the public.

It was not remarkable at the time for prosecutors to communicate with judges about their availability to handle pending cases. In many courts, judges were not assigned cases randomly; prosecutors frequently selected the judges to hear their cases. Nevertheless, it is difficult to see what purpose was served by giving the chief judge vague information about indictments expected to be filed months later, which was the sole responsibility of the prosecutor and grand jury. But in fact, there is an explanation—namely, the career aspirations of Judge Sirica. One of the upcoming indictments and trials discussed at the meeting was the anticipated prosecution of former senior aides to Nixon. The date of the indictment was particularly important.

The chief judge of a district, who is the only person with the authority to assign a case to an individual judge, must retire on his seventieth birthday. Sirica would turn seventy on March 19, 1974. It was in the interests of the prosecutor that Sirica—a hard-nosed judge whose views on the case were well known—preside. A trial judge makes many rulings on the admissibility of evidence, the permissible scope of cross-examination, and other matters, in addition to ruling on the content of the law, such as in instructions to the jury. The court of appeals reviews the trial judge's rulings of the former type, but only for an abuse of discretion. This gives the trial judge considerable leeway, and reversal on those grounds is relatively rare.[21] It was also no secret that Sirica, who had gloried in his role as presiding judge in the burglars' trial, wanted to preside over the next trial in the Watergate saga, which involved John Mitchell, H. R. Haldeman, and John Ehrlichman, who were once three of the most powerful men in Washington and who, not incidentally, Sirica had already publicly fingered as the ringleaders of the Watergate conspiracy.

PART III
1974—Days of Reckoning

The House Impeachment Committee Gears Up

To start the new year, a prominent and seasoned attorney from Boston, James D. St. Clair, was brought into the White House to head the Watergate legal team, and Wright returned to the University of Texas. As a young lawyer in the 1950s, St. Clair, a registered Republican, had been a staff assistant to Joseph N. Welch, the U.S. Army's counsel in the Joseph McCarthy hearings. He was now a respected senior partner at Hale and Dorr, a large Boston law firm. According to some, his credentials were "impeccable."[1] St. Clair had been hired at the recommendation of Charles Colson, whom he had represented. It is not known whether St. Clair had any prior experience with the criminal law. Like Haig himself and Buzhardt, St. Clair was unacquainted with the details of Watergate. Also, with the loss of Wright, Nixon had no constitutional scholar to deal with issues such as the separation of powers and presidential impeachment. Nevertheless, Nixon's defense was now run by a seasoned litigator rather than a professor or a bureaucrat.

Woodward and Bernstein's notes of their interview of St. Clair after Nixon's resignation read: "Things were in shambles, but not because of the lawyers. The reasons weren't fully understood. It was out of control. Haig said that a good trial att[orney] was needed."[2] Presumably, Nixon's new lead attorney was someone whose creed was "take no prisoners."[3] However, as events proceeded, it became clear that St. Clair's approach was far tamer. Moreover, although he lacked Haldeman's political skills, Haig, like Haldeman before him, controlled access to Nixon, and that included St. Clair.[4]

Nixon's strategy was to "stonewall" the opposition, a term he used to instruct his aides.[5] Dean described it: "The 'stonewall' strategy functioned from the very first episodes of the cover-up. It was instinctive, from the very top of the Administration to the bottom."[6] Delay, the standard approach taken by prospective defendants, was also integral to the White House strategy. It was often accompanied by a lack of respect for others, which antagonized people, including the special prosecutor.[7]

The first two months of 1974 were relatively quiet as far as the public was concerned. The Senate Watergate Committee continued to investigate and hold hearings, but on matters that did not capture the public's attention, such as unlawful campaign contributions, the Responsiveness Program (used to reward friends and punish foes), and dirty tricks by Republicans to influence the Democrats' choice of a nominee to oppose Nixon in 1972. The Watergate Special Prosecution Force accepted guilty pleas from Herbert (Bart) Porter, Egil (Bud) Krogh, and Herbert Kalmbach.

Meanwhile, John Doar hired some one hundred people to work for him on impeachment, including more than forty lawyers, most of whom were fresh out of law school. One was a young Hillary Rodham, a recent graduate of Yale Law School. The staff also included few experienced members, such as Bernard W. Nussbaum, a former assistant U.S. attorney from the Southern District of New York.[8] Other than Nussbaum, few if any of the lawyers had any trial experience, in part because of Doar's decision not to go to court to enforce a subpoena or for any other reason.[9] There were no investigators on the staff because the House Impeachment Committee did not intend to conduct field investigations. Unusually and dubiously, Doar frequently consulted old associates who had no official connection to the committee, such as Burke Marshall, former assistant attorney general in charge of the Civil Rights Division and Doar's former boss in the Department of Justice.[10] The House Impeachment Committee was staffed and ready to proceed by January 1974, although there was little outward sign of activity. Albert E. Jenner Jr., the Republicans' counsel, did little to assist the Republican cause and ended up allied with the Democrats. For example, Jenner refused to prepare a Republican version of the articles of impeachment. In fact, he later made such an impassioned speech in favor of impeachment that it brought tears to the eyes of Chairman Rodino.[11] The Republicans later removed Jenner after he seconded Doar's motion for impeachment.[12] The White House apparently had no involvement in Jenner's appointment and no contact with him once he was appointed. This was a lost opportunity and a sharp contrast to attitudes in early February 1973, when Dean told Haldeman that the identity of the minority counsel was unimportant and they needed a "real tiger."[13] Even Nixon was involved in discussions about the Republican staff.[14]

There was no major Watergate news from the White House in early 1974, other than Nixon's statement on January 30 as part of his State of the Union address that "one year of Watergate is enough." However, the White House staff did nothing, either publicly or privately, to bring the Watergate investigations to a conclusion. No one would suggest that Haig and St. Clair should have blindly followed every word of their president, but one can say with near certainty that Nixon's plea for resolution was ignored.

With the House of Representatives proceeding with its impeachment inquiry against Nixon, the WSPF addressed on how it could assist. Its efforts raised serious questions about the power and legality of the executive branch WSPF helping with a congressional impeachment, but there was little discussion of that issue. Deputy Special Prosecutor Ruth and House Counsel Doar were friends and neighbors, and they were in regular communication with each other.

The House authorized the impeachment investigation on November 17, 1973, and its self-imposed deadline for delivering articles of impeachment to the full House of Representatives or for recommending against impeachment was the end of April 1974.[15] Under the same schedule, it should have begun its hearings around February 22, 1973, three months after the committee was formed, and finished them three months later, which was also the schedule maintained by the Senate Watergate Committee. In fact, the Impeachment Committee did not *commence* its hearings until late May.

In addition to adhering to the original schedule, Nixon had good arguments for an early resolution of his impeachment, which was clearly impeding his work as president. It had been more than a year and a half since the burglars were arrested, and their trial was over. In addition, the Senate Watergate Committee had presented its evidence, and its records were available.

No one knows how Nixon would have reacted to the suggestion that he press for a quick resolution. It was not a common tactic at the time, but Nixon was frustrated by the slow pace of the investigations, and his memoirs suggest he might have been receptive. He described his state of mind in October

1973: "It had been four and a half months since Haldeman resigned; four months since Cox was named. Nothing had been resolved. The investigations dragged on."[16] Likewise, no one knows how the Impeachment Committee, the public, or the media would have reacted to a White House campaign for the immediate commencement of impeachment proceedings. There was no push by Haig, St. Clair, or anyone else for quick action. At no time does it appear that Nixon's lawyers considered whether it was in Nixon's interest to demand an early resolution.

Obviously, Nixon did not control either the WSPF or the House Impeachment (Judiciary) Committee, the two entities investigating Watergate. But that is not to say that he lacked the ability to affect the pace of their investigations, particularly the one conducted by the House committee, which was far more important to him. Nixon had allies on the Impeachment Committee, but even those members who were just leaning in his direction or were uncommitted could have been convinced that Nixon and the country deserved a rapid resolution. In fact, many liberal Democrats were anxious to proceed and said so publicly.

Matters would have worked out very differently for Nixon if the House Impeachment Committee had been pressed to hold hearings in February or even March 1974, before it received and digested the evidence.

The WSPF Indictments and "Road Map" for Impeachment

Behind closed doors, the WSPF was very busy preparing a number of indictments—including ones involving campaign finance violations, the conspiracy to deprive Daniel Ellsberg of his rights, the work of Donald Segretti and the other perpetrators of "dirty tricks," and milk producers' efforts to raise the price of milk by making large political contributions. However, the leading case by far was the one being prepared against Mitchell, Haldeman, and Ehrlichman and their alleged obstruction of justice and perjury.

James F. Neal, a former prosecutor from Nashville, Tennessee, headed the team assigned to the cover-up trial. Assisting him were young lawyers Richard Ben-Veniste, George Frampton Jr., Peter Kreindler, and several others. Because of the demands of his private practice, Neal could not spend all his time on Watergate. As a result, his colleagues on the WSPF performed critical tasks such as writing legal memoranda, interviewing witnesses, managing the tape recordings they had (and litigating for more), and even preparing proposed jury instructions months before the trial.

Nothing was more important, however, than reviewing the extensive grand jury testimony and organizing it into a coherent narrative. That was Frampton's job, and he prepared several versions of the document before finishing an important draft in mid-January. The purpose of the document was to assist in presenting evidence to the grand jury and the trial jury, and it was a partisan exposition designed for the prosecutors. Since it was an internal document, there were no restrictions on its bias or bravado.

The WSPF also carefully reviewed the public record, including the hearings of the Senate Watergate Committee. Frampton along with Ben-Veniste prepared a "road map" (in addition to creating a trial book for themselves) of President Nixon's alleged misdeeds for the purpose of assisting the House Impeachment Committee in performing a constitutional duty conspicuously assigned to it alone (although the chief justice of the Supreme Court was designated to preside at the trial of a president). After referring to the "plight" of the House Impeachment Committee and its need "to have the significance of the evidence spelled out for them in neon lights," the two WSPF lawyers set about drafting "a report to the Judiciary Committee that not only transmitted evidence but summarized and commented on it." Part of that report would be a "road map" presenting "evidence to the House Judiciary Committee."[17]

Frampton and Ben-Veniste showed their product to Deputy Special Prosecutor Henry Ruth, who approved it.[18] Assisting the impeachment inquiry became a major concern of the WSPF. In fact, Ruth considered it their "duty" to assist the House impeachment effort.[19] The WSPF, which was part of the executive branch, had prepared a crucial document for the legislative branch to use in a proceeding to impeach the president. Frampton finished his 131-page draft and gave copies to Jaworski and several of his top staff on February 7. It unabashedly favored Nixon's impeachment.[20]

The relationship between Jaworski and his staff, selected by his predecessor Cox, was marked by mutual suspicion, although Jaworski's failure to add anyone from Texas and his statements to the staff seemed to be salutary. The staff was willing to give Jaworski the benefit of the doubt, and they were able to work together effectively.[21]

Jaworski and Sirica Converse—Alone

On January 21, 1974, WSPF's in-house counsel Philip Lacovara, a brilliant and highly professional attorney, sent a memorandum to Jaworski that discussed transmitting material to the House Impeachment Committee through an interim grand jury report. The memorandum reached two significant conclusions. First, the grand jury should be informed that it could not or should not indict Nixon, who was a sitting president. Second, Lacovara agreed with another WSPF staff member, Peter Kreindler, who had prepared a memorandum about "advising the grand jury that it may return a presentment setting forth its views on the President's complicity, [and that] . . . submission of such a presentation by the grand jury would be constitutional." Lacovara's internal memorandum set out how to deal with the grand jury:

[The grand jury] should candidly be told that it is not certain how the court would respond to the submission of a presentation but should be advised that this matter will be discussed with the chief judge [Sirica]. . . .
3. If the grand jury indicates its tendency toward returning a presentment, we should schedule a conference with Chief Judge Sirica to apprise him in advance of this possible development. I would be prepared to submit a memorandum of law to him at such a meeting, if he indicated an interest in receiving it.
4. At any such meeting we should recommend that the presentment be received by him under seal, with disclosure only of the fact that the grand jury has made a submission to him, and that the White House be given ten days to review the presentment and to make objections to its filing and transmission.[22]

The memorandum was vague on the nature of the proposed conference with Sirica, and it did not discuss whether the defendants would see the "memorandum of law." Lacovara contemplated granting the White House access to the presentment at some early point, when it would have an opportunity to challenge the transmission. Copies of the memorandum were sent to Jaworski's deputy Ruth and to Kreindler and Ben-Veniste on the Watergate cover-up task force. As it turned out, the WSPF never showed Nixon's lawyers the road map or the grand jury transcripts, at least not before the trial in *U.S. v. Mitchell*. The House Impeachment Committee also denied St. Clair's request to see them.[23]

It was understood that the WSPF needed the cooperation of Judge Sirica to transmit any grand jury minutes and other legally secret material to the

House of Representatives. The WSPF apparently never believed it had the right or the power to deliver a report directly to the House Impeachment Committee, although it never articulated why the judicial branch's approval was needed to send material to the legislative branch.

Two issues concerned both Jaworski and Sirica—the judicial assignment of the cover-up case, and the transmittal of grand jury material and prosecutorial know-how to the House of Representatives. A federal prosecution in New York City of John Mitchell, Maurice Stans, and financier Robert Vesco for an unrelated offense which was filed in May 1973, was slowing down the process, and time was growing short. The cover-up prosecutors wanted the jury in the New York case to be sequestered before making their indictment public to avoid prejudicing those jurors.

The first known meeting between the WSPF and Sirica occurred on December 14, 1973. It is clear that this was not the last private meeting between Jaworski and Sirica without the opposition being present or notified. On February 11, 1974, the two met privately.[24] After that meeting, Jaworski drafted a confidential memorandum for placement in a special file (with no indication that anyone received copies). The memorandum remained secret for decades, until the government received it along with other documents from Jaworski's home in Texas after his death.

"On Monday, February 11," Jaworski wrote, "I met with the Judge at which time several matters were covered as we sat alone in the jury room. He again indicated that provided the indictment came down in time he would take the Watergate Case. . . . He expressed the opinion that these indictments should be returned as soon as possible."[25] Sirica was injecting himself into the exclusive domain of the prosecutor and the grand jury and secretly advising the WSPF when and how to file documents with the court to obtain maximum advantage. This was clearly improper and contrary to the codes that governed judicial conduct.

Jaworski's memorandum indicates that Sirica expressed some concern about the propriety of the WSPF's plan to have the grand jury file a report or presentment concerning the president of the United States. So Sirica privately counseled Jaworski on how to draft the presentment to ensure Sirica's cooperation in transmitting it to the House Impeachment Committee. He suggested that Jaworski should not urge the impeachment of Nixon but should merely recite the facts in a straightforward manner, with references to transcripts of grand jury testimony or other exhibits. The first half of the memorandum covered Sirica's reservations and advice and revealed that he considered the problem "very touchy" and warned that it might generate a negative public reaction:

> The judge commented upon the status of matters before the grand jury which led into further comments on the possibility of the grand jury considering some type of special report or presentment. The judge considered this a very touchy problem and cautioned as to what the public's reaction would be to a grand jury stepping out with something beyond its normal bounds. He cautioned that the whole effort could be tainted by something irresponsibly done by the grand jury. He stated that the public would rightfully conclude that the entire proceeding had not been judicious but simply one of wanting to hurt the President. He further said it was not the function of the grand jury but of the House Impeachment Committee to express itself on that point.

Sirica all but said that such an analysis by the prosecutor was highly questionable, if not illegal and improper. It was the job of Congress, not the grand jury, to review the law, but if the details were kept from the public, it might squeak by. Jaworski continued:

> He [Sirica] then told me that in the event I observed anything along that line being considered he thought it would be appropriate for him to meet with the grand jury *in camera*. I expressed the belief that it was appropriate for the grand jury to refer to having in its possession evidence that it believed to be material and relevant to the court to be referred to the House Committee for that purpose. He countered by stating that he believed he should be informed of the discretion that he could exercise in matters of that kind and further requested that I have a memorandum for him that covers this subject. I agreed to have this done.[26]

Sirica wanted Jaworski to spell out the extent of his powers, presumably so that he could protect himself. Although it seems clear that Sirica secretly received a copy of Lacovara's January 21 memorandum before March 1, the judge wrote in his memoirs that, as of March 1, "I had not studied the question of whether the grand jury's evidence could properly be sent to Congress."[27]

There is no doubt that this meeting took place and that Jaworski's memorandum was authentic—it contains Jaworski's handwriting. The memorandum was not in the usual format of WSPF documents with addresses, headings, and the like. It was a draft, and no other version has been found.

This suggests either that the subject matter was too sensitive to reduce to a formal memorandum or that any later versions were destroyed.

While Jaworski apparently did not inform his staff that he had discussed the matter with Sirica, he conveyed the judge's views to them. "Jaworski seemed convinced Sirica wouldn't accept a report that was accusatory of the President," members of the WSPF wrote later.[28]

Frampton rewrote what became the road map. Although it did not explicitly characterize the relevant conduct, it described that conduct and included page references relevant to grand jury testimony accompanied the road map. Typical of the statements in the memorandum are those referring to the collection of hush money:

33. On or about June 28, 1972, H. R. Haldeman and John Ehrlichman approved the use of Herbert Kalmbach to raise and distribute covert cash funds to and for the benefit of those involved in the Watergate break-in. . . .

38. In or about early December 1972 and early January 1973, H. R. Haldeman approved the transfer of money from a secret White House cash fund of $350,000 to be used for the payment to and for the benefit of the Watergate defendants.[29]

Although Jaworski apparently provided Lacovara's memorandum to Sirica at one of their *ex parte* meetings, it is virtually certain that neither the defendants in *U.S. v. Mitchell* nor the White House ever saw or knew about that memorandum. The White House would not have seen the memorandum because Nixon did not object to the transfer of materials to the House. Defendants in *U.S. v. Mitchell* would not have seen the memorandum because their objections to the transfer were very different from what Nixon's would have been. On March 18 Sirica denied the defendants' motion to prevent the House Impeachment Committee from receiving the roadmap on the grounds that, simply put, the transfer of materials had nothing to do with them and that any complaint they had could be dealt with at their trial. Sirica wrote:

The only individuals who object to such an order are defendants in the United States v. Mitchell et al. case currently pending in this court. Their standing is dubious at best given the already stated facts that (1) their mention in the Report is incidental, (2) their trial will provide ample opportunity for response to such references, none of which go beyond allegations in the indictment, and (3) considerations of possible adverse publicity are both premature and speculative.[30]

When Jaworski resigned as special prosecutor in October 1974, he took some WSPF papers (documents belonging to the U.S. government) with him.

He died in 1982. His memorandum regarding the February 11 meeting was found in his former home in 2018 and given to the National Archives. Prior to 2018, Henry Ruth, Jaworski's deputy and successor, told the Nixon Presidential Library that Jaworski had removed some papers. There were other indications that Jaworski had retained certain government documents, which the National Archives retrieved and placed where they belonged.[31] Thus, some important records were not stored in the National Archives until decades later.

Although the meetings with Sirica remained secret, Jaworski hinted about his *ex parte* activities as early as December 1974, when he told Woodward and Bernstein in an interview that "there are a lot of one-on-one conversations that nobody knows about but him and the other party."[32] This was a remarkable statement to make to reporters in the middle of *U.S. v. Mitchell*, over which Sirica presided and which did not end until January 1, 1975. There were a limited number of individuals to whom the statement could refer: Sirica and Jaworski, Rodino and Jaworski, and Doar and Jaworski. There is no indication that Woodward and Bernstein attempted to follow up on St. Clair's statement.

Jaworski's *public* accounts of his knowledge of WSPF activities were different and incomplete, to say the least. His 1975 book states: "I met with Judge Sirica at 10:30 the next morning in his chambers to go over the agenda."[33] He said nothing more, and the meeting remained off the record until decades later.

For his part, Sirica falsely stated: "Jaworski had a number of problems, and I had no idea just how he would deal with them. First, he had to make his own judgment about evidence on the tapes. . . . I couldn't know how Jaworski would view that evidence."[34] Sirica's book made no mention of any *ex parte* meetings. An examination of Sirica's papers at the Library of Congress revealed nothing on the subject, such as evidence of oral or written *ex parte* contacts with Jaworski. Missing from Sirica's correspondence file was a copy of Jaworski's letter dated December 29, 1973. To guide his conduct, Sirica preferred a memorandum prepared by the WSPF to one prepared by his law clerk (for one thing, it kept his clerk in the dark), but an examination of Sirica's files at the Library of Congress did not uncover that memorandum.

In short, in 1974 the nature and extent of the Jaworski-Sirica meetings have long been concealed from the White House and the public. The facts began to dribble out only in 2013.[35]

The WSPF Prosecutions

The mutual accommodation between Sirica and Jaworski simultaneously resolved another problem that did not directly concern President Nixon and his threatened impeachment but was nevertheless of enormous importance. Both Jaworski and Sirica were anxious for Sirica to preside over the prosecution of Nixon's former top lieutenants John Mitchell, H. R. Haldeman, and John Ehrlichman.

Sirica had hoisted his reputation on the proposition that Howard Hunt and G. Gordon Liddy were far below the pinnacle of culpable people, and he did not want to be proved wrong. Jaworski wanted the malleable and sympathetic Sirica to preside over the cover-up trial. Many of the issues the trial judge would have to decide were indisputably difficult, such as the admissibility of those Nixon tapes when no one present at the the convention could testify that the tapes accurately reflected the conversations that took place. There were numerous other issues involving the tapes, including the jury's ability to see transcripts prepared by the prosecution over defense objections that the transcripts were not accurate. The transcripts were important largely because many of the tapes were difficult to decipher, and the jury generally listened to a tape only once, unlike the prosecutors and the transcribers. Another tricky issue was the breadth of the evidence the WSPF could introduce, such as evidence of the break-in at Dr. Fielding's office. Sirica allowed the WSPF to use that incident against Ehrlichman, over objections that it was unfairly prejudicial.[36]

The timetable for ensuring that Sirica would preside over the cover-up trial was tight. Sirica would turn seventy (mandatory retirement age) on March 19, 1974, at which point he would no longer be chief judge and could not assign cases. Sirica had presided over the initial break-in prosecutions by exercising the chief judge's prerogative to assign the case to himself. Reaching the desired result required speed, and Sirica made sure Jaworski understood that. The new indictment had to be returned before he stepped down as chief judge.

Jaworski addressed the grand jury, which voted to file the indictment the WSPF had prepared, without Nixon as a defendant. The grand jury, which was unusually competant, independent, and aggressive, initially wanted to indict Nixon along with his aides, but Jaworski had decided that it could not and should not do that. The grand jury then wanted to name Nixon as an unindicted coconspirator, but Jaworski vetoed that course of action as unfair, largely because Nixon had no means to respond, and it could cause harm to the country. Ultimately, the grand jury voted to make Nixon an unindicted coconspirator but to keep that information confidential for the time being, leaving it in the hands of Jaworski. Coached by Jaworski, the grand jury authorized the WSPF to transmit a narrative of the testimony against Nixon, along with portions of the grand jury minutes, Nixon tapes, and other exhibits, to the House Impeachment Committee.[37]

Prosecutors Share Secret Grand Jury Material with the House

The WSPF did not wait for Judge Sirica's authorization to show its evidence to the House Impeachment Committee. As noted earlier, John Doar, counsel to the committee, and Henry Ruth, deputy special prosecutor, were friends. The gardens of their homes in Washington abutted each other, and Doar was a frequent dinner guest at Ruth's home. Based on the brief discussion of the subject during Ruth's 2011 interview conducted by the Nixon Presidential Library, Doar was apparently a regular visitor to WSPF offices as well, although that was not clearly spelled out. Ruth did not provide dates, but he admitted that he invited Doar to review the evidence the WSPF had developed. Ruth was asked whether Doar saw confidential grand jury minutes before the date of Sirica's order permitting it, and he responded, "I believe so."[38] Ruth acknowledged that the WSPF showed Doar the road map, which was based on grand jury testimony, while Frampton and Ben-Veniste were still working on it, which was February 1974 at the latest, since the WSPF gave the road map and exhibits to Sirica for transmission to the House Impeachment Committee on March 1. Arguably, Ruth and Doar committed a federal crime prohibited by Rule 6(e) of the Federal Rules of Criminal Procedure. The interviewer asked Ruth no follow-up questions about Doar's access to WSPF work product, secret grand jury minutes, or agreements involving the WSPF. An agreement that the WSPF would give its evidence to the House of

Representatives may have been the reason the Impeachment Committee did not hire investigators, although that is conjecture.

On February 25, 1974, the House Impeachment Committee first requested tapes from the White House, which was about the time the committee's hearings were supposed to start under the original plan. Early on, Rodino and Doar decided that the committee would not go to court to enforce subpoenas or for any other reason.[39] That decision, which surrendered a possible weapon against the White House, made the WSPF's voluntary cooperation all the more important.

Confirmation of these disclosures is contained in a book about the House Impeachment Committee by journalist Howard Fields, although he apparently did not appreciate the significance of what he wrote: "Drawing on Senate Watergate testimony, *grand jury transcripts, and suggestions from Jaworski,* Doar's staff had prepared a list of items it would request of the White House.... A five-page letter was drafted during the weekend and presented to Rodino and Hutchinson the following Monday, February 25."[40] The WSPF formally gave the grand jury minutes to Judge Sirica on March 1, and he did not authorize transmission to the House Impeachment Committee until March 18.

That action was contrary to the legal advice of WSPF counsel Philip Lacovara, who was responsible for addressing legal questions such as proper access to the work of the WSPF and the grand jury. It was also contrary to what the WSPF said publicly in February 1974. That month, Jaworski appeared on the nationally televised program *Issues and Answers.* His book quotes generously from a transcript of his statements on that program, including the following exchange, in which Jaworski concealed the relationship between the WSPF and the House Impeachment Committee:

David Shoumacher: Mr. Jaworski, to move to the other side of the Hill, have you decided how you will react if confronted with a subpoena from the House Judiciary Committee in its impeachment investigation on producing information you have?
Leon Jaworski: That is a matter for the court. That is a matter for Judge Sirica. Obviously, I don't face a dilemma. I have only one possible course that I can follow and that is to hold the evidence secret for the time being. That is all grand jury evidence.
Sam Donaldson: .... Are you telling us that you see no way for a voluntary turning over of relevant material to the House Judiciary Committee by you?

Jaworski: I see none at this time. . . . It is my obligation to contest [a subpoena], because these matters are now cloaked in secrecy in the grand jury and I have no right to release them. . . . I would be breaking an absolute rule of law if I were to do it. . . .

Donaldson: . . . . Would you entertain the idea of going to Judge Sirica along with Messrs. Doar and Jenner, the Special Counsel for the Judiciary investigation, and ask for that type of order?

Jaworski: I would not.[41]

Washington Post editor Barry Sussman wrote an excellent book, published in late 1974, which indicates that the intimate relationship between the WSPF and the House Impeachment Committee was not common knowledge. Ignorant of what was transpiring, he wrote:

But the [impeachment] committee could not count on receiving material from the special prosecutor's office, especially anything that had been the subject of grand jury deliberations, as Jaworski said he did not have the authority to release confidential grand jury records. So the Rodino Committee, now a true impeachment panel with a more solemn responsibility than any congressional committee in the hundred years since an earlier President had been impeached, was being denied material to conduct its inquiry properly.[42]

The WSPF and the House Impeachment Committee were performing a charade for the public. Sussman's book continued: "Doar asked St. Clair to submit to him at least the same documents, including tapes, that had been given to the Special Prosecutor, and he set early March for the answer, threatening a congressional subpoena for failure to comply."[43]

Led by Doar, who appeared to have the full backing of Chairman Rodino, the House committee was methodically organizing material it was receiving from other investigations (although the WSPF had done much of the work). Doar was bent on taking a nonpartisan approach that involved collecting information and presenting it as neutrally as possible to committee members and the public. He stressed that the committee was not a prosecutor; it was not partisan; it was not attempting to convince anybody. Doar instructed the staff to refrain from contact with others. At his insistence, the staff remained isolated and insulated from the outside world.[44] He considered that posture essential to gain the support of Republicans and southern Democrats, who were wary of impeaching Nixon. Matters would have proceeded differently had the relationship between Doar and Ruth been known,

The slow progress continued to disturb some of the younger Democrats on the committee, who became known as "bomb throwers."[45] They—and many others who were not members of Congress—wanted an aggressive prosecutor, not a neutral presenter of both sides of the story. They also wanted to vote on the impeachment of President Nixon. It appeared, however, that Rodino would give Doar all the time he needed.

Meanwhile, the White House announced that it would no longer voluntarily supply documents to the Impeachment Committee or to the WSPF.[46] More importantly, the White House lawyers remained strictly limited in terms of what they could do to investigate the facts. Haig wrote about what happened on May 6, 1974, before public hearings of the Impeachment Committee, after Nixon listened to the June 23, 1972, tapes: "'No one is to listen to these tapes,' he [Nixon] said. 'No one—understand, Al? Not the lawyers. No one. Lock them up.'" Haig did as he was told and locked up the tapes.[47] Haig would enforce Nixon's policy of stonewalling, which included the very people who were supposed to defend the president.

Cover-up Indictment and Transmission of a "Road Map"

On March 1, 1974, before a full and attentive courtroom, Judge Sirica unsealed the indictment of Mitchell, Haldeman, Ehrlichman, and several others for crimes involving the cover-up of the Watergate break-in, including conspiracy, obstruction of justice, and perjury.[1] The allegations covered hush-money payments to the burglars and the false statement Haldeman attributed to Nixon (claiming the president said that although raising the $1 million to pay the burglars would be no problem, "it would be wrong"). An overt act alleged in the conspiracy count of the indictment was that within hours of Nixon's March 21, 1973, conversation with Dean, the White House and its agents paid $75,000 to the burglars to remain silent.

The lengthy conspiracy count told the story of the cover-up. (Because the indictment was filed before the release of the June 23, 1972, tapes, the language with respect to those conversations was limited and vague.) Just about everyone recognized that the indictment would include the three major figures in the Nixon administration: Mitchell, Haldeman, and Ehrlichman. Others included Charles Colson; Gordon Strachan, an aide to Haldeman; and Kenneth Parkinson, a workmanlike criminal lawyer who played a narrow and marginal role as counsel to the Committee to Re-elect the President (CRP) after the burglars' arrests. Howard Hunt's lawyer William O. Bittman, a graduate of Robert Kennedy's Justice Department and a partner in a prestigious Washington firm, was not prosecuted. There was disagreement within the WSPF over the decisions to omit Bittman and to include Parkinson and Colson.[2]

The great majority of the people indicted were lawyers. The plethora of lawyers who participated in the cover-up has often been noted. Paul O'Brien, another lawyer who represented the CRP, may have escaped indictment because the U.S. Attorney's Office had granted him immunity early in its investigation. Alfred Baldwin, who monitored the bugging across the street from the Watergate Office Building, had the same result.

Jaworski told Sirica that due to the length of the trial, the WSPF recommended "that the case should be specially assigned. In his book, Jaworski wrote: "This meant that Sirica as Chief Judge could assign the case to any of the judges, including himself; later that day he assigned the case to himself."[3]

Along with its indictment, the grand jury simultaniously presented to Sirica a separate "report" in a bulging and locked briefcase and recommended that the report be transmitted to the House Judiciary (Impeachment) Committee. The contents of the briefcase were not otherwise identified by the grand jury or the prosecutors.[4] Sirica took custody of the briefcase and its contents. Impeachment committee member Edward Mezvinsky later wrote, "We knew a lot about the briefcase itself. But we knew nothing about its contents."[5] Journalist Elizabeth Drew wrote in the *New Yorker* magazine: "the speculation was that it contained information about President Nixon and was intended for the House Judiciary Committee."[6]

Knowledge of the contents of the briefcase was sparse on March 1 and in the following weeks. The WSPF said only that it was a "report." (The term "road map" was not used publicly at first.) There was no mention that the briefcase contained seven White House tapes, and there was no information about whether the exhibits included raw, verbatim grand jury testimony or paraphrases.[7] Thus, the actual transmission of the report to Judge Sirica was accomplished on March 1 with minimal disclosure to the White House or the public regarding exactly what was happening. Moreover, contrary to Lacovara's recommendation, the White House did not get to see the material. In fact, prosecutors hoped Sirica would turn the report over to the House Impeachment Committee without permitting a challenge, especially one lodged by President Nixon. Indeed, the prosecutors later said they wanted the judge to "zip" the report to the committee.[8]

The Defendants Try to Bar Transmission of the "Road Map"

Whatever the wishes of the WSPF, Judge Sirica invited the defendants in *U.S. v. Mitchell* and other interested parties to challenge the transfer of the report and briefcase containing tapes and selected portions of the grand jury minutes to the Impeachment Committee.[9] Several defendants, including Haldeman and Strachan, filed a motion asserting that if the House Impeachment Committee publicized the materials on the eve of the cover-up trial, it would prejudice the jury.[10] Indeed, the argument to prevent transmission was not based on the impropriety of the WSPF turning over the material to the Impeachment Committee. The defendants had no basis for objecting to the transfer, as none of them was the subject of impeachment. Nothing was filed on Nixon's behalf.

Sirica held a hearing on the defendants' motion. Sensing that something was wrong, Haldeman's attorney John J. Wilson wrote to Sirica on March 12, 1974 (and sent copies to all the other counsel), and asked:

Would you be willing to inform us whether you were consulted by or conferred with the prosecutors, the Grand Jury, or the foreman or other member thereof, regarding the report which the Grand Jury presented to you in open court on March 1, 1974, before such report was actually presented, or that you had notice of the Grand Jury's intention to present such a report prior to its actually doing so?[11]

Sirica simply ignored the letter. So did Jaworski. Wilson did not follow up, and it is unclear why he did not object. It may have had something to do with his long friendship with Sirica and his reluctance to think badly of him. Or perhaps Wilson recognized that he was unlikely to get any satisfaction and that pursuing the effort could be counterproductive in terms of securing the best result for his client, a valid concern. In fact, Wilson had no way of forcing Sirica to answer the letter.

On March 18, 1974, his last day as chief judge, Sirica denied the defendants' motion regarding the transfer of the report. After a short review of the history of grand jury presentments in England and in the United States, Sirica concluded, "On this historical basis, with reliance as well upon principles of sound public policy, a number of federal courts have upheld and defined the general scope of grand jury reportorial prerogatives." It was a defensible decision, although the authorities were divided. He continued:

Having considered the cases and historical precedents, and noting the absence of a contrary rule in this Circuit, it seems to the Court that it would be unjustified in holding that the Grand Jury was without authority to hand up this Report. The Grand Jury has obviously taken care to assure that its Report contains no objectionable features, and has thoroughly acted in the interests of fairness. The Grand Jury having thus respected its own limitations and the rights of others, the Court ought to respect the Jury's exercise of its prerogatives.[12]

Sirica's analysis was flawed. He wrongly concluded that the grand jury's judgment should not be questioned. Having found that the "report [was] clearly within the bounds of propriety," he saw no reason not to bow to the wishes of the grand jury and give the report to the House Impeachment Committee. At the very least, he was starting with the presumption that the transfer was proper. (So much for the Constitution and the courts' authority to decide what the law is; a grand jury decision is not entitled to any deference when there is a constitutional challenge.[13]) Sirica basically construed Rule 6(e) of the Federal Rules of Criminal Procedure as codifying common law as he saw it, and there was a "judicial proceeding," i.e., *U.S. v. Mitchell*, as required.[14]

Sirica's conclusion was based not on what the law provided but in part on what he thought made good sense: "Finally, it seems incredible," he observed, "that grand jury matters should lawfully be available to disbarment committees and police disciplinary investigations and yet be unavailable in a proceeding of so great import as an impeachment investigation. . . . Principles of grand jury secrecy do not bar this disclosure." This is not a judge construing a law written by a legislature but a judge expressing a policy preference, which is not within his province. His assertions certainly cannot be found among the axioms of statutory construction and their application to Rule 6(e).

The Case Goes to the Court of Appeals

Haldeman and Strachan filed a petition for a writ of mandamus in the U.S. Court of Appeals for the District of Columbia Circuit to prevent Sirica from turning over the grand jury material and analysis to the House Impeachment Committee. The court, sitting *en banc*, heard arguments on March 21, 1974, three days after Sirica's decision. Presumably, all the active judges on the court sat for this case because of its importance and sensitivity, although the court did not cite the rule applicable to *en banc* hearings or provide its reasoning for this unusual procedure.[15] Significantly, the court made its decision the *same day* it received the case. The court did not explain its rush to decide a question that involved the trial of some of the most prominent people in the United States, which was still six months down the road. Given its haste, the court could not possibly have researched with any thoroughness the legal issues and barely gave them a nod. "We are in general agreement with his [Sirica's view] of these matters, and we feel no necessity to expand his discussion," the court stated.[16]

One possible reason (or excuse) for the appeals court's cavalier action soon became clear when it all but dismissed the defendants' claim on the basis of an erroneous argument: "We think it of significance that the President of the United States, who is described by all parties as the focus of the report and who presumably would have the greatest interest in its disposition, has interposed no objection to the District Court's action."[17] That comment makes no sense; the rights of each person must be evaluated independently. It would be like saying a tangential defendant who received a short prison sentence could not appeal her conviction because the leading perpetrator did not do so. Moreover, the president's decision was not necessarily based on legal considerations; there was a strong political component (leaving aside incompetence). Finally, a writ of mandamus interrupted the usual process before the trial court and required a virtually unhinged decision. Calling the application "premature," the court dismissed the defendants' claim out of hand:

> We are asked to employ our extraordinary power now primarily because it is said that the District Judge, being the judge who will later try the indictment and who presently has under his control grand jury evidence, which, when and if disclosed publicly, may possibly create a climate of prejudice, in which a fair trial may not be possible, should take no chance in this regard and exercise his discretion in favor of the more cautious course. This claim is obviously, although with[in] the limits of his authority, . . . not sound policy. It almost goes without saying that this is not the kind of abuse of discretion or disregard of law amounting to judicial usurpation for which the extraordinary writs were conceived.[18]

A major part of the problem was that the appeals court was considering the prospect of future prejudice and not a simple constitutional issue. The DC Circuit's opinion also stated: "We cannot be unaware of the fact that the Special Prosecutor has concluded that his interests in successful prosecution can be reconciled with the transmittal for consideration by the impeachment process—thereby suggesting that the dangers in his estimation are not great." This suggested that the asserted views of one party to the dispute were entitled to special weight. (The defendants disagreed with the WSPF, but there was no mention of that.) There is no constitutional basis for giving greater weight to one party's interpretation of the consequences of an action.[19]

Judge George E. MacKinnon, a conservative judge appointed to the DC Circuit by Nixon, concurred in part and dissented in part in the court's decision.[20] "I concur in the implicit finding that the [defendants] have standing to seek the relief here requested," he stated, but he forcefully disagreed with giving the House committee the WSPF's slanted work product:

My view of the record, however, after the limited research permitted by the rapidity with which this court has handled the matter, convinces me that the grand jury has exceeded its authority in releasing (1) the report, (2) the so-called index, and (3) the selective evidence. The process of composing the index and selecting the evidence supporting it necessarily reflects a conscious and focused judgment by the grand jury on the credibility of witnesses and the inferences to be drawn from the totality of evidence presented to it. Moreover, potentially exculpatory material may have been excluded. For these reasons, it is my opinion that the interests of justice would not be better furthered by transmitting this grand jury report and the selective material accompanying it.... I would expunge the entire report and index and permit the House Judiciary Committee ... to have access ... to the entire grand jury proceeding under supervision by the [district] court. It would be better able to pass on credibility without having credibility prejudged for it.[21]

It is significant that MacKinnon was prepared to reverse Sirica based on the claim that publicity flowing from the report's release to the House committee might prejudice the defendants six months later *in a separate trial at which due process existed*. Nixon, who was going to be judged by the House committee and then by the full House and Senate, had a much stronger case, but his claim was not before the court. MacKinnon continued:

At oral argument the prosecutor represented that this disclosure of the grand jury material to the House Judiciary Committee and eventually possibly to the House and Senate is being made "preliminary to [and] in connection with a judicial proceeding," Fed.R.Crim. P. 6(e), in which due process of law will be available [*U.S. v. Mitchell*]. My concurrence in the release of grand jury material has taken this representation into consideration.[22]

MacKinnon seemed to be the only judge who focused on the nature and circumstances of the road map. Moreover, neither the majority nor MacKinnon discussed Nixon's far stronger claim, which did not involve a judicial proceeding accompanied by due process. Finally, all the judges wrote without knowledge of the ongoing *ex parte* Jaworski-Sirica meetings and without seeing the formidable road map and the accompanying grand jury testimony and tapes, which seems incredible in retrospect.[23]

The fifty-five-page road map was the product of an enormous amount of effort, selection, and judgment. It was unquestionably prepared in its entirety by executive branch prosecutors and not by the grand jury itself, as was traditionally the case. Grand jury testimony and other secret grand jury material that supported statements in this so-called road map had been carefully selected, organized, and identified. Though not over the top, the nonargumentative statements in the road map were incriminating—devastatingly so. Jaworski cautiously insisted that the report not be read as a brief urging impeachment,[24] but no one would construe the report and the accompanying exhibits as an impartial recitation of even the one-sided evidence the grand jury heard. Also significant, the WSPF (and grand jury) prepared the road map especially for the House of Representatives.

Nixon, His Team, and the Grand Jury Material

Nixon did not challenge the actions of the WSPF or Sirica in giving the road map, selected portions of the secret grand jury minutes, seven subpoenaed tapes, and numerous other documents to the House Impeachment Committee. On March 26 the committee obtained the material from Sirica. Strangely, three weeks earlier on March 6, Nixon had given the Impeachment Committee copies of nineteen tapes (many more than he had been ordered to turn over to the WSPF), along with other materials the White House had provided to the WSPF after the Saturday Night Massacre, including logs of conversations involving the president. A senior staff member on the House Impeachment Committee described the additional tapes voluntarily provided by the White House as "very powerful" evidence against Nixon.[25] What Nixon later wrote in his memoirs sheds little light on why he did not object to the transfer and indicates that the matter was not carefully considered:

Earlier in the year [1974] Haig told me that Jaworski had reassured him that no one currently in the White House was going to be named by the grand jury—including me. Instead, we thought, he was sending the grand jury material relating to me to Judge Sirica in a sealed report. On March 18 Sirica directed the material be sent to the House Judiciary Committee. He also stated that, contrary to recent leaks, the grand jury's report was only a straightforward compilation of evidence and drew no accusatory conclusions. . . .

The escalating pattern seemed never ending. . . . The House Judiciary Committee would prove no different from the Special Prosecutor in its insatiable demand for tapes and other materials. On March 6 I announced that we would turn over to the committee the materials we had given to the Special Prosecutor; these comprised some nineteen tapes and more that 700 documents.[26]

While the White House was standing firm in not allowing the WSPF to obtain tapes, it was facilitating their transfer to the Impeachment Committee, a much more dangerous and immediate threat. Whether he realized it or not, Nixon was setting a precedent that was potentially devastating to his future as president of the United States. He was all but ensuring his impeachment in the next few months; secret grand jury evidence would be revealed to the House Impeachment Committee and a national television audience.

The Nixon tapes had been the subject of a breathtaking fight between the White House and the WSPF, and Sirica himself had denied the tapes to the Senate Watergate Committee. The court of appeals made it clear that the Impeachment Committee had established no right to the tapes. At the very least, the White House lawyers could have severely impeded the work of the House Impeachment Committee by taking a court challenge all the way to the Supreme Court, but they did not. Perhaps Jaworski's carefully chosen words, claiming that nobody currently in the White House would be indicted, lulled the White House into a false sense of security. There is no good explanation why Nixon gave additional material to the House Impeachment Committee.

Some information is available on the thought processes that led to the White House's abject failure to challenge the transmission of the road map. In *The Final Days*, which describes events occurring in the second half of 1973 through Nixon's resignation on August 9, 1974, Woodward and Bernstein write that St. Clair, who had evidently decided not to attend the March 1 court proceedings or receive a direct report from anyone who had, read in the morning newspaper on March 2 that the grand jury "recommended that the material in the briefcase—tapes, [grand jury] testimony and documents—be forwarded to the House Judiciary Committee." St. Clair studied the indictment, including the overt acts, and mused, "If he [St. Clair] could disentangle his client from what was in that briefcase, he could beat impeachment." *The Final Days* continues:

> He [St. Clair] went to Haig and the President. It was useless to try to prevent the grand jury's report from reaching the House Judiciary Committee, he told them. They agreed. Since the committee would eventually have possession of the evidence, he continued, the White House should give the appearance of cooperation. Accordingly, on March 6, the White House announced it was voluntarily supplying the committee with all information it had turned over to the special prosecutor.[27]

It is not apparent where this account comes from, although there is no reason to disbelieve it. Haig's memoirs (which he did not write until many years later) do not specifically mention the road map, the grand jury minutes, or the events related to their transmission.[28] Nor do they appear in Woodward and Bernstein's notes of their autumn 1974 interview of St. Clair. It is unlikely that St. Clair was familiar with the arcane and complex law of impeachment or knew anything beyond the fundamentals of the separation of powers. It is unclear what St. Clair had to do with presidential public relations (recommending the "appearance of cooperation"), yet that was an important part of his reasoning. In any event, the decision was made not to challenge the transfer of the road map, and the White House chose to hand over additional material to the WSPF (and the Impeachment Committee), as well as the subpoenaed tapes.

St. Clair may have met with Nixon, but the decision to permit the WSPF to turn over its material had been made earlier. St. Clair's contribution consisted of a ratification; had he objected strongly, however, the result might have been different. Also, there is no evidence that this important question was researched or that St. Clair knew of any legal authority for the position he took with the president. In a 2011 interview, Deputy Special Prosecutor Henry Ruth said that White House lawyers told him it was "illegal" for the WSPF to give its work product and secret grand jury minutes to the House Impeachment Committee. Ruth did not say who told him this or when he was told.[29] Ruth, however, claimed it was legal because Judge Sirica had approved the transfer.[30] But that explanation does not hold up. First, Ruth made disclosures to the House Impeachment Committee before Sirica's approval; second, Sirica's decision was subject to review by higher courts, including the unpredictable Supreme Court.

Haig was in charge and wanted little interference. His memoirs read: "On May 5 [1974], a Sunday, Jaworski called for an appointment and came to see me at the White House. We met alone, as usual, in the Map Room while Jim St. Clair and a couple of Jaworski's assistants waited elsewhere."[31] That Haig alone was representing the White House in negotiations with a seasoned lawyer who had immersed himself in the facts of Watergate was preposterous.[32]

One historian wrote, "St. Clair fared as poorly as his predecessors in his access to the President. According to the President's appointments secretary and the logs, he rarely saw Nixon alone. When the two met, Haig was usually present." Haig supervised St. Clair closely and withheld information from him. There is no more glaring of an example than the fact that it was not until late July 1974 that St. Clair did not know that the tape of the crucial June 23, 1972, meetings between Nixon and Haldeman presented a serious potential problem for the president, and St. Clair later admitted that he never discussed the June 23 conversations with Nixon. St. Clair weakly explained: "There was nothing in the record hinting that June 23 was a problem. . . . It's all hindsight to say there was." He was insufficiently close to Nixon to learn the facts from him, and Haig, who had not selected him, apparently chose not to tell him that the June 23 tape could present a problem, so he relied on "the record," whatever that was.[33] In other words, St. Clair had no reliable knowledge what Haig and Jaworski were negotiating about or what the risks were in giving the WSPF additional tapes.

Haig let Jaworski know that he thought Nixon's case was weak.[34] On January 15, 1974, Jaworski wrote a memorandum concerning his discussion with Haig about the March 21, 1973, tape of Dean's meeting with the president: "Haig referred to it as terrible beyond description and was gravely concerned over the contents of the tape as described."[35] Jaworski has been quoted as claiming in mid-February 1974 that St. Clair simply agreed with everything Buzhardt suggested and as saying, "I don't think St. Clair knows what he is supposed to be doing." St. Clair trusted Haig and acknowledged that he "was unduly biased in Haig's favor."[36] St. Clair seemed to accept as gospel whatever Nixon or Haig chose to tell him and did not examine the facts for himself. Rodino called St. Clair a "puppet."[37]

The legal status of President Nixon was radically different from that of Haldeman and Strachan, who were defendants in *U.S. v. Mitchell* and were not the subject of an impeachment inquiry. The power of a federal grand jury to issue a secret report or presentment related to an impeachment inquiry and the significance of Rule 6(e) went to the heart of Nixon's arguments. If a federal grand jury was not permitted to issue such a presentment, Nixon should win a motion to bar the House Impeachment Committee from receiving the grand jury's road map. If Rule 6(e) limited a federal judge's transmission of grand jury minutes to "judicial proceedings," which it did, and if an impeachment inquiry is not a judicial proceeding, which it isn't, Nixon should win. If, as Judge MacKinnon suggested, the separation of powers prohibits the executive branch WSPF from packaging materials and sending them to a congressional impeachment committee, Nixon should win (although it is unclear that an affirmative answer to these inquiries would have helped Haldeman and Strachan). Nixon had a number of colorable arguments, the answers to which were extremely complex. He could have prevailed.[38]

There was another dimension that Nixon and his advisers should have considered—namely, the ability to argue that the impeachment process was unfair and unconstitutional because of the involvement of the executive branch WSPF—even if he was unsuccessful. A contemporary reader needs no reminder that a president's claim of unfairness would resound in Congress and with the American public. But Nixon acquiesced, with the concurrence of his advisers.

Judge Sirica's 1979 book recounted his surprise that Nixon did not challenge the transmission of the road map. He wrote: "Without that assist from the grand jury, I believe the House Committee would have taken months more to reach its decision. Perhaps, without that evidence, the decision would not have been reached."[39] Leon Jaworski's 1976 book recognized that the transmission "was without legal precedent," and he added, "I could not help but wonder what would have been the course of the Committee's labors without the benefit of the report and the evidence it documented."[40] Jaworski told Woodward and Bernstein that if the House Impeachment Committee had not received the report, the committee would have been in a "helleva shape. Indeed, without the report there probably would have been no successful impeachment."[41] Two members of the WSPF who were involved in the prosecution of the cover-up case wrote a year later, "Nixon would have had at least a plausible legal case to block the report."[42] It appears that St. Clair's indefensible failure to object had catastrophic consequences for Nixon.

Fundamental to the issue is that impeachment is the sole responsibility of the legislature, and its use of the road map may have violated the separation of powers. The Constitution does not make the impeachment of a president a joint enterprise of the legislative and executive branches. The Constitution sharply segregates the impeachment process—especially the impeachment of the president of the United States—from other matters. It could even be contended that the judicial branch has no role whatsoever in impeachment proceedings. Challenging the transmission of the report was elementary. As the Supreme Court stated only months later, "The Impeachment Clause may qualify the court's power [to] sanction non-compliance with judicial orders."[43]

St. Clair's advice to Nixon might qualify as some of the worst legal advice ever given to a sitting president. St. Clair was not a constitutional scholar. He apparently concluded off the top of his head that it would be fruitless to challenge the transmission of secret grand jury material and a selective analysis by prosecutors to Congress for use in a presidential impeachment proceeding. St. Clair's concern should not have been appearances ("the White House should give the appearance of cooperation"), and it was probably the wrong advice. Many would regard purported cooperation by the White House as a trick and as evidence of duplicity.

For his part, nonlawyer Haig described his understanding of the matter when he wrote his memoirs decades later: "The argument was made that the [impeachment] committee could not be denied whatever evidence it demanded because it was engaged in an inquiry mandated by the Constitution; executive privilege did not apply. This was an intriguing legal argument, but, as a practical matter, the Committee could issue an Article of Impeachment forthwith if Nixon refused to surrender the forty-two tapes."[44] Haig was equating proof of guilt with a refusal to incriminate oneself based on a colorable constitutional argument in the minds of members of Congress, who may have been searching for less controversial grounds on which to support Nixon.

There was a major difference, however, between Nixon's claiming executive privilege, on the one hand, and revealing the tapes, on the other. It was the difference between an argument based on principle and an attempt to explain away damaging evidence of wrongdoing. The courts might refuse to enforce a subpoena in an impeachment proceeding. But even if Nixon disobeyed a court order, he could claim it was a matter of principle. As a "practical matter" the difference between the two courses of action was enormous. It was something a good lawyer, or even an intelligent nonlawyer, would understand.

Thus, Haig was wrong. He was wrong about the "intriguing legal argument." An impeachment committee cannot overrule the Fifth Amendment privilege against self-incrimination. And the fact that impeachment "is an inquiry mandated by the Constitution" does not mean that an impeachment committee can override all privileges. A trial by jury is also mandated by the Constitution. Finally, *Nixon v. United States*, decided five months later, demonstrated that the question was a difficult one. It is not clear why someone did not pick up the telephone and speak to Professor Charles Alan Wright before the White House capitulated.

The courts rejected the claims of Haldeman and Strachan on the grounds that their interest in the transmission of the material was negligible and could be adjudicated later by the voir dire of the jury and by other means. That was not the case with Nixon. At a minimum, filing an objection to the transmission would have slowed down the ability of the House Impeachment Committee to function effectively for months, perhaps many months. That would have been enormously significant by itself. Seeking to delay an adversary is not a strategy that requires much erudition, and it is a time-honored one. It also seemed to be the one St. Clair often chose to employ, albeit inconsistently. The events of February and March 1974 alone showed the ineptness of the White House legal operation, and most of the blame falls on St. Clair, with a strong assist from Haig. For example, there is no suggestion that St. Clair or anyone else from the White House spoke to any of the lawyers for the defendants in *U.S. v. Mitchell*, many of whom represented clients who had been close to Nixon and would have cooperated.

The Media's Neglect of the "Road Map"

Television and the press, understandably, focused their attention on the indictment, which was extraordinary and unprecedented. Little was known about the material transferred to the House Impeachment Committee, and whatever information was communicated was dwarfed by news of the indictment. A sophisticated but rare account by journalist Fred Emery that later appeared in 1994 suggests the complexity of the issue:

Jaworski rose to tell Judge Sirica that the grand jury had "material to be delivered." Vlademir Pregelj, the foreman handed up two envelopes. One contained the indictment; the second what Pregelj described as a "sealed report." Judge Sirica, who had received only a few minutes forewarning, read silently the two-page "Report and Recommendations." It stated that the grand jury had heard, and listed, evidence it regarded as material to Nixon's impeachment in the impeachment proceedings....

Ben-Veniste rose and produced from under the table a bulging brown briefcase that he asked be handed up. "This is the material made reference to in the document," he said. Nobody in the public sector was the wiser, but the transmittal of the Nixon tapes, White House documents, and road map had just been made from the executive branch to the judiciary; the request was that it now be handed to the third, legislative branch, Congress, which was preparing to sit in judgment on the president.[45]

Surprisingly, historians writing decades later did not appreciate the significance of the transfer of the road map and secret grand jury testimony to the House Impeachment Committee. Stanley I. Kutler reported that Jaworski told the grand jury it could not indict Nixon. But, "as a compromise gesture, Jaworski told the grand jurors that they could give a report of the evidence and their views about the President to Judge Sirica for eventual transmission to the House Judiciary Committee.... The jurors eventually followed the Special Prosecutor's recommendation—no indictment but a report to the House." Kutler did not describe the report. Nor did he mention the attempt by Haldeman and Strachan to bar transmission of the grand jury material to the House Impeachment Committee and Nixon's failure to do so.[46] Historian Stephen E. Ambrose, who wrote extensively on Watergate, did not mention that it was the special prosecutor who supplied the House Impeachment Committee with everything it needed to impeach Nixon, and in a form that facilitated impeachment.[47]

What would have happened in the impeachment process if the *ex parte* contact between Jaworski and Sirica (or the transfer of materials from the WSPF to the Impeachment Committee) had been explored and litigated in 1974 is impossible to know, but it probably would have had a significant effect. Certainly, many members of Congress would have challenged the impeachment process. Also, there would have been cries for an inquiry in *U.S. v. Mitchell*, which may have been heeded (although public support for the defendants in the cover-up case was minimal, and Sirica was inflexible). It is possible that the indictment would have been vacated and a new proceeding instituted under new leadership.

Assisted by the fruits of the Senate Watergate Committee's yearlong investigations, the House Impeachment Committee was finally on its way, and much of its work had already been done for it. The records of the Senate Watergate Committee, however, were not organized to facilitate the work of the House Impeachment Committee, and its final report did not appear until the fall of 1974.[48] The Senate committee had focused on the Watergate break-in and cover-up in 1973. It did not look into the conspiracy involving milk prices until well into 1974, and unlike the WSPF grand jury, it never examined other possible grounds for attacking Nixon, including the bombing of Cambodia and the president's taxes. The Senate Watergate Committee was never given access to the Nixon tapes, and it never saw the grand jury minutes, which were the most significant pieces of evidence regarding President Nixon's role in Watergate. Although the Senate Watergate Committee did what it could to assist the lower house's impeachment investigation, the WSPF provided the most critical material. Arguably, Nixon could have seriously delayed, if not prevented, that from occurring.

10

Impeachment Proceedings Begin

In April 1974 Nixon settled his dispute with the IRS over his personal tax liability. At issue was the timing of Nixon's gift of his personal papers to the government, as the law governing tax deductions for such contributions became much more restrictive after July 25, 1969. Also in dispute was Nixon's sale of twenty-three acres of his San Clemente estate to friends at a price that seemed excessive. To settle the case, Nixon agreed to pay the IRS $467,000, including interest, on his 1969–72 tax delinquencies. Nixon's tax problems received extensive negative media coverage, which infuriated the president and damaged his reputation.[1] The information was also made available to the House Impeachment Committee.

Meanwhile, the more liberal members of the House Impeachent Committee were frustrated by its slow pace, even as grounds for impeachment multiplied. Among their complaints was that Doar was bending over backward to satisfy the Republicans but getting nothing in return.[2] Although mobilizing support for a subpoena against the president was difficult, many were pressing for action of any sort. Democratic leader Tip O'Neill referred to Doar as an "archivist, not a prosecutor."[3] O'Neill, along with other members of Congress both Democrat and Republican, tried to get Doar to move faster.[4] Powerful House Democrat Wayne B. Hays attacked Doar and his staff for not working hard enough and accused Nixon of stonewalling.[5] By any measure, the Impeachment Committee was moving at a crawl. One book on Watergate noted, "As time passed, the House Judiciary Committee, which had begun its work in October, 1973, fell far behind its plan. Hoping at first that its work would be completed by April, Chairman Rodino kept pushing the date back."[6]

By the time the Impeachment Committee issued its first subpoena, the Senate Watergate Committee had *completed* its public hearings. However, unlike the leak-prone Senate committee, there were no major disclosures from the House committee.[7]

The Impeachment Committee had now received three large caches of material—from the Senate Watergate Committee, from the White House, and from the WSPF—but it wanted additional tapes and other documents. However, the committee had issued no subpoenas, heard no testimony, and interviewed no witnesses (including John Dean).[8] After the White House rebuffed the committee's letter seeking more information—Rodino and Doar had acquiesced when moderates and conservatives balked at issuing a subpoena to the president[9]—it finally subpoenaed the White House for more tapes on April 11, 1974. The voting on the subpoena was unusual. The first vote, 22–16, was strictly along party lines, except for the defection of Republican Caldwell Butler, who voted to issue the subpoena. However, after St. Clair refused to agree in writing to some of the concessions, a revote led to a surprising 33–3 vote in favor of issuing the subpoena.[10] Several days later the WSPF issued its own subpoena for sixty-four additional tapes, which was eventually litigated in the Supreme Court.

Even though the Impeachment Committee staff was working as many as sixteen to eighteen hours a day, it was nowhere near ready for hearings as the committee's existence approached the five-month mark in April.[11] The staff was quietly and methodically collecting and organizing evidence, and interviews of staff members found at Nixon Presidential Library indicate that they could not have materially shortened the duration of the investigation and the hearings.[12]

At Doar's insistence, his staff was virtually nonpartisan. For example, when one staff member referred to political considerations in a meeting, Doar reacted negatively. The staff member quickly explained that he was not speaking of partisan politics but of the constitutional dimension—the "political" branches of the government.[13]

Doar, with the support of Rodino, dictated the slow schedule of the Impeachment Committee.[14] During the winter and spring of 1973–74, committee members had numerous debates over various issues, including the definition of an impeachable offense, whether a president could be impeached for the actions of his subordinates, the role of the courts in impeachment proceedings, the role of executive privilege, whether the president could be represented by counsel in the House,[15] whether the committee should call live witnesses, and whether committee proceedings should be public or conducted behind closed doors. The extent of any public presentation was a particularly contentious issue.[16] These were important debates, but they were not substitutes for proceedings to impeach President Nixon. In the absence of hard facts, the public speculated; opinions that Nixon should resign and rumors that he might resign flourished.[17]

Underappreciated is the fact that the hard-nosed attitude of those in the White House, especially St. Clair, was alienating members of Congress who were otherwise sympathetic to Nixon—southern Democrats and both conservative and moderate Republicans.[18] Maintaining good relations with Congress and prosecutors was not high on the White House agenda, but stalling, refusing to supply material, and rudeness were at times counterproductive.

The White House Releases More Transcripts

On April 28, 1974, a jury in New York acquitted Robert Vesco, John Mitchell, and Maurice Stans in an unrelated criminal case in New York City. The verdict provided a boost to the fortunes, or at least the morale, of the defendants in the Watergate cover-up case. Any benefit was short-lived, however.

The following day the White House released to the public the transcripts of forty-three tapes. These transcripts included thirteen hundred pages of conversations that led to the Saturday Night Massacre, as well as many other transcripts prepared by Buzhardt and his team to give the public a fuller picture of events (but not including the June 23, 1972, tapes). Nixon went on television with a huge stack of notebooks—purportedly the released transcripts—piled behind him. But because of delays caused in large part by Nixon's insistence that certain material be deleted, the stack consisted of blank paper.[19]

The release of the tape transcripts on April 29, 1974, was a controversial political decision over which Nixon and his aides battled, especially whether to include the seven subpoenaed tapes given to the WSPF after the Saturday Night Massacre (consisting mostly of Nixon-Dean conversations transmitted to the House Impeachment Committee along with the WSPF's road map).[20] Nixon was convinced that the September 15, 1972, tape proved that "Dean had lied when he charged that I had conspired with him for eight months on a Watergate cover-up."[21] Nixon's tendency to represent himself probably resulted in a distortion of priorities and unwarranted optimism.

According to Buzhardt's assistant Geoff Shepard, Nixon demanded unwarranted deletions of relevant material, which created problems. Shepard claimed the transcripts were ready in late December 1973 but their release was initially held up because Haig and aide Bryce Harlow realized that they had to read them first. However, no one explained why this took four months. Jaworski informed Woodward and Bernstein that Haig had told him essentially the same thing.[22]

The timing of the transcripts' release the day after the acquittal of Mitchell and Stans was unfortunate. It made the favorable verdict a one-day story. The release of the transcripts was an important event that contributed to Nixon's loss of public support. Both St. Clair and Buzhardt favored the release of the tapes because of the possibility of leaks.[23] But five months had passed without a leak from the WSPF or the White House; it was a weak argument that failed to appreciate the overwhelmingly negative consequences.

According to Nixon's memoirs, "Haig, Buzhardt, St. Clair, and I decided that because of the political realities of the situation, we had to compromise on the House Judiciary Committee's request for more tapes."[24] Nixon responded to the subpoena for the tapes themselves by stating that Rodino and senior Republican committee member Edward Hutchinson, but not the committee staff, could compare the transcripts with the tapes. The committee responded by informing the White House that it had failed to comply with its subpoena.[25]

It is significant that the White House was under no obligation to make any of the tapes public; the court of appeals had directed Nixon only to provide copies to the WSPF. Nixon's memoirs stated, "I realize that these transcripts will provide grist for many sensational stories in the Press," but "our hope was that this response might, through its sheer bulk, bring home to the American people what was being asked of me."[26] Nixon apparently failed to realize how difficult it would be to gain the public's sympathy. Haig merely wrote: "On April 29, Nixon released twelve hundred pages of transcripts from forty-six presidential conversations."[27]

Release of the Transcripts Backfires

The White House transcripts became infamous largely for a reason unrelated to Watergate. According to White House lawyer Shepard, Nixon, who was a Quaker, did not want the word "goddamn" to appear in the transcripts because he did not want to be seen as taking God's name in vain. Nixon also vetoed replacing the word with "damn" because, he said, people would make the connection. After several alternatives were rejected (Nixon did not want people to think he had used the "f-word"), they settled on "expletive deleted."[28]

Despite some imaginative editing, the White House's relatively benign version of the tapes created an uproar because of their gangster-like tone.[29] That was the case even though Nixon deleted this March 22, 1973, statement to his senior aides: "I want you to stonewall it, let them plead the Fifth Amendment, cover-up." Press coverage of the edited transcripts was pervasive and included calculations of the number of expletives deleted and suspicions that there were other deletions and substitutions.[30] The White House had become an object of ridicule.

Included among the transcripts were the Nixon-Dean conversations on March 21, 1973, when Dean told Nixon there was a cancer on the presidency yet Nixon authorized the payment of money to the convicted defendants, particularly Hunt, to ensure their silence. Significantly, the White House's version of that tape supported Dean, not Haldeman, with regard to Nixon's comment "but it would be wrong" following his statement that he could get the money to pay off the burglars. When Dean told the president they would have to pay the burglars more than $1 million, Nixon responded: "We could get that. On the money, if you need the money, you could get that. We could get a million dollars. You could get it in cash. I know where it could be gotten. It is not easy, but it could be done. But the question is who the hell would handle it? Any ideas on that?" A few seconds later, Nixon said, "You don't need a million right away, but you need a million? Is that right?" Dean answered,

"That is right." Nixon then asked, "You need it in cash, don't you? I am just thinking out loud here for a moment. Would you put that through the Cuban Committee?"[31]

Haldeman had lied under oath to the Senate Watergate Committee, and the White House had publicly confirmed it. The Nixon transcripts also revealed several minor discrepancies in Dean's Senate Watergate Committee testimony. This group of tapes included the one made on September 15, 1972, which tended to support Nixon rather than Dean on the scope of Nixon's knowledge at the time. But contrary to Nixon's expectations, Dean's discrepancies were largely ignored.

Without the release of these transcripts by Nixon, the public would not have learned of the contents until months later, during the cover-up trial that started in October 1974. That trial was not televised, and the release of the tapes was limited and controlled; tapes not played at the trial would remain secret. It was far from clear in April how much the public would learn about the tapes in the foreseeable future. The self-inflicted harm from publication of the transcripts was doubled when the House Impeachment Committee presented its more accurate version ten weeks later. Publication of the transcripts by the White House was a major turning point in Nixon's defense. He had lost the high ground. Once again the press pummeled the president.

The release of the transcripts changed history by giving the public and the media access to the damaging tapes, which also offended the public's sense of propriety. In addition to the negative public reaction, the misguided release of the tapes likely destroyed an important legal argument Nixon could have used to prevent publication of the tapes (the technical term is waiver), although no court relied on that ground.[32] The March 21, 1974, decision of the DC Circuit was based solely on the important interests possessed by federal prosecutors. Sirica had also denied Congress (the Senate Watergate Committee) access to the tapes. Now, Nixon had unilaterally conceded that the general public could see the transcripts—another largely legal decision of catastrophic proportions.

As far as St. Clair (and Buzhardt) was concerned, it might be theoretically possible to think of a public relations reason to release the transcripts to the public, but it is impossible to come up with a legal reason (good or bad) to do so. St. Clair's aggressive advocacy for the release of tapes he had not heard and transcripts he had not read bordered on legal malpractice. His position was indefensible. He acknowledged being the most enthusiastic advocate for releasing the edited transcripts, although his reasons were not clear.[33] St. Clair admitted to Woodward and Bernstein that he did not work nights (although members of his staff did). Months after Nixon resigned, St. Clair admitted to them, "Even now, I'm astonished at what I don't know."[34]

There was another inexplicable dimension to Nixon's release of the tapes. While he was releasing some tapes to the public, he was preventing his lawyers from listening to other tapes, including those of the troublesome June 23, 1972, conversations. Nixon was risking the disclosure of protected tapes based on his own impaired recollection of the conversations and his deficient understanding of the law. No one else in the White House knew how potentially damaging the release of the tapes on April 29 could be. Decisions would continue to be made ad hoc and without knowledge of all the facts or consideration of how a particular decision would affect future ones. There seems to have been no overall strategy other than the porous and perilous one to stonewall.

On May 6, 1974, after nearly two years of Watergate investigations, Nixon listened to the first two of the three tapes of his June 23, 1972, conversations with Haldeman. It seemed that Nixon was worried about the pending court case that might lead to his impeachment and prosecution, and he wanted to see what the fight was about. He apparently never discussed the content of the June 23 tapes with anyone.

Defendants Challenge Sirica's Presiding over the Cover-up Trial

Another court proceeding that warrants mention started in March 1974 and extended into July. Shortly after they were indicted, several defendants in the cover-up case filed a motion to recuse (disqualify) Sirica from presiding over their trial. As required, they filed affidavits and requested that another judge be assigned to hear the motion, as the statute permits. In essence, the defendants claimed that Sirica was biased or appeared to be biased, the statutory standard. Based on two reported instances of *ex parte* contact between the prosecution and Sirica in 1973, about which they had virtually no information, the defendants also requested an evidentiary hearing before the Calendar Committee of the district court on whether Sirica had improper *ex parte* contact with members of the WSPF. The WSPF answered that it did not oppose a hearing but provided no information about other *ex parte* contacts or anything else.[35] The American Civil Liberties Union filed a memorandum stating that a hearing should be granted.

On April 30, 1974, Sirica denied the motion to recuse himself without holding a hearing or even requesting a response from the WSPF. On the issue of bias, he quoted numerous cases holding that bias must come from matters outside the proceedings, and he concluded there was nothing of the sort in this case. On the specific request for a hearing on *ex parte* contacts, Sirica denied the motion with a carefully worded comment: "In regards to the Court's meeting with Special Prosecutor Forces personnel, there are no relevant facts to be had. These proceedings included no discussion of the evidence bearing on the guilt or innocence of any defendant in this case nor any discussion even remotely of the kind."[36]

The possibility that bias resulted from another proceeding with different defendants (or that Sirica was not being candid) was not considered. Nor was the fact that Sirica had discussed other important matters in prohibited *ex parte* contacts with the prosecutors in a case before him. Finally, the argument that this was a case of judicial bias was never effectively made. The presiding judge had made up his mind on the merits of the case and had announced so publicly. As a result, Sirica would favor the prosecution because a victory by the defendants would harm his reputation. His public announcement also tended to reduce the possibility that he would change his mind.

The defendants' motion was not, however, limited to these matters. Sirica also denied numerous motions to dismiss the indictment, to dismiss specific counts of the indictment, to sever certain defendants, and for other relief.[37]

The defendants filed a petition for a writ of mandamus with the court of appeals seeking Sirica's recusal. This was an unusual attempt to obtain a review of Sirica's ruling prior to the trial. Five of the six appeals court judges denied the petition without a hearing and without an opinion on July 7, 1974. Once again, Judge MacKinnon dissented. He reviewed the claim of bias and concluded that Sirica had "misconstrued the decisional law of this circuit." He found that the alleged factual basis for the motion to recuse Sirica was substantial and warranted further attention by the court. With respect to the claims of *ex parte* contacts, MacKinnon wrote, "The Special Prosecutor agreed in his brief that it might be reasonable to refer the matter to the Calendar Committee of the district court," which, he concluded, was the appropriate resolution.[38] MacKinnon's partial dissent suggested that the defendants were entitled to full information on the *ex parte* contacts under the salutary decision in *Brady v. Maryland* (requiring prosecutors to provide exculpatory evidence to defendants).[39] Although the assistant special prosecutors responsible for communicating with the court of appeals were apparently unaware of important facts related to those contacts, that did not absolve Jaworski, who knew the facts and apparently did not communicate them to his staff. Whether that was a carefully structured plan is unknown.

MacKinnon's opinion received praise from an unexpected source. WSPF Counsel Lacovara sent a memorandum to Jaworski and other members of the WSPF that stated: "Judge MacKinnon's opinion is an excellent and effective analysis of the reasons why Judge Sirica should not have insisted upon remaining trial judge."[40] Lacovara was a perceptive and honest realist. He would later resign over President Ford's pardon of Nixon.

Representatives Hear Evidence

Starting on May 9 and continuing for six weeks, members of the House Impeachment Committee sat behind closed doors and listened to John Doar read material obtained from the WSPF, the Senate Watergate Committee, and the White House. It had been expected that the presentation of evidence would be open to the public, yet they were kept in the dark.[41] The vote to exclude the public was 31–6, a strong bipartisan majority. The wisdom of the Democrats who voted to bar the public is open to question; denying the public access to the tapes' contents seemed self-defeating. The committee allowed St. Clair to attend as an observer, although this was probably a poor use of his time.

The material had been assembled in large volumes called Statements of Information to emphasize their tentative and neutral quality. There were no new investigations or interviews by the staff. The monotonous reading by Doar, which lasted for six weeks, nearly caused a revolt among the Democratic activists on the committee, who complained about Doar's lack of drive and progress. Nevertheless, it appears that Doar's slow education of committee members was having an effect. It was also occupying virtually all of St. Clair's time.

On May 20, 1974, while the House Impeachment Committee was listening to Doar's presentation, Sirica denied the White House's motion to quash the WSPF's subpoena seeking the production of sixty-four tapes (including the three conversations that took place on June 23, 1972, which the WSPF had included "almost as an afterthought").[42] Nixon had until May 31 to produce the tapes or to appeal. On May 24 Nixon filed a notice of appeal, seeking review in the U.S. Court of Appeals for the District of Columbia Circuit.

Hours later, however, the WSPF asked the Supreme Court to bypass the court of appeals (which had already considered a very similar motion) and order an unusual expedited hearing before the Supreme Court itself, a clever move.[43] The Supreme Court granted the WSPF's motion—a blow to Nixon— and set July 8 for oral arguments, a date when the court was ordinarily in recess and its calendar was clear. Meanwhile, the content of the tapes remained secret. Rumors abounded that Nixon would resign, as they did from time to time, but nothing came of them.

Jaworski and Haig once again tried to reach a compromise on the number of additional tapes the White House would provide, but negotiations collapsed. It was clear that Nixon was unwilling to surrender the June 23, 1972, tapes or even to let his advisers listen to them. The role of St. Clair in the negotiations, if any, has not been specified.

Nixon suffered another blow when Charles Colson, a close aide noted for his uncompromising support of Nixon, pleaded guilty on June 3 to obstructing justice in connection with the prosecution of Daniel Ellsberg and agreed to cooperate with the prosecutors.[44] From 1969 until he resigned on March 10, 1973, Colson was Nixon's special counsel and was as close to the president as anyone, with the possible exception of Haldeman. Herbert Kalmbach, Nixon's personal lawyer and fund-raiser, had earlier pleaded guilty to charges filed by the WSPF involving violations of campaign finance law, including the mishandling of the $350,000 slush fund and the illegal sale of an ambassadorship. His plea also took the White House by surprise.[45]

On June 6 the *Los Angeles Times* reported that the Watergate grand jury had secretly named Nixon as an unindicted coconspirator in the March 1, 1974, indictment, something the WSPF had already told the White House.[46] Some White House lawyers believed this was the most underhanded thing the WSPF ever did. Someone had leaked the information to the newspaper, and once again, the news devastated some of Nixon's supporters.

The close relationship between the WSPF and the Impeachment

Committee continued, including the transfer of additional material to the latter, although the details have not been revealed. On June 28 Assistant Special Prosecutor George Frampton completed an "up-to-date prosecutive memorandum laying out all the evidence against the President." Frampton considered each phase of the conspiracy charged in the indictment and cited the most important evidence of the president's participation in similar activities. In their 1977 book *Stonewall*, Frampton and Ben-Veniste explained how the WSPF accommodated Doar:

Within a few days John Doar became aware of the existence of this memorandum. Doar demanded the document and told the Special Prosecutor [Jaworski] and his deputy [Ruth] that he would recommend to the full Judiciary Committee that it be subpoenaed if necessary. Doar was told, in response, that we believed it would be unwise to have a copy of this document go to the committee physically, as it was an internal prosecution document. Since it was obviously relevant to the impeachment committee, however, Doar would be permitted to examine it in our offices if he agreed to withdraw the "threat" of a subpoena. Several late evenings that week Doar pored over the memorandum in Ruth's office, taking copious notes.[47]

Based on their discussion of events in June, Ben-Veniste and Frampton were unaware that Ruth had given Doar access to confidential materials in February. The negotiated arrangement was memorialized in three evidently staged (and secret) letters dated June 28, 1974—one each by Rodino and Ruth to Jaworski, and Jaworski's reply to Rodino.[48] The letters were made public in 2013.

It seems clear that the transfer of information was largely arranged by Ruth. It requires little imagination to conclude that the purpose of the arrangement was to conceal from Congress, the president, and the public the involvement of the WSPF (particularly Jaworski and Ruth) in the impeachment process. In other words, through Ruth, the executive branch WSPF had dubious, prejudicial, and surreptitious interactions with both the judicial branch (Judge Sirica) and the legislative branch (the House Impeachment Committee) that could potentially undermine the rights of the president as well as his top aides, who were scheduled to go to trial in two and a half months. And without a subponea the public record would be blank on the cooperation between the WSPF and the House Impeachment Committee.

During most of June and early July 1974, Nixon took two well-publicized overseas trips to the Middle East and the Soviet Union, followed immediately by a two-week stay in California. They were designed to bolster his status. As a result, he spent little time at the White House during the first half of the summer.[49] Other international matters were occupying him as well.[50] He preferred to focus on international concerns rather than a messy domestic scandal.

At home in Washington and Boston, St. Clair remained optimistic. After his argument before the House Impeachment Committee, St. Clair said, "I thought I had the case won; the argument went well; you can't fool 38 lawyers."[51] He felt the same way after his July 8 argument before the Supreme Court, saying, "I thought I would win in the Supreme Court."[52] What, if anything, he was doing to bolster Nixon's defense is unknown.

The House Committee Releases Its Transcripts

On July 9, one day after argument in the Supreme Court over the tapes subpoenaed by the WSPF, the House Impeachment Committee released its own transcripts of the tapes Nixon had made public on April 29, along with its 131-page itemization of the discrepancies. This eliminated most of the apparent inconsistencies between Dean's testimony and the tapes and overwhelmingly supported Dean's account.[53] The meticulous comparison was devastating and embarrassing to the White House. Newspaper reports linked Nixon's edited version to a continuation of the cover-up. More people wondered why Nixon had released his damaging and flawed transcripts.

The committee's transcript of the portion of the March 21, 1973, tape related to paying the burglars was more detailed and damaging than Nixon's, aside from incriminating Haldeman. In the White House transcripts, Nixon said about raising $1 million, "Let me say that I think we could get that." In the committee's version, he said, "Let me say that I think you could get that in cash."[54] Buzhardt claimed that the differences between the two versions were 95 percent due to technical difficulties and 5 percent due to Nixon's changes. Nixon had insisted on deleting some things unrelated to Watergate, such as misusing the IRS, and Buzhardt said that, surprisingly, Sirica agreed with his deletions.[55] Nixon's handling of the release of the tapes was consistent with his desire to be his own lawyer.

Later, two of the White House's principal transcribers, Richard Hauser and

Geoffrey Shepard, asserted that they had prepared the transcriptions conscientiously, without any attempt to slant or distort the tapes, and both defended the accuracy of the transcripts. Shepard later expanded his account in a book: "What seemed to happen, especially with tapes from Nixon's hideaway office in the Old EOB, was that the audio quality was so bad that various transcribers heard what they wanted to hear." Shepard was less charitable regarding deletions unilaterally made by Nixon, which were identified in the transcripts as "Material unrelated to Presidential decision-making deleted." Shepard commented, "As it later developed, some of those deletions, when compared with full transcripts of actual tapes, may not have been made in good faith."[56]

House Impeachment Proceedings Go Public

The House Impeachment Committee finally held public sessions in early July 1974 after considerable internal debate. It had been a close question whether witnesses would testify, in large part because of concern over the quality of the evidence against Nixon.[57] A total of ten witnesses testified. Dean testified on July 11, and the following day the committee released the 3,888 pages of evidence Doar had read to the representatives.[58] Suddenly, an abundance of material on Nixon's conduct became available to the public. The content of Dean's testimony was less important than the fact that the press, the public, and the House Impeachment Committee were finally hearing evidence of Nixon's misbehavior through a live and knowledgeable witness that they could watch and, in many cases, compare his testimony with tape recordings. It had been a year since Dean testified before the Senate Watergate Committee. Despite his optimism, St. Clair was not successful in shaking Dean's testimony.[59] Other witnesses who testified before the committee, most of whom the White House had proposed, had little impact.[60] The release of the transcripts and the testimony of Dean invigorated both the committee and the public.

On July 18 and 19 St. Clair and Doar argued the merits of the articles of impeachment before the House committee. It was televised and widely watched. Among other things, St. Clair stated that Nixon was not involved in any cover-up, did not urge the payment of hush money to the burglars, and had learned the facts only on March 21, 1974. Aside from misstating the record, St. Clair made a serious tactical mistake when he cited in his argument a tape the

Impeachment Committee had subpoenaed but the White House refused to provide. The committee took offense.[61] It was another public relations setback.

Committee Members Go Public

Republican committee member Charles Wiggins, a reliable source, told reporters on July 16 that he expected all the Republicans on the committee to vote against impeachment, even though several Republicans had said they wanted to hear final arguments before making a decision.[62] Then on July 22 Alabama Governor George Wallace, to whom several southern congressmen were beholden, announced that Nixon could not remain in office—a major development. Nixon spoke to Wallace by telephone and concluded: "The call took only six minutes. When I hung up the phone, I turned to Haig and said, 'Well, Al, there goes the presidency.'"[63] Three southern Democrats on the committee promptly announced that they would vote for impeachment. Perhaps most startling was that Nixon seemed to be taken totally by surprise. It was devastating news, but he kept fighting.

At about the same time, Maryland Congressman Lawrence Hogan announced his support for impeachment, the first Republican to do so. Unknown to all but a few, four moderate Republicans—Thomas F. Railsback, William Cohen, M. Caldwell Butler, and Hamilton Fish—were also on the verge of voting in favor of impeachment, another critical development. That would make the committee's vote for impeachment 25–13, or 65.8 percent. Practically from the start, Doar's goal had been to get two-thirds of the committee to vote for impeachment.[64] By then, the country was awaiting a decision by the Supreme Court on whether Nixon would have to surrender more tapes to Jaworski.

What the White House did not recognize on the eve of the Supreme Court's decision was that it had no Plan B. No one in the White House had the foggiest idea what to do if the Supreme Court ordered Nixon to release the subpoenaed tapes to the WSPF. Nixon, with the acquiescence of his lawyers and advisers, had placed the White House in an untenable position. Among other things, they had all but conceded that if they lost in the Supreme Court, the tapes would be released to the public in the worst possible circumstances. Other than Nixon, no one in the White House (or outside of it, except for Haldeman) was familiar with the contents of the June 23, 1972, conversations between Nixon and Haldeman. There was little doubt among the White House staff that something on those tapes was potentially troublesome, but that is not the same as knowing what the tapes contained. Moreover, the media and the public had not focused on the June 23 conversations. Nixon alone knew—or thought he knew—what to expect. Everyone awaited the Supreme Court's decision. St. Clair remained optimistic that Nixon would prevail.

11

The Supreme Court Rules and Nixon Resigns

On the morning of Wednesday, July 24, 1974, the same day the House Impeachment Committee was set to commence public debate on the articles of impeachment, a unanimous Supreme Court rejected Nixon's claim of absolute privilege regarding his obligation to produce the tapes. (Justice William Rehnquist recused himself, presumably because he had served in the Justice Department under Attorney General John Mitchell, who was a defendant in the cover-up trial, scheduled to begin in September.) The opinion noted the importance of a president's interest in free discussion and in the enforcement of criminal law. "It is therefore necessary in the public interest to afford Presidential confidentiality the greatest protection"—he has a "presumptive" privilege that is "constitutional" and "fundamental"—"consistent with the fair administration of justice." Nevertheless, the court ordered Nixon to turn over the tapes of sixty-four conversations to Judge Sirica, who would deliver portions relevant to the Watergate investigation to the WSPF for use against criminal defendants.[1] That was the heart of the opinion. The other language, though important, did nothing to help Nixon. It was a Pyrrhic victory of sorts for Nixon.[2]

The public knew little about what was happening in the White House, but it was roiling. On the day of the Supreme Court's ruling, Nixon and a few senior aides, including Haig, Ziegler, and St. Clair, were in California. The tapes and the president's other lawyers and staff members, including Buzhardt, who was recovering from a heart attack he suffered on June 13, were in Washington. Almost immediately after learning of the court's ruling, Nixon telephoned Buzhardt and said, "There is one tape in particular that I want your opinion on. It's the one for June 23, 1972. I want you to listen to it right away, then call Al [Haig] and tell him what you think." Nixon also told Buzhardt there was a "problem" with that tape, and Buzhardt thought he was referring to a national security problem.[3] Haig largely corroborated Buzhardt's account.[4] Nixon had listened to that tape on May 6, 1974.

That morning, Buzhardt became the third person to learn the contents of the June 23 conversations. He found the tape of Nixon and Haldeman's morning conversation devastating, but he listened a second time to make sure. Buzhardt then telephoned Haig and said, "This is the smoking gun."[5] Buzhardt also called St. Clair with the news, although St. Clair's assessment was more optimistic.[6] According to Haig, "St. Clair's attitude was confident, even breezy." Haig added, "There was no doubt in my mind, then or now, that he [Nixon] believed that personal considerations were secondary because his own fate had already been decided by the defection of the Southerners."[7]

The term "smoking gun," in this context, meant that the tapes indisputably established Nixon's guilt. Synonyms to describe the evidence they contained include "definitive," "dispositive," and incontrovertible." This did not bode well for potential challenges regarding the tapes' import—or Nixon's future. Buzhardt told Haig they could not turn over the tapes or the transcripts to the WSPF, as they were too damaging. They could do so only if Nixon pardoned everyone and then resigned. Haig was very pessimistic, and he ordered speechwriter Raymond Price to prepare a resignation speech.[8]

But when Haig and St. Clair reported to Nixon, Haig said the president "listened with a dubious air, voicing no agreement. This seemed significant to me but not earthshattering. Obviously, there was something on the tape that bothered Nixon." He said, "'You'd both better listen to the tapes yourselves when you get back to Washington. The we'll get together with Fred and talk again.'"[9] Woodward and Bernstein have a different account: "The President seethed. Buzhardt was completely off base, he said. Everything that was on the tape had been disclosed in his previous statements. . . . Buzhardt was probably tired, and he was still ill from his recent heart attach; besides he was given to panic."[10]

St. Clair was something of a Cassandra. He later told Woodward and Bernstein that he had privately concluded Nixon would have to resign but apparently did not tell anyone else. It is difficult, however, to give credence to St. Clair's take on the situation. He did not listen to the June 23 tapes in July 1974 (there was no transcript yet), and whatever comforting comments he made at the time did not change the equation. According to Woodward and Bernstein, St. Clair said, "There was nothing in the record hinting that June 23 was a problem. . . . It's all hindsight to say there was. . . . It is fortuitous that they found a smoking gun. [The] June 23 tape was not bad; what was bad was that it was not disclosed."[11] A lead lawyer's reference to the "record" may be considered bizarre, and St. Clair did not explain his last sentence.

The overwhelming feeling among those involved with Nixon's plight was pessimism. One person who took a comparatively benign view of the June 23 conversations was Leonard Garment, but he did not speak to Nixon in those final months.[12] Buzhardt never wavered in his conclusion that the tape was terminal, but he had no direct access to Nixon. Haig generally agreed with Buzhardt's conclusion but was more circumspect. Nixon and St. Clair were less pessimistic, but they seemed to be prepared for the worst, and their cautious optimism did not gain traction. The main topics of discussion in the White House were who should listen to the tapes, whether they should be transcribed, what should be given to the WSPF and others, and how to manage Nixon's resignation. There was no discussion about what the June 23, 1972, tapes meant or how to counter them. There was no doubt as to their meaning. Haig incredibly told Woodward, "You only have to read it [the transcript] once."[13]

Meanwhile, the media pressed the White House for a response. Eight hours passed while the White House debated whether to make a public statement. In the end, St. Clair asserted that the president was a firm believer in the law. The delay in the White House's response and St. Clair's unilluminating language did not inspire confidence. In July 1974, in polls taken before the country knew the contents of the June 23, 1972, tapes, 57 percent and then 66 percent of respondents favored Nixon's removal from office. Nixon's approval rating had dropped from a high of 68 percent after his reelection to about 20 percent.[14]

The House Impeachment Committee Votes

The committee began its public debate on impeachment on the evening of July 24 and completed it on July 25.[15] The initiative moved back and forth between the proponents of impeachment and the defenders of Nixon. The latter's call for "specificity" backfired when Democratic members bombarded the Republicans with overwhelming details about Nixon's improprieties. It was a commanding performance.

On national television, the thirty-eight committee members discussed their solemn duty to judge the president fairly. Some of the presentations were memorable, including one by Barbara Jordan, who reminded the country that when the Constitution was written, "We, the people" did not include her African-American ancestors. During the committee debate and votes, Chairman Peter Rodino presided with quiet dignity. He was humble. He was fair. He was concerned. He was even tortured. His stature had grown enormously. A national television audience absorbed the weeklong presentation, and the tide was strongly against the president.

All twenty-one Democrats on the committee voted for the first three articles of impeachment, and seven of the seventeen Republicans voted for at least one of them. Article I concerned the Watergate cover-up;[16] Article II related to Nixon's misuse of federal agencies, including the IRS; and Article III cited his failure to cooperate with the House Impeachment Committee. The committee rejected proposed articles of impeachment related to Nixon's income tax returns, the secret bombing of Cambodia, and corrupt contributions to Nixon's reelection campaign by milk producers.[17] It seemed to many that the often-disparaged committee members voted their consciences after a careful analysis of the facts.

Impeachment in the full House of Representatives was moving ahead, with formal proceedings likely to begin in August, probably August 19. As the public waited, the Impeachment Committee prepared its formal report, which would go to the full House. Still to come was the release of new and presumably harmful Nixon tapes. Impeachment by the full House of Representatives seemed certain to the White House and many members of the public, and the question was what the Senate would do because it only required a majority of the House, while it required sixty-seven of the 100-member Senate.[18]

On July 26 Sirica met with the lawyers in court and pressed St. Clair to deliver the tapes. His questioning established that St. Clair had not listened to any of the tapes. Sirica's memoirs quote his exchange with St. Clair:

"Well, do you mean to say that you would go before the Judiciary Committee up there and make statements you have made up there and the arguments without being fully acquainted with all of the material in those tapes that they are talking about?" I asked.

St. Clair tried to dodge the question. . . . St. Clair objected that he was not "a good listener" and said he had neither the time nor the expertise to listen to the tapes. I found this unbelievable. . . . He said the president would have permitted him to hear the tapes, but he never had bothered. I couldn't imagine a lawyer defending a client without knowing every possible detail of the case.[19]

Sirica speculated that either "St. Clair simply trusted President Nixon totally, or . . . he had some fear of finding out the truth that the tapes contained."[20] There were other possibilities, including that St. Clair was lazy, that he feared he might become a witness if he listened to the tapes, and that he wanted to distance himself from Nixon. In any event, St. Clair's deficiencies harmed Nixon. As a result, the White House hastily gathered the subpoenaed tapes and began to deliver them piecemeal to the WSPF.

During the seventeen days following the Supreme Court's decision, Buzhardt and most other senior aides were primarily concerned with the mechanics of ending the Nixon administration.[21] Others spent their time counting Nixon's supporters and opponents on the House Impeachment Committee, in the full House of Representatives, and in the Senate, rather than analyzing the reasons for his dwindling support and strategizing how to counter the negative evidence.[22] Another concern was Nixon's state of mind. He had been under enormous strain. One caveat among the senior staff was that no one should encourage Nixon to resign, which would only cause him to resist the idea. The staff also discussed how to get him to make a decision.[23]

There were only a handful of relevant predictions and computations. How would the vote go in the House Impeachment Committee? Which Republicans on the committee would remain loyal to Nixon? Would any southern Democrats support him? Did he have a chance to win in the whole House of Representatives if two-thirds of the committee voted to recommend impeachment? If Nixon was impeached, did he have the thirty-four votes he needed in the Senate to prevent a conviction? Could he sweep any southern Democratic senators into his column? Was it conceivable that Republican stalwarts and longtime friends and supporters Senator Barry Goldwater and Representative Robert P. Griffin would abandon him?

The disorganization in the White House was apparent to many, but the extent of the rivalries among the aides and the disrespect they had for one another received little notice. Contributing to both problems was the staff's limited interaction with Haig, who was spending considerable time with Nixon, and their resulting isolation. This state of affairs is revealed in Woodward and Bernstein's interview with James Lichtenstein, deputy to Dean Burch, whose primary role was congressional liaison.[24]

Speculation over the tapes and Nixon's future led to concerns about foreign policy. "Without alluding to [Secretary of State Henry] Kissinger's strained relations with Nixon and the distance Kissinger had placed between his own image and the President's all during Watergate," Haig wrote in his memoirs, "the situation is terminal," and "Nixon's presidency is over."[25] Kissinger was relieved that Nixon was considering resignation.

When Were the "Smoking Gun" Transcripts Prepared?

Confusion remains over when the first June 23 conversation was transcribed and reviewed, which is curious, given the importance of that event. Nixon decided on August 4, 1974, to release the transcripts to the public, so when the major participants first knew the contents of that key conversation is significant. Haig admitted that he never listened to any tape, which some consider remarkable. He explained in an interview: "You know, the first thing I was told by counsel, Fred Buzhardt, was, 'Al, don't ever touch a tape. Don't ever be alone in the same room with a tape and don't ever, ever listen to a tape.' . . . All I ever did was take advice from Fred Buzhardt, who[m] I trusted implicitly and explicitly, and in every way you can, and it was well placed."[26]

According to Haig's memoirs, "On my order, Buzhardt had caused a transcript of the June 23 tape to be made, and I read this as soon as I reached my office on Monday morning, the twenty-ninth [of July]."[27] However, other evidence suggests that he read the transcript days later. Woodward and Bernstein's notes of their interview of Buzhardt show that Haig first read the transcript on Thursday, August 1, and that no transcript existed earlier than that date: "Aug. 1 when Fred took the transcript to Haig, Haig was sitting at his table and 'he had a strong reaction and indicated he was going back to [Vice President Gerald] Ford.'"[28] Thus, according to Buzhardt, Haig first saw the transcript shortly before he briefed Ford on the afternoon of August 1.

Ford's account of his August 1 conversation with Haig places the availability of the transcript even later. According to Ford's published account, Haig told him on August 1, "He hadn't seen the evidence [the new tapes] himself, but he'd been told about it by people who had.... The tapes were being transcribed. Eventually, he'd have copies, but he didn't have them yet." Ford added that the tapes "showed that Nixon knew about the cover-up six days after the break-in at the Democratic National Committee headquarters and that he'd been deceiving the American people ever since."[29] But that was not the position of President Nixon, Haig's superior.

That same day, Nixon informed Ford that he intended to resign, although later events indicated that Nixon might still change his mind.[30] As a result, Ford remained uninvolved in any decision making, as he had a conflict of interest and was frequently out of Washington.[31]

Haig told Nixon on August 1 that it was vital to act quickly. "It might be better to resign tomorrow night [Friday, August 2].... Your enemies will try to create the perception that you're resigning because of the uproar. Your friends will be put in a very difficult position."[32] Haig saw no reason to delay what he considered inevitable. But Nixon was not prepared to make the ultimate decision.

Kissinger's memoirs place the completion of the transcript even later. He wrote: "On Friday, August 2, he [Haig] told me that Nixon was digging in his heels.... Haig did not show me a transcript, saying it was just then being prepared."[33] Thus, according to Kissinger, there was still no transcript on August 2, nine days after the Supreme Court's ruling and three days before the president's final decision regarding the tapes. Key people were debating Nixon's future without knowing the most relevant facts.

Apparently providing no explanation as to their meaning, on August 2 the White House showed the June 23 transcripts to the president's "chief defender," Republican Congressman Charles Wiggins, who represented a portion of Nixon's old congressional district. Wiggins was an able attorney who headed the president's legal defense in the House Impeachment Committee. (He subsequently became a distinguished judge on the U.S. Court of Appeals for the Ninth Circuit.) Wiggins told Haig and St. Clair that the conversations doomed Nixon's presidency. A few days later, Wiggins told reporters that the conversations established "beyond a reasonable doubt that on June 23, 1972, the President personally agreed to certain actions, the purpose and intent of which were to interfere with the FBI investigation of the Watergate break-in." Wiggins believed those facts were "legally sufficient" to sustain "at least one count against the president of conspiracy to obstruct justice," and Nixon should resign.[34]

That weekend at Camp David, Haig, St. Clair, and Patrick Buchanan (but not Buzhardt, who was "in the doghouse," as he put it[35]), occasionally joined by speechwriter Raymond Price, debated what to do. Nixon did not see St. Clair at Camp David, where the president's future was being decided.[36] That key group was largely political, with the emphasis on what to communicate to the public. Everyone understood that Nixon had to fully disclose the contents of the June 23 tapes soon. That seemed to be the only option, as Nixon had released the first batch of tapes to the public and St. Clair had described to the House Judiciary Committee the contents of the tape Nixon refused to release.[37]

At the urging of Buchanan and Press Secretary Ziegler, on Sunday afternoon, August 4, Nixon decided to delay taking any action until the following day so he could see how the public reacted to the release of the tapes and his accompanying statement.[38] It was a slim reed, but probably a rational one. They scrapped the idea of Nixon addressing the nation when he released the tapes in favor of providing a written statement with the transcripts. Haig, Ziegler, and Price (all nonlawyers) were the main architects of the statement, although a few minor changes may have been made the next day. Apparently, they paid little if any attention to the effect this statement might have on Nixon's possible prosecution after he left office.

Nixon Releases the "Smoking Gun" Transcripts

Work at the White House started early on Monday, August 5. Discussions and speculation continued at multiple levels, including among Nixon's daughters and their spouses, who opposed resignation but had been kept largely in the dark. Buchanan informed senior staff about recent events and told them that the White House would be releasing a damaging tape that day. Haig showed Nixon the accompanying statement, which the president reluctantly approved.[39] That afternoon, excerpts from the tapes were read to senior staff for the first time.[40] White House staff briefed congressional leaders and members of the House Impeachment Committee. The atmosphere was grim.

Buchanan was tapped to tell Nixon's daughters and sons-in-law that the president would resign shortly. (There was little mention of Pat Nixon in the accounts.) Buchanan convinced the family that the public would learn that Nixon had been lying for more than two years and he could not survive in office. Moreover, Buchanan believed the tape showed that Nixon was "using the CIA to restrict the FBI's investigation to the break-in in the days immediately following," and he probably conveyed this interpretation to the family.[41]

When the White House released transcripts of the three June 23, 1972, tapes late on the afternoon of August 5, 1974, Nixon did not address the press or the public. The self-incriminating statement that had been prepared for him by his aides embraced the worst possible interpretation of the tapes and surrounding events and acknowledged that Nixon had withheld information from his lawyers and his staff. The first subject of the written statement was Nixon's pronouncement that his staff and counsel had been gulled and were innocent of any wrongdoing:

Among the conversations I listened to [on May 6, 1974] were two of those of June 23 [1972]. Although I recognized that these presented potential problems, I did not inform my staff or my counsel of it, or those arguing my case, nor did I amend my submission to the Judiciary Committee in order to include and reflect it. At the time, I did not realize the extent of the implications which these conversations might now appear to have. As a result, those arguing my case, as well as those passing judgment on the case, did so with information that was incomplete and in some respects erroneous. This was a serious act of omission for which I take full responsibility and which I deeply regret.

Nixon's statement then turned to his conversations with Haldeman. The staff tried to put a good face on these conversations, but Nixon's advisers did not understand the events of June 23 and, as a result, accepted the conventional wisdom that Nixon was trying to suppress the investigation of the Watergate break-in rather than trying to protect the anonymity of pre–April 7, 1972, campaign donors, many of whom were Democrats. Thus, Nixon mistakenly focused on protecting "persons connected with the re-election committee" rather than on anonymous donors and whether the CIA "could be compromised by a full F.B.I. investigation of Watergate":

In a formal written statement on May 22 of last year, I said that shortly after the Watergate break-in I became concerned about the possibility that the F.B.I. investigation might lead to the exposure either of unrelated activities of the C.I.A. or of sensitive national security matters that the so-called "plumbers" unit at the White House had been working on because of the C.I.A. and plumbers' connections of some of those involved. I said that I therefore gave instructions that the F.B.I. should be alerted to coordinate with the C.I.A. and to insure that the investigation not expose these sensitive national security matters....

The June 23 tapes clearly show, however, that at the time I gave those instructions I also discussed the political aspects of the situation, and that I was aware of the advantages this course of action would have with respect to limiting possible exposure of involvement by persons connected with the re-election committee.

The next paragraph was a curious mixture of doom and defense:

I recognize that this additional material I am now furnishing may further damage my case, especially because the rules of evidence will be drawn to it rather than to the evidence in its entirety.... [Keep in mind that] Acting Director Gray of the F.B.I. did coordinate with Director Helms and Deputy Director Walters of the C.I.A. The C.I.A. did undertake an extensive check to see whether any of its covert activities would be compromised by a full investigation of Watergate. Deputy Director Walters then reported back to Mr. Gray, that they would not be compromised.

Though far from crystal clear, Nixon accepted the interpretation of his June 23 conversations with Haldeman as instructing the CIA to convince the FBI to stop its entire investigation of the Watergate break-in (and related matters). It seems inescapable that Nixon, with the participation of his aides, chose to resign based on a severe misinterpretation of the evidence. The tapes of the conversations were considered a "smoking gun" by many, but they added little if anything to Nixon's improprieties. The release of the tapes should not have significantly changed the playing field.

The Media Reacts

Nixon still retained some hope on the evening of August 5, partly because some of the initial media reports were benign.[42] Why this was the case is not clear. It may have been the difficulty of parsing the exchanges between Nixon and Haldeman, although Nixon's statement left little doubt about the essential thrust of the conversations. The timing of the release gave the media little time to digest the material. Buzhardt's assistant Geoffrey Shepard gave an account to the Nixon Presidential Library and revealed that not until Buzhardt telephoned members of the media and explained the tapes to them did their significance become clear, although there is no corroboration of

Shepard's statement.⁴³ I emailed Shepard in April 2024 for clarification, and he replied:

As I recall, Buzhardt told me the next morning, August 6th, that it was taking the media a little longer to focus on the critical part of the June 23rd tape than he had expected, so—at about 8 pm—he decided to move things along and made a couple of phone calls.

He didn't tell me how many or to whom. From his point of view, it was only a matter of time until they realized what was on the transcript—the meaning of which he believed to be self-evident. I doubt that he told anyone else about these calls, with the possible exception of Al Haig or (much less likely) Jim St. Clair— both of whom have passed away.⁴⁴

It was not the job of Nixon's lawyers, especially the one responsible for the tapes, to "move things along" and help the media interpret the evidence against Nixon in the worst possible way. Subsequent reports tied the tapes to a comprehensive cover-up of the break-in at DNC headquarters in the Watergate Office Building. The cover-up, not Nixon's two years of lying, was most important to the media.

The front-page banner headline of the August 6 edition of the *New York Times* read: "NIXON ADMITS HALTING INVESTIGATION OF WATERGATE 6 DAYS AFTER BREAK-IN."⁴⁵ The story by John Herbers began: "In a sharp setback to his fight against impeachment, President Nixon admitted today [August 5] that six days after the Watergate burglary he ordered a halt to the investigation of the break-in for political as well as national security reasons and that he kept evidence from his lawyers and supporters on the House Judiciary Committee."⁴⁶

The *Washington Post*'s page-one headline on August 6 was: "PRESIDENT ADMITS WITHHOLDING DATA; TAPES SHOW HE APPROVED COVER-UP." The story by Woodward and Bernstein read:

President Nixon personally ordered a cover-up of the facts of Watergate within six days after the illegal entry of the Democrats' national headquarters on June 17, 1972, according to three new transcripts of Mr. Nixon's conversations released by the White House yesterday.... [T]ranscripts show that the President directed to hide the involvement of his aides in the Watergate break-in through a series of orders to conceal details about the break-in known to himself but not the FBI.

The *Wall Street Journal*'s headline was: "TAPES SHOW NIXON KNEW OF COVER-UP IN JUNE 1972 AND APPROVED AT LEAST PART OF IT FROM THE

BEGINNING." The article by Carl H. Falk started: "President Nixon tried to turn off the Watergate investigation after learning it was leading to the top levels of his re-election committee, the latest presidential transcripts show."

The *Los Angeles Times*, which played a significant role in uncovering the facts related to Watergate, ran a front-page story by Robert L. Jackson titled "TAPES PORTRAY EFFORT BY HALDEMAN TO HALT FBI PROBE." It stated that Nixon and Haldeman "were involved in a plot to obstruct the FBI's probe of the June 17, 1972 break-in as early as six days after the burglary."

The *Washington Star* gave Nixon's release of the tapes broad coverage on August 6, including two stories on page one. "TAPES DETAIL COVER-UP" by Barry Kalb began: "After two years of unrelenting controversy, it has suddenly become clear that President Nixon tried to cut short the Watergate investigation six days after the June 17, 1972, burglary . . . [and] that Nixon's re-election manager and staff were behind the burglary and wiretapping of Democratic National Committee headquarters in the Watergate." The other story, by James R. Polk, read: "Only six days after the Watergate break-in, President Nixon was told that money received by one of the burglars had been traced back to the re-election campaign committee."

Many other newspapers carried similar front-page stories. No leading newspaper referred to the role of campaign contributors. These accounts perpetuated the incorrect belief that the White House designed the cover-up to protect individuals running the Nixon reelection campaign.[47]

Newspaper coverage of the June 23, 1972, conversations constituted an extraordinary failure on the part of journalism, caused in large part by Nixon's unpopularity and by the wording of the statement drafted by his lieutenants to accompany the transcripts of the tapes. Although there were mitigating circumstances, including deadline pressures and the White House's failure to provide guidance, a close reading of the June 23 transcripts along with Senate Watergate Committee testimony regarding that day's events should have produced more accurate coverage. Whether that would have made a difference at the time or historically is impossible to tell.

The "Smoking Gun" Tapes End the House Debate

Members of Congress reacted negatively to the release of the transcripts. All ten Republicans on the House Impeachment Committee who had previously supported Nixon announced they would vote for impeachment. They reported their views individually in the final report of the House Judiciary Committee and then concluded, "We believe that the charges of conspiracy to obstruct justice, and obstruction of justice . . . may be taken as substantially confessed by Mr. Nixon . . . and corroborated by ample other evidence in the record."[48] They seemed to be considering primarily the statement Nixon released on August 5, 1974, rather than the transcripts of the tapes.

The committee was now unanimously against Nixon. It seemed indisputable that the full House of Representatives would vote to impeach Nixon. In the White House, any hope that the media and the public would interpret the June 23 tapes charitably evaporated.

Nixon had almost nothing to tell sympathetic members of Congress. In the absence of intellectual and substantive arguments, he relied on personal and political ones. But his status as president, his consistent loyalty to the Republican Party and its candidates, and everything else he had done in the past quarter century for the country and the party could not hold back the storm that developed once the public realized that Nixon had lied to them for more than two years and had concealed a despicable and unacceptable act: he had used the CIA to influence the FBI—sacred institutions to many—for his own personal purposes and to save his political hide. That conduct went to the heart of his fitness to govern the country, and Nixon had no answer.

Nevertheless, the administration continued to operate. At a cabinet meeting at 11:00 a.m. on Tuesday, August 6, Nixon announced that he did not intend to resign. Leaders in a parliamentary system did that, he said, not in a presidential one. Moreover, he was not guilty of any impeachable offense. His announcement to the cabinet was communicated to the media. Whether Nixon was having second thoughts or displaying pique is unknown.[49]

Nixon Resigns

Nixon was under enormous pressure. His son-in-law Edward Cox told a senator that Nixon was drinking and not sleeping, and Cox was worried about his father-in-law's health.[50] According to Woodward and Bernstein, Haig and Buzhardt had a pessimistic talk on the morning of August 7; the discussion ranged from how to get Nixon to resign to concern about whether he might commit suicide.[51]

Haig and Dean Burch, White House liaison with the Republican Party, met with Senator Barry Goldwater, who advised them that Nixon had no chance of winning in the Senate.[52] Senators Goldwater and Hugh Scott and Congressman John Rhodes, all top Republican leaders and friends of the president's, met with him in the Oval Office at about 5:00 p.m. on August 7. They told him he had only fifteen to eighteen votes in the Senate, although by then, Nixon had made the decision to resign.[53]

Over dinner that evening, Nixon told his family that he was definitely resigning. He would give his resignation speech to the country the following evening, and his resignation would be effective at noon on August 9. On the evening of August 8, Nixon announced his resignation on national television by saying, "I no longer have a political base in Congress." He did not address the morality of what he had done.

Nixon gave a farewell speech in the White House to his staff and supporters on the morning of August 9. His final address did not mention the events that drove him to resign. He irrelevantly focused on money, seeming to justify the rampant abuse of power that characterized his tenure in office on the grounds that neither he nor his appointees improperly pocketed any money during the five and a half years of his presidency. He said:

As I pointed out last night, sure, we have done some things wrong in this Administration, and the top man always takes the responsibility, and I have never ducked it. But I want to say one thing. We can be proud of it—5½ years. No man or woman came into this Administration and left it with more of this world's goods than when he came in. No man or woman ever profited at the public expense or the public till. That tells something about you.

Nixon chose a peculiar note on which to conclude his political career.

In the end, Nixon did not pardon anyone, including himself, during his last days in office. He left his supporters and himself dangling. He, his family, and a few aides departed for California at around 10:00 in the morning. At noon on August 9, 1974, Gerald Ford took the oath of office as president. Nixon's decisions to comply with the Supreme Court's July 24, 1974, ruling and to resign without the assurance of a pardon can be considered statesmanlike; he avoided a serious constitutional crisis.

It would be ironic if, as clearly seems to be the case, the people at the top of the Nixon pyramid were trying to protect the identities of anonymous donors to Nixon's campaign when they enlisted the CIA to restrict the FBI's investigation on June 23, 1972. The Department of Justice had decided not to investigate campaign contributions and had made this known to the White House, so there would have been limited damage, if any, to the anonymous donors. The investigation could have stopped at Dahlberg and Ogarrio, neither of whom faced criminal liability. Basically, the former was a known Nixon fund-raiser, and the latter, acting in Mexico, was helping a client and a friend. As it was, the names of the donors were not revealed for months. But even disclosure of the names of all the anonymous donors in June 1972 would not have wounded Nixon deeply, and the donors would have gotten over it.

Thus, Nixon, Haldeman, Ehrlichman, Mitchell, and Stans apparently engaged in a massive and self-destructive cover-up for an honorable and altruistic reason—namely, to live up to their commitment to the maintain the anonymity of pre–April 7, 1972, donors. There was little self-interest on the part of Nixon and his campaign. Nixon could not run again. The donors were mostly Democrats, and a show of Democratic support could only have helped him. Nevertheless, they were determined to keep their promises, however difficult it was to do so. There was no way they could have foreseen the extent of the problems their dedication would create. What finally transpired was unimaginable to the White House in June 1972.

These were not stupid or naïve individuals (they were virtually all men). The FBI was involved in one of the largest investigations in its history soon after the burglars' arrests. FBI officials immediately under Gray had no desire to restrict the investigation. The White House realized that Gray could not control the FBI, so it is unclear what good it would do for Walters to convince Gray to do something he could not accomplish. Given the mystique of the CIA, the effort might have worked, or it might not have. The leadership of the FBI was not on good terms with the CIA and would have been skeptical of any suggestion by the CIA that it abandon the entire investigation. And attempting to do so would have created another firestorm with uncertain consequences. The FBI plowed ahead with its investigation, having made what seemed to be merely a cosmetic course alteration.

12

A Missed Opportunity
Representing Nixon

By the end of 1973, almost every person who had been present in the White House in 1971 and 1972 or involved in the 1972 reelection campaign in a senior capacity had departed. Gone from the White House were Chief of Staff H. R. Haldeman, Chief Domestic Adviser and former Counsel John Ehrlichman, Special Counsel Charles Colson, White House Counsel John Dean, and assistants Dwight Chapin, Gordon Strachan, and others. Gone from the defunct reelection committee were Director John Mitchell and Deputy Director Jeb Magruder. Gone from the defunct Finance Committee to Re-elect the President were Chairman Maurice Stans, treasurer Hugh Sloan, and fund-raiser and Nixon's personal lawyer Herbert Kalmbach.

A New White House Team

The key lawyers now representing Nixon were J. Fred Buzhardt, who had been transferred from the Defense Department in May 1973 at the urging of Alexander Haig, and James St. Clair, Colson's former attorney, who arrived in early January 1974 from Boston. They had assistants, but nowhere near the scores of lawyers who investigated and prosecuted Nixon and his aides and served as staff members of congressional committees. These new individuals on Nixon's team had not been involved in the Watergate scandal from the beginning a year and a half ago. For most of them, their main job was first the protection and then the transcription of the White House tapes. Although Leonard Garment remained with Nixon in 1974, he was not involved in Watergate matters.

Nonlegal senior members of the team were Chief of Staff Haig, whom Nixon appointed in May 1973 after Haig had spent several years working with Henry Kissinger on foreign policy. Ronald Ziegler, a former Disneyland guide and assistant to Haldeman, assumed the post of press secretary in 1969 at the age of twenty-nine. He had no experience as a reporter or working in public relations or communications. Speechwriter Raymond Price was occasionally consulted. Although Ziegler and Price were in the White House in the first half of 1972, they did not have significant roles in the reelection campaign or in dealing with the Watergate scandal. Patrick Buchanan had been with Nixon since 1966 but played a minor role in 1974, until he spent the administration's final weekend at Camp David.[1] By July 1974, Nixon was spending far more time with Haig and, to a lesser extent, Ziegler than with anyone else, and neither of them had participated in the relevant events of 1972 or could offer legal advice.

That Nixon had inadequate legal representation was no secret among White House insiders. Former White House Counsel Garment noted in 1997, "So why was the White House stumbling along with a handful of lawyers while 'they' had a cast of hundreds?"[2] (He offered several explanations: Nixon had proclaimed his innocence and presumably did not need a large legal team, government rules limited the use of government lawyers, and assembling a large contingent of outside lawyers involved a number of problems, including financial ones.) Another important reason not fully appreciated was that it took the senior member of the White House a long time to recognize that the cover-up entailed serious criminal elements.

Little attention has been paid to Nixon's inadequate representation, in large part because no one believed that better representation would have mattered. The analysis in this book shows the importance of the quality of Nixon's legal representation, not only in March 1974, when the WSPF (via Sirica) gave grand jury material and a road map to the House Impeachment Committee, but also at other points in the saga, including the public dissemination of tape transcripts and the handling of the "smoking gun" tapes in August. It also places some responsibility on Nixon, who was a lawyer himself but used his attorneys poorly.

Several destructive events occurring in the first months of 1974 have been described. The White House gave tapes that had not been subpoenaed to the Impeachment Committee, undermining later claims of confidentiality. Haig negotiated with Jaworski without the participation of lawyers. The grand jury's report was turned over to Sirica without a murmur and without the involvement of anyone from the White House, which made no objection to the transmission even after the defendants in the cover-up case challenged it. A cascade of tapes was released to the public on April 29, without any indication that the legal implications of doing so had been considered. In addition, no lawyer was reviewing the library of remaining Watergate tapes that had not been transferred to the WSPF for the purpose of mounting a defense to the allegations against Nixon. Nor was anyone thinking in terms of an overall strategy to protect the president.

Information Deficits Undermine the White House

There is no evidence that members of Nixon's new team made a serious effort to bring themselves up to date after April 30, 1973—an enormous task. Although they were being bombarded almost daily with information about the Watergate scandal, Nixon's chief advisers were not personally familiar with earlier events, such as the circumstances surrounding the change in campaign finance laws on April 7, 1972. Moreover, many of the lawyers were occupied with the tapes in one way or another. Buzhardt said that in late July 1974, when St. Clair listened to the tapes of the Nixon-Haldeman June 23, 1972, conversations, he was not familiar with the names Dahlberg and Ogarrio.[3] The information deficit was palpable.

Haig's reaction to the transcripts was that Nixon was guilty. He wrote: "Out of this conversation [June 23, 1972] came the attempt to end the FBI investigation of the Watergate burglary by ordering Vernon Walters, Deputy Director of the CIA, to inform FBI Director Patrick Gray that the break-in was a CIA operation justified for reasons of National Security. This was a lie."[4] Haig did not know the facts, and he seriously misrepresented the contents of the "smoking gun" tape. No one from the White House claimed the Watergate break-in was a CIA operation. Around the time Haig first read transcripts of the tapes in early August 1974, he was telling Nixon's top supporters that the president "could not remain in office because he could not govern."[5] This did not make it easier to mount a defense in Congress. Nixon's closest adviser had all but capitulated, although neither Nixon's opponents nor the public was aware of it.[6]

One of the problems facing Nixon's advisers during the first week after the Supreme Court decision was that they were basing virtually their entire reaction to the "smoking gun" tape on Buzhardt's evaluation after listening to it; they were receiving information secondhand from a source that was not in the White House when the conversation occurred. Only Buzhardt, who was recovering from a heart attack, had listened to the principal June 23 tape (or read a transcript of it), and he did not listen to the other two June 23 tapes for days.[7] Nixon's advisers misunderstood the tape from the start, and they never recovered from this misconception. They operated under the assumption that Nixon and Haldeman had asked the CIA to stop the FBI investigation into the Watergate break-in.[8]

Nixon had consulted Buzhardt on a number of earlier issues, including the criminal investigation of Agnew in 1973 and the handling of the June 20, 1972, tape with the eighteen-and-a-half-minute gap. However, apparently because Buzhardt expressed his candid view that the June 23 tapes were devastating, Nixon banished him, and the two did not speak to each other between July 24 and August 7, 1974, with one possible exception.[9] Thus, when St. Clair and Buzhardt tried to see Nixon on July 31, 1974, he refused to meet with them.[10] There is no evidence that Haig tried to intervene with Nixon.

Haig, who spent more time with Nixon than anyone else, never listened to the June 23 tapes and did not read a transcript of the Nixon-Haldeman meetings until August 1 at the earliest, which was after he had participated in numerous discussions about Nixon's strategy.[11] Haig was concerned that if he listened to the tapes he might become a witness in the impeachment process, and he otherwise wanted to keep his hands clean.[12] In 1974 no one was closer to Nixon or had a greater influence on him, yet Haig, for his own personal reasons, intentionally deprived himself of information that might have helped Nixon.

There is no evidence that St. Clair listened to more than the few tapes he was ordered to hear, and it took him until the end of July 1974 to do that. St. Clair accepted Nixon's restrictions on his access to information even though he was aware that Nixon, whose reputation as a truth teller was not good, might be withholding information or even lying to him.[13] Remarkably, St.

Clair seemed comfortable making representations to the House Impeachment Committee and the courts regarding things he knew he was ignorant of. None of the other people who were talking to Nixon had heard the tapes.

A book on the Nixon presidency includes the following statement St. Clair made to the authors: "I am satisfied that I was furnished all the information that I wanted to know—and then some. There was only one tape that I was not furnished with until nearly the end of the proceedings, which led ultimately to his resignation."[14] This remarkable statement was apparently made in all seriousness by St. Clair. Nixon's advisers' personal concerns and lack of curiosity, not their analyses, determined the release of the tapes to the public and other strategies. St. Clair also made this enigmatic statement to the authors: "The June 23rd tape seemed so crucial because it was made so crucial," suggesting that he knew they had mishandled its release.[15] The book's authors did not quote any statement by St. Clair on the meaning of the June 23, 1972, tapes. St. Clair, who died in 2001, allowed himself to be interviewed very few times.

At a hearing held in the district court on Friday, July 26, Judge Sirica pressed St. Clair to produce the subpoenaed tapes, as ordered by the Supreme Court. Over St. Clair's objections, Sirica also ordered him to listen to the tapes. When the lawyers returned to the White House after the hearing, Buzhardt expected St. Clair to listen to the June 23 tapes immediately and was amazed when St. Clair said, "Not now."[16] Instead, St. Clair took off for a long weekend in Cape Cod "to get some rest" (and play in a golf tournament), leaving that same Friday and returning on Tuesday, July 30.[17] Therefore, he did not listen to the June 23 tapes before July 30, 1974 (there was no transcript yet).[18] Two days after the crucial June 24 Supreme Court decision and hours before the House Impeachment Committee would decide President Nixon's fate, Nixon's lead counsel had not examined critical evidence that would soon be delivered to the opposition. St. Clair apparently did not communicate with Haig or anyone else during his weekend at Cape Cod. Yet somehow he managed to convince some people that he was working hard.[19]

St. Clair's mini-vacation took place in the midst of crucial debates in the White House about Nixon's strategy and prospects. To say that these issues required immediate and undivided attention is an understatement. The House committee voted on the first article of impeachment on July 26, the day St. Clair left Washington. One possible reason for St. Clair's action is that he wanted to create as much distance as possible between Nixon and himself. That is not how a lawyer should behave.

The evidence suggests that St. Clair was not effective himself and did not make effective use of other lawyers.[20] He was never sufficiently knowledgeable about the facts and background of Watergate. He spent days at the closed Impeachment Committee sessions listening to Doar read the evidence rather than working on a response. There is no indication that he had any of Nixon's lawyers prepare an analysis of the June 23 tapes and the relevant circumstances surrounding them.

John J. Chester, a well-connected lawyer from Columbus, Ohio, started working for Nixon in January 1974 and thought that *he* would be number two behind St. Clair. Attorney General William Saxbe (appointed after Elliot Richardson resigned) recommended Chester. Chester worked extensively on legal issues related to the standards for impeachment before working on litigation involving the tapes; he was in charge of preparing the White House's briefs. But at times Chester found himself with nothing to do. When Nixon released the tape transcripts on April 29, 1974, Chester was not consulted. When the Supreme Court ordered Nixon to surrender additional tapes on July 24, Chester was shut out of the ensuing discussions. Finding himself essentially excluded from the effort to defend Nixon, Chester submitted his resignation effective August 1, 1974.[21]

A conversation that took place on August 3, 1974, reveals that St. Clair failed to use the lawyers under him, including his deputy:

St. Clair's deputy, [Jack] McCahill, had not been able to track his boss down for several days. When St. Clair finally stopped by McCahill's office that afternoon [July 30], the deputy had some questions: "How's it going? What's on those tapes?"
"Some interesting things," St. Clair responded.
"How interesting?"
"Very interesting," St. Clair said, and he walked off.[22]

Late on the morning of August 5 St. Clair finally told McCahill what was on the June 23 tapes. However, St. Clair falsely informed him that Nixon was going to contest the impeachment effort all the way, withholding the fact that Nixon had accepted the statement his aides had pressed on him at Camp David. According to McCahill, he and St. Clair never discussed whether Nixon was guilty.[23] Apparently, none of the handful of lawyers who worked for St. Clair ever discussed Nixon's defense with him.[24]

Every Man for Himself

Nixon's legal representation was poor for reasons other than his lawyers' failure to learn the facts. St. Clair, who did not work evenings, used his time badly, such as spending hours listening to Doar reading the evidence. He failed to ask his staff to do essential investigations. Lawyer Richard Hauser absented himself for family reasons and then left the defense effort before Nixon resigned.[25] Chester, apparently through no fault of his own, did little in the final months.

Perhaps as significant as the absence of knowledgeable and conscientious advisers was that some of them were primarily concerned with their own status and professional survival rather than Nixon's. In fact, some aides in the White House wondered at the time whether St. Clair's focus was the president or himself, although it is unknown how widespread this concern was.[26] When St. Clair learned that the June 23, 1972, conversations between Nixon and Haldeman were far more incriminating than he had represented to the House Impeachment Committee at a critical hearing in July 1974, his reaction was noteworthy. He and Haig pressed Nixon to tell the world that his aides were unaware of the damaging contents of the June 23 tapes—that Nixon had deceived them and that he alone was responsible for the false statements. Indeed, St. Clair threatened to resign if Nixon did not exonerate him.[27] In other words, Nixon's advisers, particularly St. Clair, protected themselves at the expense of their client, even as the future of the president of the United States hung in the balance. St. Clair was not seeking protection against an ethics investigation conducted after the conclusion of a case; he was concerned about protecting himself in the middle of an attack on his client and on the eve of the case's resolution. There may be times when a lawyer or adviser should resign or threaten to resign, but it is difficult to think of any situation in which a lawyer should sacrifice his client to serve his own interests.[28] Even Haig concluded that St. Clair was focused on himself at the end: "St. Clair was particularly concerned that he had seriously misled the House Impeachment Committee on July 18 when he told them that the June 23 conversations were innocuous as far as Nixon was concerned."[29] According to Haig and others, St. Clair believed the evidence on the June 23 tape was so significant that he worried a further delay might result in a charge of obstruction of justice against himself, despite his ignorance of the tape's text, especially since he had mischaracterized the extent of Nixon's knowledge to the House Impeachment Committee.[30]

Haig's memoirs quote a portion of the inculpatory statement drafted by Nixon's advisers and released along with the June 23 tapes:

> Among the conversations I listened to [in May 1974] were two of those of June 23. Although I recognized that these presented problems, I did not inform my staff or my Counsel of it, or those arguing my case, nor did I amend my submission to the Judiciary Committee in order to include and reflect it. At the time, I did not realize the implications which these conversations might now appear to have. As a result, those arguing my case, as well as those passing judgment on the case, did so with information that was incomplete, and in some cases erroneous. This was a serious act of omission for which I take full responsibility and which I deeply regret.[31]

Haig's next words were: "That got everybody but Nixon off the hook." Precisely. He wrote, "The consensus of the group was that Nixon would have to concede in his statement that he had listened to the incriminating tape almost three months before but had kept what he heard to himself." Haig explained to Nixon: "'The lawyers will jump ship if I ask them to change it.' I explained how St. Clair and the others felt and what a struggle it had been to produce even this draft." When Nixon objected to the language, Haig assured him, "'This is the best we can do,'" although Haig later wrote that the statement, though accurate, "seemed to me to go too far."[32] St. Clair and perhaps others would have resigned if the statement did not protect *their* interests. Two Watergate prosecutors called the statement "tantamount to an admission of guilt."[33]

Nixon accepted full responsibility not only for the content of the transcripts but also for withholding them from his advisers and the public. He weakly claimed that his lawyers had "incomplete, and in some cases erroneous [facts]. This was a serious act of omission for which I take full responsibility and which I deeply regret." That was his only explanation, other than noting his insistence on "a full investigation and prosecution of those guilty" in a conversation with Patrick Gray on July 5, 1972. Rather than make any effort to explain that the tape did not mean what everyone thought it meant, the statement all but foreshadowed the forthcoming Armageddon.

When Nixon sought candid advice, he received little help. When Nixon decided to delay a decision on resigning until he could assess the reaction to the release of the June 23 tapes on August 5, he asked Haig whether he thought he was making a mistake. Haig cited his answer in his memoirs: "I replied that it was not my place to make judgments on such matters. The decision was his alone, but whatever he did must have the support and agreement of everybody he loved and respected."[34] When Nixon asked Buzhardt, a devout Baptist, what he thought the right thing to do was, Buzhardt replied that he could not make or recommend moral judgments, citing the Bible's admonition against judging others.[35] St. Clair's advice on whether Nixon should resign varied from day to day.[36] And he left Washington to play in a golf tournament in the middle of the crisis. No wonder Haig said Nixon was living in his own private world.

Nixon's staff created another public relations disaster by releasing the entire June 23 transcripts rather than a redacted version. Nixon's memoirs ruefully noted: "In the rush to produce copies of these transcripts for distribution to the press, some personal references were carelessly and unnecessarily left in."[37] The transcripts quoted Nixon as saying, "The ... Jews, they're left wing." He also offended Italians by saying, "Well, I don't give a shit about the lira." About a loyal senior aide, Nixon said, "He just doesn't have his head screwed on right. . . . He just opens it up and sits there with egg on his face."[38]

Members of Nixon's team attempted to minimize their exposure in other ways. They tried to make it seem that they had learned about the content and significance of the June 23, 1972, tapes only shortly before their release to the public on August 5, 1974, rather than ten days earlier (when Buzhardt listened to and disclosed the tapes' contents). When Representative Charles Wiggins asked St. Clair on August 2 when he first learned of that evidence, his answer implied that he had become aware of it only in the last day or two, rather than admitting "that they had been warned urgently about the tape nine days earlier, before the House Judiciary Committee had taken its first vote."[39] Members of the WSPF wrote, "Unknown to us, some of the President's closest advisors had learned about the June 23 tapes more than a week before."[40] Haig's memoirs support this statement.[41]

Nixon's Team Goes It Alone

Other events demonstrated the closed-mindedness of the White House. It appears that Haig's first contact with Wiggins about impeachment occurred on August 2, when he showed the transcript of the June 23 tape to the congressman. There is no evidence that anyone from the White House talked to Wiggins before that date, even though he was crucial to Nixon.[42] Furthermore, Haig's memoirs mention Edward Hutchinson, the ranking Republican member of the committee, only to identify him to readers.[43] There is no suggestion that Haig or anyone else met with Hutchinson during the impeachment process. It appears that no representative of the president was monitoring, much less supporting, the loyal Republicans on the House Impeachment Committee.

The White House was defending the president from impeachment, but it was making no effort to understand what the House Impeachment Committee was doing or to influence its loyal members in any way. It apparently had no insight into the views of moderate Republicans like William Cohen of Maine and Thomas Railsbach of Illinois, who were undecided. The status of the committee should have been central to the White House strategy. This was the responsibility of Nixon's staff.

It is not clear why Nixon's top advisers failed to communicate with sympathetic members of the House Impeachment Committee. Arrogance, lack of imagination, ignorance, incompetence, timidity, hopelessness, and laziness are all possibilities. It was a major failing and essentially inexplicable in view of the extensive contacts the White House had with Republicans on the Senate Watergate Committee and staff a year earlier. Whether taking advantage of these contacts would have changed the outcome is, of course, unknowable. But there were members of the committee minority who would have been willing to help.

By the time of the Supreme Court's decision on July 24, 1974, it was clear that the June 23, 1972, tapes were critical to Nixon's case. According to Woodward and Bernstein's subsequent interview with Haldeman's lawyer John J. Wilson, Haig called Haldeman around that time and asked what he remembered about the June 23 conversations. Apparently, that was the first time the White House contacted Haldeman about the facts. Haldeman testified he did not remember the details of his June 23 meetings with Nixon, which was hardly a surprise. That was the end of the effort to reach Haldeman.[44] The White House should have approached Haldeman months earlier, not at the last minute. Haldeman understood the context of the June 23 tapes better than anyone else, and unlike Ehrlichman, he continued to hold Nixon in high regard.⁴⁵ Nearly two years had passed since the conversations took place, and his memory was limited, so they should have played the recording for Haldeman. During the trial of *U.S. v. Mitchell*, Haldeman remembered the true nature of the June 23 conversations when his recollection was sufficiently refreshed. But that was months too late to help Nixon.

It is also strange that Haig, rather than one of the lawyers such as St. Clair or Buzhardt, reached out to Haldeman. Interviewing witnesses is standard practice for lawyers preparing for a trial or other proceeding. The effort to talk to Haldeman was too little, too late. Once again, Nixon's lawyers and advisers failed him.

It seems that no one contacted Maurice Stans, who was deeply involved in 1972 and was anxious to tell his story. He had been acquitted by a New York jury and presumably would have told the truth, if asked. He was knowledgeable about the role of campaign financing in the case, but Haig's sole mention of Stans in his memoirs was to note his acquittal.⁴⁶ Someone should have enlisted his help.

It is true that the defense team was dealing with a difficult client who refused to tell his lawyers what he knew and would not allow them to investigate the facts necessary for his defense. There is, however, no record of anyone objecting to the restrictions imposed by Nixon or threatening to resign because of them.⁴⁷ Nixon refused to listen to the tapes when asked to do so by Buzhardt. He would not even talk to Buzhardt. He was isolating himself from the facts.

This was not an ordinary situation, but the people on whom Nixon relied were not ordinary either. Lawyers and advisers are not supposed to hide from the facts.⁴⁸ Nor are they supposed to disappear, physically or mentally, when they are needed most. Because of St. Clair's largely self-inflicted ignorance of the facts, he misrepresented them when arguing before the House Judiciary Committee, if not elsewhere. St. Clair seemed awed by the trappings of the presidency. Pusillanimity is not desirable in a senior presidential aide.

Nixon and his advisers learned nothing of importance between July 24, 1974, when the Supreme Court ordered the release of the tapes, and his decision to resign seventeen days later. Nothing new happened, no new witnesses were uncovered, and no one considered an innovative approach. Nixon had nothing in the way of intellectual arguments to stave off his impending removal from office. In the absence of anything else to hold on to, he let the increasingly depressing perspectives of those around him decide his future.

No one in the White House fully appreciated one important fact: although there was general agreement that the June 23 tapes were damaging, perhaps terminally so, there was no discussion of what the president had done to warrant his removal from office. There was no serious attempt in the White House to articulate what on the tapes was the problem, much less how to cope with it.[49] Easiest to understand was the negative reaction to the admission that Nixon had lied for more than two years about his involvement in Watergate. The discussions on the tape demonstrated his shoddy character and indicated that he was unworthy of serving as president. But that was not what caused him to resign.

There is strong evidence that on June 23, 1972, Nixon and Haldeman were not conspiring to halt the FBI investigation into the break-in at the Watergate Office Building but were talking about protecting the identities of the anonymous donors to Nixon's reelection campaign, a far less serious and dramatic accusation. There were reasons why Nixon's lawyers should have discounted his words on that date, including Haldeman's testimony during the Senate Watergate Committee hearings that the conversation was hurried (and confused) and should not be equated with a formal presidential statement.

Accounts of Nixon's defense in the summer of 1974 ignored the importance of maintaining the anonymity of early campaign contributors. No one considered that Nixon and Haldeman must have realized by June 23 that it was foolhardy to try to protect members of the Committee to Re-elect the President (CRP) and the Finance Committee to Re-elect the President (FCRP); they knew the money could be traced from the FCRP to the burglars. But those arguments were not made. No one considered the obvious: that stopping the FBI investigation of the Watergate break-in was impossible.

The precise responsibilities and prerogatives of a lawyer (or a nonlawyer adviser) who is misled by a client during the pendency of a proceeding are not clear, but the actions of St. Clair (and probably Buzhardt and Haig) cannot be characterized as acts of moral courage. True, they were in a difficult spot, but it is difficult to feel sorry for them. They were on the firing line, standing in front of and protecting the president of the United States, and they ducked; they put their personal reputations first. In doing so, they left the president exposed and essentially on his own and unprotected. They would have been criticized for a while no matter what they did, but that goes with the job of representing the president (and many other clients). It was a pusillanimous performance unworthy of experienced people dealing with an unimaginable crisis involving one of the most important people in the world. It was a rigorous test, and they failed.

Had there been competent lawyering, it is likely that the White House would have quietly delivered the June 23 tapes to the WSPF along with dozens of others, and no one outside the prosecution would have been the wiser. Congress and the public would have learned the content of the tapes only when the prosecution played them at the trial of Mitchell, Haldeman, and Ehrlichman. Any tape not played would remain confidential. As the next chapter demonstrates, the "smoking gun" tape played a relatively modest role in the cover-up trial, despite the spectacle it provoked on August 5 and 6. At the very least, its contents probably would not have been known for months, maybe a year or more.[50] The White House should have been poised to contradict any claim that the June 23, 1972, tapes showed that Nixon sought to stop the FBI's investigation as opposed to protecting some anonymous donors.

Of course, it is unknown how effective that explanation would have been. But it can safely be said that the reaction would not have been worse than it was on August 5 and 6, 1974. It would be an exaggeration to say the "smoking gun" tape would have been lost in the wealth of information introduced at the trial, but it is clear that its impact would have been reduced.

No one should view this book as an exoneration of Richard Nixon. His conduct was deplorable, and he repeatedly lied to the American people and manipulated his staff to serve his personal interests. He may have violated the law in multiple respects. But he was entitled to competent and conscientious representation by individuals who were dedicated to the interests of their client.

13

The Cover-up Trial

After Nixon resigned on August 9, 1974, two important topics on the public's mind were Gerald Ford's presidency and what would happen to Nixon. Resisting advice to the contrary, Ford kept most of Nixon's advisers in place. He needed to govern, and he was absorbed by the tasks of finding a vice president and deciding whether to pardon Nixon.

The White House was in turmoil, as the changeover was sloppy and the staff was bickering over power.[1] Haig stayed on for a month before resigning in September to become the head of NATO. On August 20 Ford nominated Nelson Rockefeller as vice president, but he did not take office until December 19, 1974. Within a month, and before Ford pardoned Nixon, Ford pardoned conscientious objectors to the Vietnam War, which he announced in a speech before the Veterans of Foreign Wars. He described the act as one of Christian charity, but it confused his supporters.[2]

Ford's unexpected pardon of Nixon on September 8, 1974, did little to explain why Nixon had resigned. Ford did not specify what crimes or potential crimes he was forgiving; he granted Nixon "a full, free, and absolute pardon" for any and all federal crimes he "committed or may have committed or taken part [in] during the period from January 20, 1969, though August 9, 1974." Nixon made no statement in response to the pardon. Some said that Nixon's acceptance of the pardon was, in effect, an admission of guilt. But that was a sentiment, not a legal determination. I would ask the reader to consider just one question: If you were wrongly accused of a serious crime, looking at the prospect of spending years bankrupting yourself and your family to defend yourself, and facing years in prison if you were wrongly convicted, wouldn't you accept an unconditional pardon? In any case, the reaction to the pardon was overwhelmingly negative.[3] The public wanted Nixon to be held accountable.[4]

The trial of Mitchell, Haldeman, Ehrlichman, and two others (Robert C. Mardian, a colleague of Mitchell's, and Kenneth W. Parkinson, an attorney hired by the CRP after the burglars' arrests) was considered an anticlimax after the pardon.[5] Some thought it was wrong to prosecute Nixon's aides after their leader escaped judgment. But the trial went ahead with haste—Sirica agreed to just a one-month delay because of the publicity surrounding Nixon's resignation and Ford's pardon.

Those who saw any part of the trial itself probably number in the low thousands, and they had to endure weeks of an often dull, slow-moving presentation to get the full picture. Reading the ten thousand–page trial transcript is an alternative, but not an appealing one. It is not easy to locate and is not an easy read.[6] Few have tried. What follows is a summary of the trial transcript as it relates to the "smoking gun" tape. All in all, it did almost nothing to alter the conventional interpretation of that tape. As noted earlier, the *ex parte* contacts between Jaworski and Sirica remained secret for decades.

John Dean Takes the Stand

The trial started before Judge John J. Sirica and a jury on October 8, 1974. Jury selection took nearly a week. When he gave the opening statement for the government on October 14, 1974, Assistant Special Prosecutor Richard Ben-Veniste devoted two sentences to the June 23, 1972, Haldeman-Nixon tapes and took the position that the criminal activity of those in the White House was broader than the break-in at the Watergate Office Building and its cover-up. The prosecution wanted to present as much evidence as possible that Nixon and his aides had engaged in other improper or illegal acts.[7] Whether to allow this evidence was a judgment call. Sirica could admit or exclude the evidence at his discretion. He chose to admit it.

John Dean was the first and unquestionably the principal government witness, and he performed the same vital role he had played at the Senate Watergate Committee hearings. Under questioning by Assistant Special Prosecutor

James F. Neal, he described the early days of the cover-up, his conversations with FBI Director Gray, and his conversation with Mitchell on the evening of June 22, 1972, about the role of the CIA and anti-Castro Cubans in the Watergate break-in.[8] Dean testified that on the morning of June 23, 1972, he relayed to Haldeman what Gray and Mitchell had told him the evening before. Gray was getting conflicting information about the CIA's involvement in Mexico. Dean said, "I reported to Mr. Haldeman that the FBI was pursuing the Dahlberg and Ogarrio checks and I also alluded to the fact that Mr. Gray seems to think this is all tied in with the CIA."[9] Dean's testimony reminded Haldeman that the Department of Justice (DOJ) had assured the White House that its investigation would not involve campaign financing and that the DOJ understood that the contributors to the reelection campaign had nothing to do with the future trial of the burglars.

Although the identity of the persons or organizations (the CRP and FCRP) that supplied money to the burglars was relevant, the identity of the people who had contributed money to the CRP and FCRP was not, and nothing about them was offered or admitted into evidence. The burglars did not know or care where the money they received from Sloan came from. It did not matter to them whether the money came from a donor to the reelection campaign, was a lottery prize, or had been stolen from a bank.

Dean was clear that the campaign contributions were not integral to the Watergate break-in or to the prosecution of the burglars; only "an accident of circumstance" brought the two together.[10] Dean's emphasis on the lack of a link between the contributors and the break-in did not please the prosecutors; they preferred to keep the cover-up as all-encompassing as possible.[11] The examination and cross-examination of Dean brought out the distinction between the break-in and campaign financing, but not forcefully. Haldeman, if no one else, should have realized that Dean was testifying truthfully, and Haldeman should have informed his attorney that, if asked, Dean would corroborate the explanation in Wilson's opening statement and the later testimony by Haldeman. Although competent lawyers generally do not ask a hostile witness a question to which they do not know the answer, this was an exception.

If asked, Dean would have testified that the FBI was not supposed to be investigating campaign finance violations and the DOJ had assured the White House that it was not going to engage in a fishing expedition. Dean had informed Haldeman of this, so arguably, the White House had a right to try to keep the FBI in line. In other words, the evidence suggested that Nixon and Haldeman intended to stop only the part of the FBI inquiry that was beyond the scope of the legitimate investigation into the Watergate break-in. In fact, in January 1974 an internal memorandum written by an assistant Watergate prosecutor interpreted the June 23, 1972, conversations as relating to the interviews of Ogarrio and Dahlberg, essentially taking the view that the discussion between Nixon and Haldeman was about campaign contributions.[12]

Events that immediately followed the meeting of Haldeman, Ehrlichman, Helms, and Walters, though mentioned by Dean, could have been emphasized more by the defendants' lawyers. Walters spoke with Gray, which caused the FBI to delay its questioning of Dahlberg and Ogarrio but did not otherwise affect the investigation.[13] Based on Walters's request, Gray temporarily canceled FBI interviews that could have ascertained the original source of the cash possessed by the burglars, but little else.

The Nixon tapes played an important role in the cover-up trial. The WSPF's principal challenge was getting the tapes admitted into evidence. The defendants objected to the admission of all tapes, but the question of their admissibility was a relatively easy one when the prosecution had a witness who could testify that the tape recordings accurately reproduced the conversations themselves. Dean authenticated the tapes of his September 15, 1972, conversations with Nixon and Haldeman, when Nixon praised him for his efforts, and his March and April 1973 conversations, when Dean explained the cover-up to Nixon and tried to convince him to end it. The prosecution played these tapes while Dean was on the witness stand.

Far more difficult for the WSPF was getting other tapes, such as the conversations between Nixon and Haldeman, admitted when it had no witness to testify as to their accuracy. This dispute between the prosecution and the defense began weeks before the trial started and continued for weeks afterward. Ultimately and unsurprisingly, Sirica admitted all the tapes offered by the prosecution based largely on chain-of-custody and circumstantial evidence.[14] Almost as significant, Sirica gave the jury transcripts of the tapes prepared by the prosecution, but he did not admit the transcripts into evidence, whatever that was worth to the defense.[15]

The most important tapes at the cover-up trial were not the June 23, 1972, conversations between Nixon and Haldeman or the later ones between Nixon and Dean. Most significant were tapes of the April 1973 conversations that discussed paying hush money to the burglars and having Mitchell take the blame.[16] Nixon would never be a defendant, and Dean had already pleaded guilty; Haldeman was only one of five defendants at the cover-up trial, and Ehrlichman was relying on his absence from the June 23, 1972, meetings to support his defense that he was not a major player in the cover-up. The payments were a more spectacular action than stifling an investigation by one federal agency through the use of another federal agency.

Haldeman Interprets the "Smoking Gun" Conversation

Haldeman testified in his own defense right after John Mitchell's defense, which occurred several weeks after Dean testified.[17] Mitchell never wavered in his loyalty to Nixon. Haldeman had a strong motive to minimize his criminality, but he too continued to protect Nixon.[18] Even though his credibility was questionable, Haldeman was uniquely knowledgeable about the events of June 23, having spoken with Dean, Nixon, and the CIA director and deputy director within days of the burglars' arrests. (In fact, no one but Haldeman spoke to more than one of those four on June 22–23.)

Haldeman maintained that the Allen and Andreas checks that were converted into $100 bills were unrelated to the Watergate break-in. Nothing about those donations could shed any light on the break-in, he argued. If there were a problem with the contributions and how they were handled, that would come under the rubric of possible campaign finance violations. But that distinction was not easy to explain to the jury. Haldeman summarized his telephone conversation with Dean about the FBI investigation that immediately preceded his conversation with Nixon on June 23:

In general Mr. Dean told me that the FBI investigation was leading to or had uncovered some tracing information that led to money that had been contributed to the campaign by a Mr. Dahlberg and by some Texans and that there was concern on his part that the investigation would lead to the money source. He also informed me that the FBI was confused as to where to go, what was happening on the case, what they were uncovering, and had a theory that this might be a CIA operation.[19]

Haldeman next answered his lawyer's questions about his subsequent meeting with President Nixon:

I told the President that Mr. Mitchell had suggested and Mr. Dean had confirmed or agreed to a proposal that Mr. Walters talk with Director Gray of the FBI and go into the question of not pursuing the investigation of the source of the checks to the President or raising the embarrassment of those checks to the President which were, of course, not related—the donations were not related to the Watergate matter at all.[20]

Notably, Haldeman used the word "source" here to refer to the contributors to the reelection campaign, as he did elsewhere. He also referenced the donors.

On cross-examination, Haldeman repeated his point that whoever originally donated the money that ended up in the hands of the burglars was irrelevant to the latter's prosecution. It was undisputed that the money in the burglars' possession had come from the FCRP. Minutes later, Ben-Veniste confronted Haldeman with the conventional wisdom—namely, that Nixon and Haldeman were trying to protect the CRP and FCRP:

Mr. Haldeman, weren't you telling the President the FBI was going into some areas that were productive to the FBI investigation . . . but that you didn't want them to go into because you knew that the money could be traced back to the Committee to Re-elect the President because Mr. Stans had given the checks to Mr. Liddy who in turn had given them to Watergate burglar, Bernard Barker, who had been arrested and this was a direct link for the first time in the investigation showing the Committee to Re-elect the President on one side and the burglars on the other?[21]

What Haldeman actually said to Nixon was, "Their investigation is now leading into some productive areas, because they've been able to trace the money, not through the money itself, but through the bank, you know, sources the banker himself. And, and it goes in some directions we don't want it to go." He did not mention the FBI. Haldeman disagreed with Ben-Veniste's version of the facts and stated:

Mr. Stans was . . . very concerned about the names of donors not being revealed. . . . This was a problem that was very acute . . . this is something the President would have been immediately familiar with. . . . Mr. Nixon was extremely anxious that the names [not] be made public to the point of requesting that donations of those who didn't want their names made known be returned to the donors so the balance could be made public because he thought it was a political liability to have this issue of unknown donors hanging over us during the course of the campaign.[22]

Haldeman then returned to another point—namely, that protecting the identities of the anonymous donors was a significant issue in the spring of 1972:

> The question of whether to reveal these names or not was a front-burner issue, if I may put it that way, and Mr. Stans took a strong position they must not be revealed. That being a sensitive area there was concern on our part, on the President's part about the question of whether specific donors would be revealed and the Dahlberg one was one of the more highly sensitive ones because his check was a contribution from Mr. Andreas in Minnesota who was a close friend and supporter of Senator Humphrey's and the revelation of his donation would have been deeply embarrassing to him and to Mr. Stans.... [T]hose contributions would be made known because of the fact their contributions had been turned over to Mr. Liddy who turned them over to Mr. Barker to have the checks cleared through his bank account so the sources would not be uncovered.[23]

Haldeman explained that when he spoke to the CIA leaders on June 23, 1972, he had two very different concerns, only one of which had to do with the anonymous donations. A separate concern was national security. "The other purposes of the meeting were those that I recall as having been raised by the President as relating to the Bay of Pigs, the investigation of other non-Watergate matters, and so forth."[24] But the relationship between the cover-up and the Bay of Pigs remained unclear, perhaps because it was unclear even to Haldeman, which he eventually explained (quoted later).

Haldeman's account omitted an important misconception that made the connection between the contributions and the burglary more concerning at the time. There was no question that Liddy gave Barker the checks to cash at his bank and that Liddy turned the cash received from Barker over to the campaign treasury, where it was commingled with other cash in the FCRP's safe, as Sloan testified. On June 23, 1972, many in the White House and on the campaign staff believed that the anonymous donors had dealt directly with the burglars and had more to fear from their conduct than was in fact warranted. None of the contributors believed they had done anything other than make a legal, confidential contribution to Nixon's reelection campaign through proper channels, and none of them had. But there was some connection, and that raised suspicions and confusion at the time.

While Haldeman's testimony about the handling of the cash was close to the mark, he had testified previously to the grand jury and three congressional committees that he had no recollection of discussing the fact that money found in Barker's possession had a connection to Mexico.[25] Ben-Veniste confronted Haldeman about his prior inconsistent testimony. Haldeman's response was that his memory had been refreshed by seeing a transcript of his taped conversation with Nixon, an answer that Ben-Veniste mocked, even though it was a reasonable and plausible explanation.[26] Haldeman's recollection was also refreshed by Dean's earlier testimony, but he may have been reluctant to say that.

Ben-Veniste then accused Haldeman of confessing to obstruction of justice. The prosecutor's reasoning was that Haldeman had testified that he used a government agency, the CIA, to take steps to avoid an embarrassment to Nixon's political campaign—something that was not in the national interest but in Nixon's political and partisan interest.[27] Unfortunately for Haldeman, Ben-Veniste argued, from the standpoint of the law, using the resources of the federal government to protect contributors to Nixon's reelection campaign was just as wrong as using the manpower and resources of the federal government to protect the burglars and the FCRP.[28] (More on this in the next chapter.)

John Wilson, Haldeman's attorney, objected, stating that the indictment did not allege that the defendants had obstructed justice in the manner claimed by Ben-Veniste. The indictment did not mention, Wilson argued, the confidentiality of campaign donations made before April 7, 1972, so the cross-examination went beyond the scope of the indictment. Judge Sirica ruled against Wilson based on the indictment's general language.[29] Once again, Sirica made an important ruling in favor of the government that was effectively immune from appellate review. Questioning resumed, and Haldeman denied trying to obstruct justice, but he was not doing well.[30]

"Now, there weren't any national security aspects to your conversation with Mr. Nixon . . . about . . . calling the CIA in, were there, Mr. Haldeman?"

"I think there were," Haldeman insisted.

"If this was national security, then why did the President suggest an alternative way of curtailing this area of the investigation which wouldn't even involve the CIA?"

Haldeman replied: "Now, if we are back to apples and oranges again, there are two areas here, one is the question of the checks; and the other is the question of national security."[31]

Nixon's interjection of the Bay of Pigs as a way to get the CIA's cooperation was difficult to explain, even for Haldeman. (At the trial, Ben-Veniste called the Bay of Pigs an afterthought.[32]) It was not easy to say that the president of the United States was twisting the arms of the leaders of the CIA, however subtly, to get them to intervene in the FBI's investigation (if that was the reasoning behind Nixon's mention of the Bay of Pigs).

"Now, isn't it a fact, Mr. Haldeman," Ben-Veniste continued, "that the entire reason for bringing the CIA into this matter was to obfuscate the fact that it was the White House and John Mitchell and the CRP that wanted this investigation curtailed?"

"No," insisted Haldeman.[33]

"So what happened was you came upon the fact that Hunt had been involved in the Bay of Pigs, which was twelve years old at that time, and that is what it was going to be hung on, not any mention about the fact that this pursuit of this investigation would link up the CRP with the burglars but pin it on the fact that twelve years ago Hunt had been involved in the Bay of Pigs, and then tell them, well, this is a comedy of errors, do you see that?"

"Yes," Haldeman said. He was following Ben-Veniste's train of thought, which was a recitation of the conventional wisdom.

"Does it say that?"[34]

At this point, for the first time in the various Watergate proceedings, someone publicly tried to clarify Nixon's reference to the Bay of Pigs in his conversation with Haldeman. To many observers, the Bay of Pigs was an ancient and irrelevant distraction and could not be the reason the White House asked the CIA to limit the FBI's 1972 investigation. Hunt, who had been involved in the Bay of Pigs invasion, had been convicted of breaking into the DNC, which Ben-Veniste tried to exploit. Haldeman gamely tried to explain how the 1961 invasion of Cuba fit into the present picture:

Yes, it says that, and may I explain? There is a constant reference here to the Bay of Pigs being twelve years earlier. The event of the Bay of Pigs was twelve years earlier. The investigation and concern about the Bay of Pigs was very current. It was current in the sense that I later learned, I didn't know at this time, but I presume the President did—that, for example, when Mr. Hunt was working at the White House, Director Helms of the CIA was very concerned that Mr. Hunt not have any access to anything relating to this Bay of Pigs episode during the time he was working at the White House because the White House at that time was engaged in trying to compile all of the facts regarding the Bay of Pigs episode....

The question of the Bay of Pigs in this context was raised by President Nixon and not by me, as I have frequently testified in earlier forums.

Haldeman's statement regarding Helms's concern about Hunt working in the White House seems to be true, but it was not clear how relevant it was. In other words, Haldeman may have used Hunt's presence in the White House as an excuse to explain the president's mention of the Bay of Pigs. Years later, Haldeman admitted that he did not understand Nixon's reference to the Bay of Pigs.

Ben-Veniste wanted to move away from national security matters and asked: "Mr. Haldeman, isn't it a fact that the whole reason for this was political and with whatever criminal overtones [there] were to it, and the President said, I don't want them to get any ideas we are doing it because our concern [is] political?" Ben-Veniste would not be harmed by another Haldeman denial.

But Haldeman was ready for him: "As far as I was concerned, there were no criminal overtones to it. The original proposal made at John Dean's suggestion by me to the President in the morning was as a result of the concern about tracing the source of the funds. The other points raised by the President at that meeting and in another meeting were in other areas, as the tapes show."[35] Once again, Haldeman rejected the conventional wisdom, albeit unclearly. He had no satisfactory answer to Ben-Veniste's charge that he and Nixon were directing the CIA to take action to protect the identities of anonymous donors to Nixon's campaign, a partisan and political objective rather than a national or governmental one, but arguably less serious than trying to upend the entire FBI investigation into the Watergate break-in.

Despite Haldeman's difficulty explaining the facts to the jury, he was on the right track. Putting Haldeman's and Dean's testimony together with the three June 23, 1972, conversations between Nixon and Haldeman demonstrates that the "smoking gun" tape was about protecting anonymous campaign contributors, but that was not easy to see or explain. And, as Ben-Veniste said, it was not relevant as a matter of law in *U.S. v. Mitchell*.

The Defendants Learn Their Fate

Mitchell's main defense was that he had not approved Liddy's intelligence plan and had no idea who eventually implemented the operation or how they did so. He minimized his role in the cover-up and claimed he had been a force for moderation.

Ehrlichman argued that any conspiracy did not involve him, and he wanted Nixon to take the witness stand to support his position. After all, he did not know about the recording system and did not participate in the critical Nixon-Haldeman conversations on June 23, 1972. He had little to work with, and it was a game effort. Ehrlichman, who was estranged from his former boss, seemed to have no qualms about embarrassing him and subpoenaed Nixon as a witness to bolster his defense. After extended arguments and Nixon's examination by physicians, Sirica ruled that the president, who was in California suffering from phlebitis, was too ill to testify, even by way of a deposition.

Six months after the trial, representatives of the WSPF and two members of the grand jury questioned Nixon in California on June 23 and 24, 1975. Nixon claimed Andreas's contribution was returned to him on June 19, 1972. No one asked Nixon about the content of the June 23, 1972, tapes.[36] Nixon's testimony was limited because he could be asked questions only about matters pertaining to investigations that were still in progress.[37]

On January 1, 1975, the jury convicted Haldeman, Mitchell, Ehrlichman, and Mardian of conspiracy and obstruction of justice; the first three were also convicted of perjury. The jury acquitted Parkinson, the largely neglected attorney for the CRP who was represented by Jacob Stein, a prominent Washington attorney. The indictment of Parkinson was probably a miscarriage of justice, as he had far less involvement in the cover-up than some of the other attorneys.[38] These include Hunt's attorney William Bittman, who was deeply involved in payments to the burglars, and Paul O'Brien, another CRP attorney who was given immunity early in the proceedings.[39]

The Media Coverage

Because federal law prohibited the broadcasting of the cover-up trial live or the recording of it it for later viewing—unlike the hearings of the Senate Watergate Committee and the House Judiciary Committee—very few people are familiar with the testimony given at the trial. Many people, including the authors of books on Watergate, have had to rely on daily newspaper coverage of the trial.

That coverage included several gaffes by Judge Sirica, which were far more entertaining than Haldeman's testimony. For instance, Sirica said it would have saved a lot of trouble if Mitchell had thrown Liddy out of his office early in 1972, and he announced that he was not going to apply the rules of evidence rigorously (he later explained that this was because of the centrality of the charge of conspiracy, which involves many exceptions to the standard rules of evidence). But most of all, the newspapers described the testimony of the witnesses, starting with the two weeks John Dean spent on the witness stand and continuing through the many other witnesses called by the prosecution, and, finally, the recordings of the White House conversations.

The WSPF's position on the June 23 conversation, as reported by the *New York Times*, was not emphasized. Its short statement on November 16, 1974, promoted the conventional interpretation: the White House and campaign officials realized immediately after the break-in that a thorough investigation would uncover the link between the campaign and the burglary, so they conspired to obstruct the inquiry through a "cover story" and payoffs to the seven men who had participated in the break-in. The cover story was that the FCRP had given the money to Liddy for legitimate campaign purposes, but Liddy used the money to break into the DNC. Although it could not say so, the White House welcomed the involvement of the reelection campaign because it diverted attention from the White House, a connection that Hunt's involvement strengthened.

Haldeman's testimony started on December 3, and the next day the *New York Times* ran a story on page 23 with the rather bland but accurate headline "Haldeman Rebuts Prosecution on Meaning of Tapes." (Most of its coverage of the trial began on page 1; this article did not.) The newspaper reported that Haldeman claimed the White House had approached the CIA for the purpose of protecting campaign contributors. Haldeman admitted to the jury that this was the first time he had offered this explanation and that he had testified incorrectly before the Senate Watergate Committee. The account of his defense, such as it was, was a one-day story. No other defendant focused on the campaign contributors.

The *Washington Post*, which also gave the trial daily and usually front-page coverage, reported that Nixon told Haldeman "not to pursue the source of these [checks from Dahlberg and Ogarrio] to the point of embarrassment to the donors" because "the donations weren't related to Watergate at all."[40] At another point, the *Post* discussed the goal of the cover-up: "All he [Haldeman] was trying to do was protect the anonymity of the donors who had made the contributions."[41] But these two sentences were virtually the only things the *Post* had to say on the subject of Haldeman's motives during nearly three months of trial coverage. Moreover, these two references were buried in the middle or near the end of the story on the inside pages of the newspaper. The *Post*, of course, did not explain the reason for its relatively brief coverage of Haldeman's defense, which was overshadowed by the extensive evidence of large payments of cash, offers of clemency, and lying that occupied the pages of the newspaper.

The Appeal

On appeal, the DC Circuit, again sitting *en banc*, filed a lengthy opinion that upheld the convictions of Mitchell, Haldeman, and Ehrlichman but reversed Mardian's conviction because Judge Sirica had required him to proceed with a junior attorney when his principal attorney, David Bress, became ill and was forced to retire.[42] The admissibility of the Nixon tapes and the motion to disqualify Sirica were major portions of the opinion, as was pretrial publicity in general. Judge MacKinnon voted to affirm in part and reverse in part. His dissent was confined to the issue of pretrial publicity in general and to the conviction on the hush-money charge based on insufficient evidence and flaws in Sirica's instructions to the jury.

It is unlikely that Dean's and Haldeman's testimony caused any perceptible change in the almost universal conclusion that on June 23, 1972, Nixon used (or misused) the CIA to try to stop the FBI's investigation of the break-in at DNC headquarters in the Watergate Office Building. Whether history would correct that conclusion remained to be seen.

PART IV
The Aftermath

14

Thoughts on Prosecuting Nixon

After just one month in office, and with no advance warning to anyone other than his closest aides, on September 8, 1974, President Ford granted a total and unconditional pardon to Richard Nixon for all federal crimes he committed or may have committed while president. The pardon created an uproar, particularly since Nixon had not admitted to any criminal conduct.

Many Americans wanted Watergate Special Prosecutor Leon Jaworski to obtain an indictment against Nixon, forcing the former president to defend himself against major criminal charges. The potential charges involved not only crimes related to the cover-up of White House activities, burglaries at the Watergate Office Building and the office of Dr. Lewis Fielding, bribery, and the subornation of perjury but also the bombing of Cambodia, Nixon's income tax returns, and bribery in connection with the price of milk. It would have occupied the country for months if not years.

This chapter focuses on whether Nixon committed a federal crime on June 23, 1972, related to his conversations with Haldeman that directly precipitated his resignation more than two years later.[1] A significant minority of the House Impeachment Committee fixated on the issue of whether Nixon had committed a crime: "The language of the Constitution indicates that impeachment can be only for serious criminal offenses."[2] For them, a criminal case against a president was the gateway to his impeachment and removal from office. A minority of congressmen held this view, and it continues to be the minority interpretation of the constitutional language. Republican Representative Delbert L. Latta noted that, given the June 23, 1972, tapes coupled with Nixon's statement on March 6, 1974, "obstruction of justice would be an impeachable offense [and] would have been sufficient to vote affirmatively on these two Paragraphs [in Article I]. . . . However, at the time the vote was taken in the Judiciary Committee in this matter, this evidence of direct presidential involvement had not been revealed and was not before us."[3]

The prosecution is responsible for filing charges and then presenting its evidence to the trial judge and jury. At some point, the presenters of the hypothetical *U.S. v. Nixon* would have had to decide what Nixon did on June 23 that was illegal. The prosecutors got away with some fudging in *U.S. v. Mitchell*, but John Dean—reinforced by H. R. Haldeman, the other party in the conversations with Nixon—made it clear that he thought the June 23 discussion of approaching the CIA was about protecting anonymous donors to Nixon's 1972 campaign and not about stopping the FBI from investigating the Watergate break-in.

Nixon's lawyers certainly would have examined the "smoking gun" tape closely, in light of the testimony of both Dean and Haldeman. They also would have spoken to Haldeman, Dean, and Maurice Stans before the trial. Moreover, Haldeman and Stans almost certainly would have been witnesses for Nixon, and they would have testified—probably along with a reeducated and revitalized Nixon—that the concern on June 23, 1972, was confined to anonymous donors to Nixon's reelection campaign. Whatever position the WSPF took in *U.S. v. Nixon*, it would be clear that Dean had approached Haldeman after speaking with John Mitchell and Stans and that he was conveying their concern that the FBI investigation was turning toward Mexico and would inevitably disclose the campaign contributions of Robert Allen and his friends.

The Criminal Law

The WSPF would not have filed an indictment against Nixon until after the conclusion of the cover-up trial. Trials and appeals take time; four or five years, including consideration by the Supreme Court, would be a conservative estimate for the prosecution of a former president. Federal decisions as of the end of the 1970s state what the applicable law would have been in a prosecution of Nixon, assuming he was convicted and went through the appeals process. The federal criminal charges discussed at the time, which still appear to be the only crimes possibly related to Nixon's conduct on June 23, were obstruction of justice (defined in 18 U.S.C. § 1503) and conspiracy (defined in 18 U.S.C. § 371). The principal allegation would have been that Nixon conspired to endeavor to impede or obstruct a federal proceeding, which was the charge levied against his top aides. The applicable words of section 371 are: "If two or more persons conspire to commit any offense against the United States, or to defraud the United States, or any agency in any manner or for any purpose, and one or more of such persons do any act to effect the object of the conspiracy, each shall be . . . [punished]."

To prevail, a prosecutor must satisfy the jury that the prosecution has proved all the elements of the crime beyond a reasonable doubt. The elements of conspiracy under section 371 are an agreement, the potential violation of a federal statute, the requisite knowledge or intent, and an overt act on the part of one of the conspirators in furtherance of the conspiracy (that act itself need not be illegal).[4] Participation in a conspiracy must be voluntary, although it is not necessary that a conspirator know all the details or objectives of the conspiracy or even the identity of all the coconspirators named by the grand jury or the prosecutor.

A prosecutor in *U.S. v. Nixon* would have had a relatively easy time with some of these elements. Nixon and Haldeman unquestionably agreed to try to influence the CIA, and Haldeman committed an overt act in furtherance of the conspiracy—namely, meeting with the CIA director and deputy director.[5] The most controversial issue under section 371 would be Nixon's state of mind; to convict, the jury would have to find that he had the requisite knowledge and intent. There also may have been unique questions because, as president of the United States, Nixon was in charge of the executive branch of the government that he was accused of obstructing.

Two alternatives present themselves. One, which is superficially attractive, would be to accuse Nixon of conspiring to defraud the United States or one of its agencies rather than conspiring to violate a law.[6] However, the argument that a president defrauds the United States by using the federal government for his personal or political purposes seems too broad to form the basis of a prosecution of a president. Nixon directed one executive branch agency to tell another executive branch agency to limit an investigation. Whether a president violates section 371 if he uses money to bribe the head of an agency to take, or refrain from taking, action need not concern us, as there is no evidence of that occurring. The question is whether a president violates section 371 if he tells an agency in the executive branch to do something that, on its face, is not illegal. The answer seems to be no. The charge that Nixon conspired on June 23, 1972, to defraud the United States could not be sustained because there would be doubt as to his motives. Consequently, the prosecution would have to prove a conspiracy to violate a federal law.

Clearly, the best option was obstruction of justice under section 1503, which on June 23, 1972, read: "Whoever ... corruptly ... influences, obstructs, or impedes, or endeavors to influence, obstruct, or impede, the due administration of justice, shall be punished." Some of the elements would be easy to prove. To "endeavor" means to undertake any effort to accomplish a purpose the section was enacted to prevent.[7] It connotes a lower threshold of purposeful activity than to "attempt."[8] This provision may be violated without actually succeeding in the endeavor.[9] Nixon clearly endeavored to limit an FBI investigation, at least to some extent.[10]

More difficult would be meeting the requirement that there be an endeavor to obstruct the "due administration of justice"—namely, a pending judicial proceeding. The prosecution would have to prove the existence of a pending judicial proceeding, knowledge by the defendant that the proceeding was pending, a corrupt interference in or endeavor to interfere with a pending proceeding, and a specific intent to obstruct justice. Not all federal courts have agreed on when a proceeding is pending, but even in the 1970s, they all agreed that there must be a pending judicial proceeding. An FBI investigation is not considered a judicial proceeding.[11] The FBI does not administer justice; it is an investigative body. Moreover, Nixon could argue that because the Department of Justice had assured the White House that the FBI would not investigate campaign contributors, the FBI was acting beyond its authority, at least insofar as it related to Nixon's state of mind. Although this argument would be unnecessary, it would make Nixon's position more palatable to a jury.

If a federal grand jury is actively investigating a crime, there is a pending judicial proceeding; there is no requirement that the grand jury must have heard witness testimony. If a subpoena has been issued on behalf of a grand jury, its investigation is pending, even though the subpoena was issued by the prosecutor supervising the grand jury and the latter was unaware of it.[12] Indeed, according to some authorities, there was not even a requirement that a subpoena be issued, which was probably the law at the time.[13]

Obstruction of Justice

President Richard M. Nixon did not engage in a conspiracy on June 23, 1972, for the fundamental reason that he never sought to obstruct a judicial proceeding. He (and H.R. Haldeman) sought to engage the CIA to limit the scope of an FBI investigation, which is not a judicial proceeding. Nixon was concerned about leaks of the FBI investigation, which had been taking place. FBI agents were on the verge of investigating confidential contributions to the 1972 Nixon re-election campaign and the White House was attempting to stop that. There is no suggestion in his conversations with Haldeman that he was concerned about the grand jury or any forthcoming trial. In this connection it is significant that the White House approached the CIA to influence the FBI rather than direct their attention to the Department of Justice, which was responsible for presenting cases to the grand jury and then trying them in court. In 1972 endeavoring to misdirect the FBI was not an obstruction of justice.

The fact that Assistant Attorney General Henry Petersen told John Dean (who told Haldeman) that the Department of Justice was not investigating campaign contributions strengthens Nixon's position on the import of the taped conversations. Members of the "conspiracy" knew they had no reason to influence a grand jury. The FBI was below the Attorney General of the United States. The White House was simply not concerned about the grand jury and trial in June 1972.

Nixon's injection of national security and the Bay of Pigs into his discussion with Haldeman was irrelevant on this issue. Nixon's adding that dimension to the discussion related only to motivating the CIA to approach the FBI. In fact, the injection of national security into the picture, if anything, made it less likely that a grand jury would be informed. Similarly with the activities of E. Howard Hunt. His escapades were far from anything that would be presented to a grand jury in the middle of 1972. Associating any of the actions of the White House or campaign with the CIA and national security could help the White House.

Even in 1972, decades before the Supreme Court expanded the protections given to the president in *Trump v. U.S.*, Nixon could have argued that his giving directions to the FBI, which was part of the executive branch, did not violate the law, although he had little authority to back his position. He did have one argument that might have given a court pause, namely, that he was doing no more than keeping the FBI's investigation within its proper bounds, although it would have required imaginative lawyering to make that argument. In any event, convicting Nixon of obstruction of justice for his statements on June 23, 1972, would have been difficult, if not impossible.

What Nixon Knew and When He Knew It

It is worth noting that even if the June 23 conversations are somehow construed more broadly to include obstructing the grand jury, the prosecution faced major barriers in proving that Nixon violated section 1503. The reason is that while a grand jury was beginning to investigate the Watergate break-in, Nixon had insufficient awareness of it to be guilty of obstructing a judicial proceeding. Moreover, at no time were the payments made by Kenneth Dahlberg (Dwayne Andreas) or Manuel Ogarrio (Robert Allen) before the grand jury. Proving that Nixon was aware of the grand jury proceedings would have been much more difficult than proving that he was aware of a criminal case in the district court.[14] Nothing about a grand jury appeared in the *New York Times*, the *Washington Post*, or the *Washington Star* in the period June 20–23, 1972, although the *Star* contained two references to an "FBI subpoena," one to the Republic Mutual Bank in Miami, and one to the Watergate Hotel in Washington, where some of the burglars were staying. This almost certainly referred to grand jury subpoenas served by the FBI.[15] A reference to grand jury subpoenas also appeared in Nixon's multipage daily news summary, albeit in one brief sentence. The news summary for President Nixon on June 23, 1972, included the following paragraph, although it is not clear where the writer obtained his information about the alleged subpoena of Mrs. McCord:

Break-in suspect Barker was "tenaciously" after Dem Conv. Hall blueprints 8 months ago, says the *Star* on p. 1. Also reported are 2 calls from McCord to Bob Mardian the week before the break-in. Mardian denies knowing McCord tho the *Star* says the 2 men did know each other in '69–'70. . . . *Mrs. McCord has been subpoenaed before the grand jury*. It was also learned $90,000 drawn from a Mexican bank was deposited in Barker's Miami account. He later withdrew a similar amount [emphasis added].[16]

The question would be whether Nixon read this paragraph before his first meeting with Haldeman on June 23 (the tapes indicate he did not read it between the first and second meetings). Here, the prosecutors would receive an unusual break. Nixon's diary indicated when he was given the summary: "On Friday, June 23, 1972, I had breakfast with Jerry Ford and [Congressman] Hale Boggs, who were leaving on a trip to the People's Republic of China. After breakfast I went to the Oval Office and *Alex Butterfield, one of Haldeman's assistants, brought in several routine papers and documents.* Then Haldeman came in as he did every morning, unhurried, ready to begin the day."[17]

Even if the prosecution established that the "routine papers and documents" included the news summary, it would still have to prove that Nixon read it; no one provided him with an oral briefing. Unexpectedly, the end of the first June 23 tape seemed to prove that Nixon read the news summary before he met with Haldeman:

Haldeman: The FBI guys working the case had concluded that there were one or two possibilities, one, that this was ... either a White House operation and they had some obscure reasons for it, non-political ... or it was ... Cubans and the CIA. And after their interrogation of ... Colson, yesterday, they concluded it was not the White House, but are now convinced it is a CIA thing....

President: Yeah, *when I saw that News Summary item,* I, of course, knew it was a bunch of crap, but I thought, ah, well it's good to have them off on this wild hair thing because when they start bugging us, which they have ... [emphasis added].[18]

Nixon did not otherwise describe the news item, but newspapers on June 23 indicated that the arrested Cubans were known to be interested in Democratic candidate George McGovern and may have engineered the break-in to learn more about the Democrats' involvement with Castro. Nixon's scoffing at the idea made sense, given his substantial knowledge on June 23 (as evidenced by tapes of earlier conversations). He did not seem to be referring to anything involving the CIA.

Nixon had another engagement, namely, that the grand jury was not investigating campaign contributions, as well as other arguments related to a charge based on the violation of campaign finance laws. That was the position of Assistant Attorney General Henry Petersen. Assistant U.S. Attorney Earl Silbert, the principal prosecutor, viewed the ultimate source of the money possessed by the burglars and the roles of Dahlberg and Ogarrio as not material to the prosecution of the seven men involved in the break-in, and he presented no evidence on that subject to the grand jury or at trial. Instead, this matter was explored by Silbert and the FBI, not the grand jury, when trying to figure out why those checks were in Barker's bank account, and it was all sorted out relatively quickly.[19]

There is additional evidence on this question. Silbert began dictating a diary in late July or early August 1972, using FBI reports and notes when he lacked personal knowledge. His diary has never been published, but Silbert's dictations have been transcribed (a very rough and unedited draft, apparently by someone in the U.S. Attorney's Office). It is massive, running some 910 pages of double-spaced text and exceeding 200,000 words. Pursuant to Rule 6(e) of the Federal Rules of Criminal Procedure, which imposes secrecy on all federal grand jury proceedings, the National Archives carefully vetted Silbert's diary and redacted all material related to the grand jury. The fact that some 4,300 words in the diary are devoted to Silbert's explanation of the handling of the Ogarrio and Dahlberg money indicates that this material was not addressed by the grand jury, given the National Archives' care and caution with regard to potential Rule 6(e)–related material.

Another argument that probably would have been unsuccessful was seemingly precluded by court cases available in the 1970s. In at least three cases, a court of appeals held that a defendant (whether an attorney or not) violated the law by urging a witness not to recall something or to invoke the Fifth Amendment if the motive was to shield the defendant's own wrongful conduct.[20] Whatever the rights of a suspect, a person advising him is in a weaker position.

It should be kept in mind that Judge Sirica would not have presided over the hypothetical case of *U.S. v. Nixon* in 1975. Judge George L. Hart Jr. succeeded Sirica as chief judge. Hart, a law-and-order judge, tended to be lenient with well-connected defendants. For example, he presided over the prosecution of former Attorney General Richard Kleindienst, who pleaded guilty to lying to a Senate committee about the antitrust case against International Telephone and Telegraph, a misdemeanor. Hart sentenced Kleindienst to thirty days in jail and a fine of $100 and then suspended the sentence, which most people would consider lenient. Of course, it is impossible to know whether Hart would have assigned the case to himself or how he would have handled the prosecution of Nixon.

No one should construe this book as exonerating Nixon, even from a charge that he violated the criminal law during his tenure as president. The trier of the facts would have to examine the evidence minutely. One should not be hasty, however, in assuming that Nixon's sordid record in connection with Watergate and related (and unrelated) matters would smoothly translate into a successful prosecution for the violation of federal law, including his statements on June 23, 1972. Be that as it may, it is clear that no one will ever know.

15

Fifty Years of Misunderstanding

The public's perception of the "smoking gun" tape was solidified on August 5 and 6, 1974, when the media portrayed Nixon and Haldeman as trying to stop the FBI's investigation into the Watergate break-in rather than trying to protect the anonymity of pre–April 7, 1972, campaign donors, some of whom were prominent Democrats who had been promised their identities would not be disclosed. Events in the following months did nothing to change anyone's mind. In fact, many considered acceptance of a pardon an acknowledgment of guilt.

In the five decades since the scandal, some two hundred books about Watergate have been published, a number of them best sellers. These books did not scrutinize the "smoking gun" tape. Likewise, there was little critical examination of the process and events that led to Nixon's resignation and to the conviction of his senior aides. This chapter examines a sampling of the leading books published between 1974 and 2024, some by participants in the events, but most by journalists and historians.[1]

Probably the most noteworthy book to emerge in the aftermath of Watergate was Bob Woodward and Carl Bernstein's *The Final Days*, a careful examination of the last weeks of the Nixon administration and the events leading up to them. Although it made an important contribution, the book virtually ignored the meaning of the "smoking gun" tape, leaving the traditional interpretation of events undisturbed. This is not surprising, as the authors built their careers on investigating the Watergate break-in and its aftermath and were instrumental in forming public opinion. "The [first June 23] tape established that Haldeman intended to use the CIA to impede the investigation of Watergate," they wrote.[2] That statement is simplistic at best. *The Final Days* also included a chronology of events that was more specific about the Nixon-Haldeman conversations. The entry for June 23, 1972, read: "The President and Haldeman formulate a plan to have the CIA impede the FBI's investigation into the Watergate break-in," repeating the conventional wisdom.[3] That statement is not accurate. Ben Bradlee, executive editor of the *Washington Post* during Watergate, made an even stronger comment: "The [June 23, 1972,] tape proved that Nixon had approved the plan for the CIA to call off the FBI's Watergate investigation, and that he lied when he said he hadn't."[4]

The famous chronicler of presidential campaigns Theodore H. White published a widely anticipated book in 1975. It, too, incorrectly asserted that "on the advice of said John Mitchell, relayed by John Dean to Bob Haldeman, Richard Nixon used the Federal machinery—namely, the CIA—to obstruct and halt the FBI investigation of the break-in."[5] Another prominent journalist, Clark R. Mollenhoff, was more accurate but did not provide any detail: "[The tape] established clearly that within five days of the break-in President Nixon had known of the involvement of the re-election committee and had directed some phases of the initial obstruction of the FBI."[6]

The members and staffs of the Senate Watergate Committee and the House Impeachment Committee produced several books. Neither body received the "smoking gun" tape in connection with its official duties, but there was no reluctance to comment on its meaning. Unfortunately, the interpretations were universally wrong. For example, the Senate Watergate Committee's Chief Counsel Samuel Dash wrote: "Nixon conspired with Haldeman six days after the Watergate break-in to use the CIA to head off the FBI investigation of the break-in."[7] A Democratic member of the House Judiciary Committee published a book in 1977 that reached a similar conclusion: "The transcripts, recounting conversations between the President and H. R. Haldeman, then [on June 23, 1972] his chief of staff, showed Nixon personally ordering that the CIA be enlisted to obstruct the FBI investigation of the Watergate break-in."[8] A 2024 biography of Peter W. Rodino Jr. referred to "a conversation six days after the Watergate break-in during which [Nixon] authorized H. R. Haldeman to use the CIA to derail the FBI's investigation, a clear obstruction of justice."[9]

In their book *Stonewall: The Real Story of the Watergate Prosecution*, Assistant Special Prosecutors Richard Ben-Veniste and George Frampton Jr., both of whom actively participated in the cover-up trial, perpetuated the misconception that Haldeman approached the CIA "in order to obstruct the FBI's Watergate investigation."[10]

Leon Jaworski's book described a telephone call from Haig on the morning of August 5, 1974. He repeated what Haig told him about the Nixon-Haldeman conversations on June 23, 1974:

"They talk about getting the FBI out of the investigation by using the CIA—having the CIA say it was a national security matter. . . . "

All three of us on the line knew that Haldeman and Ehrlichman had tried to use the CIA to halt the investigation.

"We didn't know it," Haig said. "He didn't tell us about it. He didn't tell anyone."[11]

At the time, the reference to "the investigation" could only mean the investigation into the break-in at the DNC offices.

Judge John J. Sirica was the nominally impartial jurist who presided over *U.S. v. Hunt et al.* and *U.S. v. Mitchell et al.*, but he sided with the prosecution. He also sided with conventional wisdom. After quoting from the transcript of the first June 23 tape, he wrote in his book: "Here was the 'smoking pistol' the investigators had been looking for—the direct, undeniable evidence that from the very beginning Nixon had been in on, had approved, had condoned and supported the attempt to bury the Watergate mess out of sight of the prosecutors, the courts, Congress, and the public."[12] Sirica made an unusually aggressive and incorrect formulation, including placing Nixon at the start of the cover-up.

Nixon's detailed memoirs reveal that he was confused about important aspects of Watergate and did not recall many of the events immediately following the burglars' arrests on June 17, 1972. "As I understood it, unless we could find some way to limit the investigation the trail would lead directly to the CRP, and our political containment would go by the boards."[13] Nixon referred directly to neither the break-in nor the interests of the contributors; his ultimate fear was disclosure of the roles of the CRP and FCRP, both of which were implicated within days of the arrests.

H. R. Haldeman's 1978 book *The Ends of Power* all but abandoned the detailed argument he made at his trial in late 1974. Rather than develop his somewhat mitigating argument that the White House and the Nixon reelection campaign were concerned with protecting the anonymity of contributors, he wrote simply: "On June 23, 1972 ... I had requested that the CIA attempt to stop the FBI investigation of the Mexican bank through which the CRP checks had been laundered." He continued cryptically and without specificity:

> I thought our objective was to prevent the Watergate investigation from spilling over to other areas. Not to obstruct the process of justice in pursuing Watergate itself. As Dean saw it, we had no intent to impede the Watergate investigation itself—only to avoid the very real possibility that it would lead the investigators, and later the Congressional inquiry, into these "other things," which were not a part of the Watergate crime, and thus not a legitimate part of the investigation of that crime.[14]

Books and statements by Nixon's later team were no better; they were probably worse.[15] Several books by or about key people were drastically wrong. Alexander Haig, Nixon's chief of staff starting in May 1973, wrote of the first June 23 Nixon-Haldeman conversation: "Out of this conversation came the attempt to end the FBI investigation of the Watergate burglary by ordering Vernon Walters, Deputy Director of the CIA, to inform FBI Director Patrick Gray that the break-in was a CIA operation justified for reasons of national security." The CIA's refusal "to cooperate smothered the cover-up in its cradle."[16] That statement is false—remarkably so. The CIA cooperated briefly and had no role in the demise of the cover-up, which should be attributed to John Dean and the Nixon tapes. Thomas Powers's biography of CIA Director Richard Helms states that Helms believed the White House wanted to blame the CIA for the break-in.[17] That is not corroborated by the June 23, 1972, conversations between Haldeman and Nixon.

A biographer of Republican Senator Howard Baker, vice chairman of the Senate Watergate Committee, inaccurately wrote that "on 23 June 1972 [Nixon] ordered H. R. Haldeman to direct the CIA to block the FBI probe of the bugging."[18] The bugging of the DNC, which was discovered immediately after the arrests of the five burglars on June 17, produced nothing of significance and was irrelevant to the cover-up. Journalist Tom Brokaw wrote: "Nixon instructed his chief of staff, Bob Haldeman, to have Richard Helms, director of the CIA, tell the FBI to break off the investigation into Watergate because it was a national security matter."[19]

Most historians waited a dozen or more years to weigh in. Their interpretations of the "smoking gun" tape, however, were by and large traditional and superficial. For example, Stanley Kutler wrote obliquely, "The June 23 tape offered a definitive answer to [Senator] Howard Baker's questions [about what the president knew and when he knew it], put just over a year earlier: the President knew. He knew that he had instigated a cover-up and thus had participated in an obstruction of justice almost from the outset of events." There is no evidence that Nixon *instigated* anything in connection with Watergate, including the cover-up. Kutler did not say what Nixon tried to cover up. His use of the phrase "*almost* from the outset" was correct but unenlightening.[20]

Historian Stephen E. Ambrose recognized that the statement accompanying the release of the June 23 tape "put the worst possible interpretation on the June 23 tape for Nixon" and that some of Nixon's advisers seemed more interested in protecting themselves than in protecting the president. However, he did not mention that the Nixon-Haldeman conversations involved maintaining the anonymity of the pre–April 7, 1972, donors. Ambrose wrote, "Haig told Kissinger that the smoking gun had been found; the June 23 tape left no doubt that Nixon was familiar with the cover-up and may have ordered it."[21]

With one notable exception, books written in the twentieth century missed the fact that the "smoking gun" tape was about protecting anonymous contributors to Nixon's reelection campaign and not about shutting down the FBI's investigation into the Watergate break-in. Maurice Stans, former secretary of commerce and chairman of Nixon's Finance Committee to Reelect the President, sought to resurrect his damaged reputation. He discussed the tape in the context of his fund-raising efforts: "The specific act was his [Nixon's] attempt to thwart the FBI investigation of the Mexican money by blocking the path of the probers. We now know that all the FBI could have done and did do was trace it back to Robert Allen."[22] Stans was knowledgeable, and his remarks were accurate. His statement went unnoticed.

By the end of the 1970s, only sixty of the hundreds of hours of recordings had been made public. Stanley Kutler added a large cache of transcriptions in 1997.[23] John Dean noted the limited availability of the Watergate tapes, particularly the ones from immediately after the break-in, so after the turn of the century he personally arranged to transcribe the balance of the tape recordings related to Watergate. His 2014 book *The Nixon Defense* concluded that the conventional wisdom concerning the events of June 23, 1972, was incorrect.[24] He reported that the conversations he had with Haldeman and those between Haldeman and Nixon were about protecting the anonymous contributors to the reelection campaign that the out-of-control FBI was improperly investigating. His book also brought his and Haldeman's testimony at the cover-up trial to the public's attention.

Interestingly, some of those who have endorsed Dean's 2014 interpretation of the "smoking gun" tape are conservatives who were sympathetic to Nixon and rejected the description of Dean as a conscientious whistleblower who decided to tell the truth after actively participating in the cover-up. To many of them, Dean was a turncoat and a self-promoting liar; however, they accepted his interpretation of the June 23 tapes largely because it reflected less badly on Nixon than did the conventional interpretation. Books published in the twenty-first century by Geoffrey Shepard, who worked for Buzhardt from 1973 to 1974, and by Roger Stone endorsed Dean's view of the "smoking gun" tape with pleasure.[25] Few others have considered recent developments, especially the meaning of that important evidence.[26]

Two recent books on Watergate ignore current scholarship and add little to the knowledge about the scandal. Former assistant Watergate prosecutor Jill Wine-Banks writes: "They hoped to persuade the CIA officials to tell the acting director of the FBI not to follow the money—because the money trail would reveal that CREEP had paid the burglars. The tape proved that Nixon was directly involved in the cover-up from the start, a clear and obvious obstruction of justice."[27] Both sentences are wrong. The most recent book devoted to Watergate (as of this writing) is also one of the longest. Author Garrett M. Graff notes, "If they [Nixon and Haldeman] could get the CIA ... to wave Pat Gray off, they may be able to block the whole thing." He later states, "The White House had intended to stonewall the investigation from the start. And Nixon was in on it."[28] These two books ignore that the cover-up started before anyone talked to Nixon, apparently spontaneously instigated by middle-level White House and campaign staff, and that Charles Colson had already submitted to an FBI interview the day before June 23, which Nixon accepted after the fact. Virtually the only sources Graff cites on that subject are books by members of the WSPF.[29] Graff never before reported on the events of Watergate and apparently did not interview anybody with firsthand knowledge, including Dean.

By and large, authors have not asked, much less answered, the most important questions: What made the June 23 tape a "smoking gun"? What, specifically, were Nixon and Haldeman trying to accomplish on June 23? Authors have not even considered how a fledgling deputy director of the CIA who was an outsider (Walters) could succeed in getting the new acting director of the FBI (Gray), also an outsider who was resented and undermined by his deputies, to stop an "out-of-control" army of FBI agents. Most authors have readily accepted that the White House believed Gray could shut down a massive and well-publicized investigation of a burglary in the District of Columbia simply because a check remotely connected to the burglary had an alleged connection with a (nonexistent) CIA operation in Mexico, a neighboring and friendly country. Looking at it from the perspective of half a century later, the conventional wisdom is deeply flawed.

As a result, authors have not asked what Nixon specifically did that led to his unprecedented resignation. The few who attributed Nixon's departure to the tapes that proved he was a liar from the start had an easier job than those who gave a more specific and narrower reason that did not hold up, but the former were in the minority. Once it is recognized that Nixon did not know about the break-in at Dr. Fielding's office until many months later, had no advance knowledge of the Watergate break-in, did not originate the cover-up, did not approve in advance the payments to Hunt, and did not lie to investigators, including the FBI, the issue becomes more complex and less clear.

Conclusion

The history of the United States in the 1970s and beyond might have been very different had Nixon been graced with excellent lawyers and advisers—and had he accepted their advice. Starting in early 1974, Nixon made extraordinary mistakes and was the victim of mistakes made by others who were supposedly on his side. Those major mistakes include the failure to challenge the transmittal of a "road map" for impeachment, grand jury testimony, and the Nixon tapes to the House Judiciary (Impeachment) Committee. Nixon and his advisers released transcripts of tapes to the public that the courts had limited to federal prosecutors. Nixon did not allow his lawyers to listen to or prepare transcripts of crucial tapes, including his three conversations with Haldeman on June 23, 1972, and otherwise hindered his legal team.

The facts do not absolve Nixon, but they suggest that he was not as culpable as many believe. He had virtually nothing to do with the break-in at the office of Dr. Lewis Fielding, Daniel Ellsberg's psychiatrist; he had no advance knowledge of the Watergate break-ins; he did not originate the cover-up that immediately followed the arrests of the five burglars on June 17, 1972; and he was not attempting to stop the investigation of Watergate when he and Haldeman spoke on June 23, 1972. The defense put forward in 1974 was far weaker than it would have been if Nixon had obtained first-rate legal representation. Although he cannot be seriously faulted for the composition of his legal staff, his inclination was to withhold facts, and he did not encourage his lawyers to prepare the best defense possible.

The interpretation of Watergate has been erroneous in some respects and simplistic in others. Acceptance of the following facts is necessary for an accurate understanding of Watergate:

- Nixon almost certainly had no advance knowledge of the burglary of Fielding's office until March 1973 or the break-ins at the Watergate Office Building. He did not learn the details until after June 17, 1972. Apparently, the information given to Nixon on the Fielding break-in was limited and slow to be revealed for months after June 17.
- The cover-up of the reelection campaign's involvement in the Watergate break-in was spontaneous and immediate, beginning within minutes of the June 17 arrests. It involved Alfred Baldwin, James McCord, G. Gordon Liddy, E. Howard Hunt, and Jeb Magruder of the campaign staff and Gordon Strachan, H. R. Haldeman, John Ehrlichman, and John Mitchell of the Nixon administration. Nixon did not originate the cover-up, and there is no firm evidence that he participated in the cover-up before June 23; there is likewise to evidence that he did anything to discourage it.
- For unknown reasons, the FBI's initial investigation into the Watergate break-in was inept and inadequate, particularly its failure to obtain search warrants for the vehicle and home of James McCord, even though a search of his room at the Watergate Hotel had found significant incriminating material.[1]
- The tapes of the three conversations on June 23, 1972, were no "smoking gun." The principal concern at the time was protecting the anonymity of pre-April 7, 1972, donors to the Nixon reelection campaign. On June 23 the White House's knowledge of the Watergate burglary was still limited, and Nixon was ignorant of most of the details. He seemed distracted and was most concerned about the CIA and foreign policy, not the break-in. Participants in the White House promptly forgot the reason for the June 23 conversations, which says something about their importance.
- By June 23, 1972, it was a practical impossibility for the White House or anyone else to stop the FBI's massive investigation of the break-in at the Watergate Office Building.
- On June 23, 1972, the White House had little to fear from an FBI investigation of the Watergate break-in.
- Events taking place after June 23, such as the actions taken by the FBI,

CONCLUSION [189]

confirm that the purpose of those conversations was to stop the unauthorized FBI investigation into contributions to the Nixon campaign.
- The decision to upgrade Patrick Gray's status from acting to permanent director of the FBI was a serious and inexplicable error. The blame falls mainly on Ehrlichman, who knew about Gray's vulnerabilities yet said nothing to Nixon. In fact, Gray's nomination in February 1973 was an important step in Nixon's downfall.
- Nixon incriminated himself in his conversations with John Dean in March 1973, but he was not responsible for the payment of hush money to Hunt after the March 21 conversation.
- The cover-up was in serious danger of collapsing in the spring of 1973—when Dean decided to cooperate with authorities—because of the difficulty of raising cash to pay off Hunt, Liddy, and others implicated in the Watergate break-in. It is unclear what would have happened if other unrelated events had not intervened.
- After Haldeman, Ehrlichman, and Dean departed the White House on April 30, 1973, Alexander M. Haig Jr., J. Fred Buzhardt, and James D. St. Clair were appointed to replace them. None of them were knowledgeable about Watergate, and they were not devoted to Nixon.
- Arguably, the conditions the Senate Judiciary Committee imposed on Elliot Richardson during his confirmation hearings in May 1973 with respect to the president's ability to fire a special prosecutor were unconstitutional.
- Although Dean made remarkable disclosures before the Senate Watergate Committee in June 1973, the evidence to prosecute Nixon, Haldeman, and Ehrlichman was grossly insufficient in June 1973.
- Starting in December 1973, Judge John Sirica and Special Prosecutor Leon Jaworski had improper secret meetings where they established the scenario for Sirica to preside at the cover-up trial of Mitchell, Haldeman, and Ehrlichman and for the WSPF to funnel secret and privileged information to the House Impeachment Committee.
- Jaworski and his deputy Henry Ruth began funneling secret grand jury information to the House Impeachment Committee in February 1974 or earlier, before Judge Sirica authorized the transfer of information on March 18, 1974.
- When the indictment of Mitchell, Haldeman, and Ehrlichman was filed on March 1, 1974, the WSPF and the grand jury transferred secret grand jury

information, WSPF work product, and White House recordings to Sirica (pursuant to a secret arrangement) for him to transfer to the House Impeachment Committee. The WSPF and Sirica provided virtually no information about the content of the transferred materials. Some information was available at the time and several days later, when Sirica invited any interested party to file an objection to his turning over the material to the House Impeachment Committee.

- Because of the incompetence and arrogance of Nixon's aides, especially St. Clair, the White House did not object to the transfer of secret grand jury information from the WSPF to the House Impeachment Committee. This was an astonishing failure; Nixon had substantial grounds for objecting, and his failure to do so surprised many participants. Without the material provided by the WSPF, the House Impeachment Committee would have been unable to make its presentation when it did. The failure to object may have been responsible for Nixon's resignation. (Although defendants in *U.S. v. Mitchell* objected to the transfer, their grounds for objection were much weaker than Nixon's, and they lost.)
- The U.S. Court of Appeals for the District of Columbia Circuit, with the exception of Judge George MacKinnon, rubber-stamped Sirica's rulings, although in many cases its scope of review was limited.
- Although under no obligation to do so, the White House publicly released tapes it had been directed to provide only to the WSPF, which undermined the claim that the tapes were confidential. The White House also gave the WSPF tapes it was not court-ordered to provide.
- Once the White House recording system was revealed on July 16, 1973, Nixon prevented his lawyers and advisers from listening to the tapes or obtaining information essential for the protection of his interests. Neither the lawyers nor the other advisers objected to this arrangement. Equally important, there is no evidence that Nixon's team ever attempted to organize a defense for him.
- The White House made no effort to influence the appointment of Republicans to the House Impeachment Committee staff and failed to effectively coordinate its Republican members.
- Nixon's lawyers and advisers did not analyze the situation in early 1974 and made no objection to the agonizingly slow pace of the Impeachment Committee, which was not ready to hold hearings until May 1974.

- Only Nixon listened to any portion of the June 23 tapes prior to July 24, 1974.
- Haig, a nonlawyer who had limited knowledge of the details of Watergate, negotiated with the more sophisticated and knowledgeable Jaworski.
- When the Supreme Court ordered Nixon to surrender important tapes to the special prosecutor on July 24, 1974, St. Clair, Nixon's principal lawyer, all but abandoned any effort to defend the president. In fact, he took a four-day vacation to play golf in the two-week interval between the Supreme Court's order and Nixon's decision to resign.
- Even after the Supreme Court's ruling, Nixon and his lawyers and advisers made no effort to analyze the tapes or prepare a defense. They blindly accepted that Nixon and Haldeman had conspired to stop the investigation into the Watergate burglary. When they spoke to senators and others about the tapes, they provided no defense or explanation.
- Haig apparently listened to none of the White House tapes. St. Clair apparently listened only to the June 23 tapes, but not until about a week after the Supreme Court ordered the White House to give the tapes to the WSPF and several days after Sirica ordered him to do so. It does not appear that anyone else listened to the tapes.
- The White House apparently did not make a transcript of the June 23, 1972, conversations until August 1 or 2, 1974, more than a year after the recording system was revealed, eight or nine days after the Supreme Court ordered that the tapes be provided to the WSPF, and just days before Nixon made his final decision to resign—a decision based on those tapes.
- Nixon's lawyers and other close advisers pressured him to release what amounted to a broad confession when he released transcripts of the June 23, 1972, tapes. Then they insisted that Nixon exonerate them when he resigned.
- To the extent that Nixon's resignation was the result of efforts to protect anonymous contributors to his reelection campaign, it was largely an altruistic act that was unlikely to benefit Nixon to any significant degree.
- Putting the trial of Mitchell, Haldeman, and Ehrlichman in the hands of Judge Sirica was a travesty. He had gambled his reputation on the proposition that people senior to Hunt and Liddy, including Mitchell, Haldeman, and Ehrlichman, were implicated in the Watergate scandal. Given a trial judge's broad discretion, there is no way they could have received a fair and unbiased trial with Sirica in charge.

- The true import of the June 23 tapes did not come to light until the cover-up trial, when Dean's testimony explained their true nature and Haldeman remembered that his concern on that date was protecting the identity of anonymous and mostly Democratic contributors to the Nixon campaign. This revelation was barely mentioned in the press or otherwise noted.
- Haldeman did not confess to the crime of obstruction of justice during *U.S. v. Mitchell.*
- It would have been impossible to convict Nixon of any crime related to the Watergate break-in itself. He probably did not commit a substantive crime, and although the evidence of his participation in a criminal conspiracy was not overwhelming, it was almost certainly sufficient to permit a jury to find him guilty based on the recorded conversations with his senior aides in March and April 1973.
- For all his misconduct and mistakes, it is important to recognize that Nixon believed in and accepted the legal and political system. He ultimately obeyed court orders and resigned when impeachment by the House of Representatives and conviction by the Senate seemed certain. Though he was bitter and uncompromising at times, he never attacked the country's institutions or claimed that his opponents acted in bad faith. He accepted his fate if not with grace, at least without challenge. There is no evidence that anyone in the White House, including earlier aides, made any attempt to intimidate Dean or otherwise prevent him from testifying.
- For decades after Watergate, virtually everyone, including those involved in the criminal activity and those investigating or prosecuting it at the time, accepted the conventional wisdom that the cover-up that started after the burglars' arrests was directed at stopping the FBI's investigation into the break-in at the Watergate Office Building. This interpretation was repeated in books by the participants, by people involved in the investigation, by journalists, and by historians.

When bits and pieces of evidence are combined and analyzed carefully, a different picture of Watergate emerges. Much of this evidence, which did not exist or was unavailable until the last dozen years, has been largely ignored by mainstream publishers but has appeared in a few books published by the conservative press. This evidence includes WSPF records, the notes of Bob Woodward and Carl Bernstein, and interviews conducted by the Nixon

Presidential Library. Although this new information does not exonerate Nixon, the facts present a substantially different picture than the one that has been accepted for more than half a century. I have tried to establish that the record is more complex and nuanced than we realized. It is time to correct history.

ACKNOWLEDGMENTS

This book dates back to a memorandum John Dean wrote in 2011 about the "smoking gun" tape and the issues involved in prosecuting ex-President Nixon. Dean sharpened his analysis of the "smoking gun" tape in his book *The Nixon Defense*, published in 2014. In 2022 Dean proposed that he and I collaborate on something, and I suggested that we write a book that included other issues I had researched. But demands on Dean's schedule meant that he could not devote as much time to the project as he wanted, and he urged me to continue alone. This book borrows from Dean's work, and he generously provided assistance to ensure its accuracy. However, he bears no responsibility for the opinions or characterizations expressed herein; those are mine alone.[1]

I made substantial revisions and additions to Dean's original memorandum, principally with regard to the Senate Watergate Committee and the events of March 1974 involving the WSPF and Judge John Sirica. I also greatly expanded his comments on newspaper and book accounts of the Watergate scandal. I based portions of the book on my research and my experience as assistant chief counsel to the Senate Watergate Committee, but I relied primarily on the printed record.

I want to express my gratitude to those under whom I worked on the Senate Watergate Committee: Chairman Sam Ervin and Chief Counsel Samuel Dash. The Library of Congress, the National Archives (Robert Reed), the Nixon Library (Timothy Neftali and Ryan Pettigrew), and the Harry Ransom Center at the University of Texas at Austin (Stephen Mielke) provided important source material from their invaluable collections of documents. Richard (Rick) Wallace, former director of the Harry Ransom Center, did the investigation and research that supplied Woodward and Bernstein's notes for their two books on Watergate as well as later material, particularly involving Alexander Haig, that became part of the collection.

I also received significant help from the custodians of the records of the Senate Watergate Committee. Over the past fifty years, Gordon Freedman and, more recently, Don Rayno, who were on the committee's staff from 1973 to 1974, have maintained and developed the committee's files. The committee made all its records available to the general public when it filed its final report in late 1974.

I want to express my thanks to the University Press of Kansas for the considerable work its members undertook to improve by book. In particular, I want to thank David Congdon, Andrea Laws, and Erica Nicholson for their efforts with respect to this volume. To say that it was done highly professionally would barely scratch the surface of their contributions.

APPENDIX A

List of Participants

Adler, Renata	Assistant to Doar
Agnew, Spiro	Vice president of the United States
Allen, George	Texas Democrat and contributor to CRP
Andreas, Dwayne	Regional chairman, FCRP
Armstrong, Scott	Investigator, Senate Watergate Committee
Baker, Howard,	Deputy chairman, Senate Watergate Committee (R)
Baldwin, Alfred	Monitor of bugged conversations
Barker, Bernard	Cuban burglar
Ben-Veniste, Richard	Assistant special Watergate prosecutor
Bernstein, Carl	*Washington Post* reporter
Bittman, William	Lawyer for Hunt
Bork, Robert	Solicitor general
Boyce, Eugene	Assistant majority counsel, Senate Watergate Committee
Bradlee, Ben	Editor, *Washington Post*
Bray, Jack	Attorney for Strachan
Bress, David	Attorney for Mardian
Buchanan, Patrick J.	Special assistant to the president
Bull, Stephen	Assistant to Haldeman
Burch, Dean	Assistant to the president
Butler, M. Caldwell	Member, House Judiciary Committee (R)
Butterfield, Alexander	Deputy White House Chief of Staff, Secretary to the cabinet
Buzhardt, J. Fred	Special White House counsel to the president
Castro, Fidel	Leader of Cuba
Chapin, Dwight	White House appointments secretary
Chester, John J.	Assistant to St. Clair
Cohen, William	Member, House Judiciary Committee (R)
Colson, Charles W.	Special counsel to the president
Cox, Archibald	Watergate special prosecutor
Cox, Edward	Nixon's son-in-law
Cox, Tricia Nixon	Nixon's daughter
Cushman, Robert	Deputy director, CIA
Dahlberg, Kenneth	Regional chairperson FCRP
Dash, Samuel	Chief counsel, Senate Watergate Committee
Davis, Evan	Assistant counsel, House Judiciary Committee
Dean, John	Counsel to the president
Diem, Ngo Dinh	President of South Vietnam

Doar, John	Impeachment counsel, House Judiciary Committee
Dorsen, David M.	Assistant chief counsel, Senate Watergate Committee
Doyle, John	Press chief, WSPF
Edminsten, Rufus	Deputy chief counsel, Senate Watergate Committee
Ehrlichman, John D.	Assistant to the president (domestic affairs)
Eisenhower, David	Nixon's son-in-law
Eisenhower, Julie Nixon	Nixon's daughter
Ellsberg, Daniel	Defense Department analyst
Ervin, Sam	Chairman, Senate Watergate Committee
Felt, Mark	Associate director, FBI
Fielding, Fred	Deputy counsel to the president
Fielding, Dr. Lewis	Ellsberg's psychiatrist
Ford, Gerald R.	Vice president and president of the United States
Frampton, George, Jr.	Assistant Watergate special prosecutor
Garment, Leonard	Counsel to the president
Gessell, Gerhard	Judge, U.S. District Court
Glanzer, Seymour	Assistant U.S. attorney
Goldwater, Barry	Senator (R)
Gray, L. Patrick, III	Acting director, FBI
Griffin, Robert P.	Senator (R)
Gurney, Edmund	Member, Senate Watergate Committee (R)
Haig, Alexander H., Jr.	White House chief of staff
Haldeman, H. R. (Bob)	White House chief of staff
Hamilton, James	Assistant chief counsel, Senate Watergate Committee
Harlow, Bryce	Advisor to the president
Hart, George L.	Chief judge, U.S. District Court
Hauser, Richard	Assistant to Buzhardt
Helms, Richard M.	Director, CIA
Higby, Lawrence	Assistant to Haldeman
Hogan, Lawrence	Member, House Judiciary Committee (R)
Holtzman, Elizabeth	Member, House Judiciary Committee (D)
Humphrey, Hubert H.	Vice president; candidate for president (D)
Hunt, Dorothy	Wife of Howard Hunt
Hunt, E. Howard	White House Plumber
Hutchinson, Edward	Ranking member, House Judiciary Committee (R)
Inouye, Daniel	Member, Senate Watergate Committee (D)
Jaworski, Leon	Watergate special prosecutor
Jenner, Albert E., Jr.	Republican lawyer, House Judiciary Committee
Jordan, Barbara	Member, House Judiciary Committee (D)
Kalmbach, Herbert W.	Personal lawyer to Nixon
Kennedy, John F.	President of the United States
Kissinger, Henry	National security adviser to the president; secretary of state

Kleindienst, Richard	Attorney general of the United States
Kreindler, Peter	Assistant special prosecutor
Krogh, Egil (Bud)	Co-head, White House Plumbers
Lacovara, Philip A.	Counsel, WSPF
LaRue, Fred	Assistant to Mitchell, CRP
Latta, Delbert A.	Member, House Judiciary Committee (R)
Lenzner, Terry F.	Assistant chief counsel, Senate Watergate Committee
Lichtenstein, James	Assistant to Burch
Liddy, G. Gordon	Counsel, FCRP
MacKinnon, George E.	Judge, U.S. Court of Appeals
Magruder, Jeb Stuart	Deputy chairman, CRP
Mardian, Robert C.	Assistant to Mitchell, CRP
Marshall, Burke	Adviser, WSPF
McCahill, Jack	Deputy to St. Clair
McCord, James	Chief of security, CRP
McGovern, George	Senator; candidate for president (D)
Mezvinky, Edwin	Member, House Judiciary Committee (D)
Mitchell, John N.	Attorney general; campaign manager, CRP
Mitchell, Martha	Wife of Mitchell
Montoya, James	Member, Senate Watergate Committee (D)
Muskie, Edmund	Senator; candidate for president (D)
Neal, James F.	Assistant Watergate prosecutor
Neftali, Timothy	Director, Nixon Presidential Library
Nixon, Pat	First Lady
Nixon, Richard M.	President of the United States
Nussbaum, Bernard W.	Assistant counsel, House Judiciary Committee
O'Brien, Lawrence	Chairman, DNC
O'Brien, Paul	Lawyer for CRP
Ogarrio, Manuel	Mexico City lawyer
O'Neill, Tip	Speaker, House of Representatives (D)
Parkinson, Kenneth W.	Lawyer for CRP
Petersen, Henry E.	Assistant attorney general, criminal division
Porter, Herbert L.	Assistant to Magruder
Price, Raymond A.	Speechwriter for the president
Railsback, Thomas F.	Member, House Judiciary Committee (R)
Rebozo, Charles G.	Friend of the president
Rehnquist, William J.	Associate justice, U.S. Supreme Court
Rhodes, John J.	Congressional leader (R)
Richardson, Elliot	Attorney general of the United States
Rient, Peter	Assistant Watergate special prosecutor
Rockefeller, Nelson	Vice president of the United States
Rodham, Hillary	Assistant counsel, House Judiciary Committee

Rodino, Peter W., Jr.	Chairman, House Judiciary Committee
Ruckelshaus, William D.	Deputy attorney general
Ruth, Henry S., Jr.	Deputy Watergate special prosecutor
Sanders, Donald	Assistant chief minority counsel, Senate Watergate Committee
Saxbe, William	Attorney general
Scott, Hugh	Senator (R)
Segretti, Donald	Friend of Chapin and Strachan
Shepard, Geoffrey	Assistant to Buzhardt
Silbert, Earl	Assistant U.S. attorney
Sirica, John J.	Chief judge, U.S. District Court
Sloan, Hugh	Treasurer, FCRP
Stans, Maurice H.	Chairman, FCRP
St. Clair, James D.	Special counsel to the president (Watergate)
Stennis, John	Senator (R)
Strachan, Gordon	Assistant to Haldeman
Sussman, Barry	Editor, *Washington Post*
Talmage, Herman	Member, Senate Watergate Committee (D)
Thompson, Fred D.	Chief minority counsel, Senate Watergate Committee
Titus, Harold	U.S. attorney
Trump, Donald J.	President of the United States
Vesco, Robert	American financier
Vorenberg, James	Harvard Law School professor
Wallace, George	Governor of Alabama
Walters, Vernon A.	Deputy director, CIA
Weicker, Lowell	Member, Senate Watergate Committee (R)
Wiggins, Charles	Member, House Impeachment Committee (R)
Wilson, John J.	Lawyer for Haldeman and Ehrlichman
Wine-Volner, Jill	Assistant special Watergate prosecutor
Woods, Rose Mary	Personal secretary to the president
Woodward, Bob	*Washington Post* reporter
Wright, Charles Alan	Special counsel to the president (Watergate)
Young, David	Co-head, White House Plumbers
Zeifman, Jerry	Counsel, House Judiciary Committee
Ziegler, Ronald L.	Press secretary to the president

APPENDIX B

Reconstructed Transcript of Dean-Haldeman Conversation, June 23, 1972

Dean: I had a meeting last night with Pat Gray, who told me of the latest. I checked to see if you were in your office but learned you had gone to a meeting and dinner with the board of trustees of the Kennedy Center. So I called Mitchell, and he requested I bring this to your attention this morning.

Haldeman: You've got my full attention.

Dean: Well, the FBI is following every lead. Liddy and Hunt left tracks everywhere they went, and most everything they did. As I told you they have traced the numbers on the new $100 bills they found on the burglars and in their hotel room to banks in Philadelphia and Miami. The Philadelphia bank was a dead end. But the Miami bank is where Bernard Barker did his real estate business, so they looked at his account and discovered he had processed checks for $114,000. Some five checks—

Haldeman: But I thought they couldn't trace the money.

Dean: They didn't trace the bills per se, other than to Barker's bank, which caused them to look at his bank account, where they discovered he had cashed five checks. Gray told me the amounts but I didn't write them down. The cashier's check to Dahlberg was $25,000; he was one of Maury Stans' guys, from Minnesota. Mitchell said Dahlberg contacted Stans and wanted to know why the FBI wanted to talk to him. He's flying to Washington today to meet with Stans. I understand that Dahlberg and his money have nothing to do with Watergate. But apparently what happened is that Liddy, as counsel to the finance committee, used Barker to cash his checks and—

Haldeman: This sounds like they are investigating campaign law violations, which Gray was not going to pursue.

Dean: Bob, the investigation is out of control. Pat Gray is somewhat flustered by the situation, but he doesn't have a clue about how to control the Bureau, so it's not under control. Not only have they found Dahlberg but also $89,000 in a cashier's check out of a Mexican bank.

Haldeman: Yeah, Mitchell said something about that yesterday. It's Texas money, but they aren't sure whose. I gather it's like the Dahlberg money. Liddy used Barker's account to convert it to cash.

Dean: That's my understanding. They, the FBI, have requested that their agent in Mexico City contract the guy, Ogarrio, who wrote the checks, and do it today. Mitchell said this is a problem. They don't know who this Ogarrio is or why he wrote this check, only that all these people were promised anonymity. Mitchell says the FBI is barking up the wrong tree. He's concerned they're looking for ways to embarrass the president, not to mention his supporters.

Haldeman: God, this thing is a mess.

Dean: Bob, you can't believe how bad it is. It is hard to believe how foolish Liddy and Hunt were. Everything was bungled. Gray also told me an informant had come into their Miami office. He runs a camera shop, develops photographs, a regular commercial operation. He said he had been reading in the Miami newspapers about the Cubans being arrested at the DNC, and when he saw the names, one name clicked: Bernard Barker. He said Barker had dropped off several rolls of film in early June to be developed. He said the pictures were photos of documents, taken while someone was holding down letters on the floor, you could see the rug in the photo, and the letterhead on one or more of the documents was the Office of the Chairman of the Democratic National Committee, Larry O'Brien.

Haldeman: So is the FBI investigating campaign activities?

Dean: That's not supposed to be the focus of their investigation. But they are running out leads way beyond what is necessary and getting into political stuff. Petersen agreed that they would not go on a fishing expedition, and campaign law violations were not going to be pursued. It is my understanding that Petersen told Harold Titus that they only had jurisdiction to investigate the break-in and bugging. But it appears, as I told Mitchell, that neither Petersen nor Titus are providing any guidance, so the FBI is running out any and every lead wherever it takes them. Gray has no control of the investigation or the leaks that are coming out of it.

Haldeman: That's obviously a problem. So what do we do about it?

Dean: Well, Mitchell says he's now pretty concerned. He told me that LaRue and Mardian had debriefed Liddy, and Mardian is convinced that these guys may have had help from the CIA. Mitchell thinks it started when they were working for Ehrlichman. Mitchell said he had no idea about the things Ehrlichman was doing on the Ellsberg case.

Haldeman: I don't know anything about that, and frankly, don't want to know.

Dean: Well, Mitchell thinks with the FBI going every which way, that this investigation is at the brink right now, and it can go one of two ways: Either it's going to open up everything, and that will be an even worse disaster, or it can be closed down, contained, and not get into unrelated matters like the source of the Mexican money.

Haldeman: It doesn't seem anyone knows how to do that, however.

Dean: Mitchell and I talked about that. Pat Gray told me, based on the evidence and leads so far, that the agents working the case have several working theories of what happened. Until Colson convinced them he was not involved, they suspected it could be a White House operation. Gray thinks it could have been a set-up job by a double agent, and I am not sure he is wrong on that. Or it was someone in the reelection committee who was responsible. Another real possibility, given the people involved, is that it was a CIA operation. Frankly, I am not sure any of those theories are totally wrong, or mutually exclusive.

Haldeman: What's Mitchell think?

Dean: I told him I think Gray is looking for a way out. He called Helms, who told him there was no CIA involvement, but Gray still thinks they've run into a CIA operation, and given the bad blood between the agencies, the CIA is not talking.

Haldeman: The president just buzzed me. What's the bottom line?

Dean: Mitchell's most worried about the Mexican money. They don't know what it involves. He thinks you should call Bob Walters—

Haldeman: Who's Bob Walters?

Dean: The new deputy director at the CIA—

Haldeman: That's Dick Walters.

Dean: That's correct. Sorry. Mitchell suggested you call him and tell him you don't know where this FBI investigation is going, but the White House needs some help, and the CIA may need some help as well. I agree that the investigation is out of control, and the Hoover legacies at the FBI have their own agenda. So have Walters talk to Gray, remind him of their interagency delimitation agreement, that they are not to get involved in each other's business.

Haldeman: I understand. Got to go. We'll talk later.

APPENDIX C

Haldeman's Notes of Conversation with Dean

MEMORANDUM

Dean 6/23   THE WHITE HOUSE
            WASHINGTON   HIGH PRIORITY

invest. out of control — they doesn't know what to do
they've found Dahlberg
      also $ out of Mex. bank.
      we know who the depositors were today
informant came into Miami
      photog devel films for Barker - six DNC
Peterson - Titus - no guidance

is at brink right now —
      either up open all up — or be closed
FBI conv. it's CIA - Cits test. cleared him
Gray looking for way out - called Helms
call Walters in —
      they don't know where going - need some help
      have him talk to Gray

APPENDIX D

Transcript of Three Nixon-Haldeman Conversations, June 23, 1972

First Conversation (No. 741-2), Oval Office, 10:04–11:39 a.m.

Haldeman: Now, on the investigation, you know, the Democratic break-in thing, we're back to the—in the, the problem area because the FBI is not under control. Because Gray doesn't exactly know how to control them, and they have, their investigation is now leading into some productive areas, because they've been able to trace the money, not through the money itself, but through the bank, you know, sources the banker himself. And, and it goes in some directions we don't want it to go. Ah, also there have been some things, like an informant came in off the street to the FBI in Miami, who was a photographer or has a friend who is a photographer who developed some films through this guy, Barker, and the films had pictures of Democratic National Committee letterhead documents and things. So I guess, so it's things like that that are going to, that are filtering in. Mitchell came up with yesterday, and John Dean analyzed very carefully last night and concludes, concurs now with Mitchell's recommendation that the only way to solve this, and we're set up beautifully to do it, ah, in that and that . . . the only network that paid any attention to it last night was NBC.

President: That's right.

Haldeman: Who did a massive story on the Cuban thing, and all that.

President: Right.

Haldeman: That the way to handle this now is for us to have Walters call Pat Gray and just say, "Stay the hell out of this, this is, ah, business here we don't want you to go any further on it." That's not an unusual development—

President: Um huh.

Haldeman: And, uh, that would take care of it.

President: What about Pat Gray, ah, you mean he doesn't want to?

Haldeman: Pat does want to. He doesn't know how to, and he doesn't have, he doesn't have any basis for doing it. Given this, he will then have the basis. He'll call Mark Felt in, and the two of them, and Mark Felt wants to cooperate because—

President: Yeah.

Haldeman: —he's ambitious.

President: Yeah.

Haldeman: Ah, he'll call him in and say, "We've got the signal from across the river to, to put the hold on this." And that will fit rather well because the FBI agents who are working the case, at this point, feel that's what it is. Is the CIA.

President: But they've traced the money to whom?

Haldeman: Well they have, they've traced to a name, but they haven't gotten to the guy yet.

President: Who is it, is it somebody here?

Haldeman: Ken Dahlberg.

President: Who the hell is Ken Dahlberg?

Haldeman: He's, ah, he gave $25,000 in Minnesota, and ah—

President: Well—

Haldeman: —the check went directly in to this, to this guy Barker.

President: Maybe he's a, ah, he didn't, I mean, his, his base is Stans.

Haldeman: Yeah. It is. It is. It's directly traceable and there's some more through some Texas people in, that went to the Mexican bank which they can also trace to the Mexican bank, they'll get their names today. And [pause].

President: Well, I mean, ah, there's no way I'm just thinking if they don't cooperate, what do they say? They, they, they were approached by the Cubans. That's what Dahlberg has to say, the Texans too. Is that the idea?

Haldeman: Well, if they will. But then we're relying on more and more people all the time. That's the problem. And ah, they'll stop if we could, if we take this other step.

President: All right, fine. Right.

Haldeman: —and they seem to feel the thing to do is get them to stop?

President: Right, fine.

Haldeman: They say the only way to do that is a White House instruction. And it's got to be to Helms and, ah, what's his name? Walters.

President: Walters.

Haldeman: And the proposal would be that Ehrlichman [coughs] and I call them in—

President: All right, fine.

Haldeman: —and say, ah—

President: How do you call him in, I mean, you just, well, we protected Helms from one hell of a lot of things.

Haldeman: That's what Ehrlichman says.

President: Of course, this is a, this is, ah, Hunt, you will, that will uncover a lot of, see, you open that scab there's a hell of a lot of things and that we just feel that it would be very detrimental to have this thing go any further. This involves these Cubans, Hunt, and a lot of hanky-panky that we have nothing to do with ourselves. One thing I want to know, did Mitchell know about this thing to any much of a degree?

Haldeman: I think so.

President: Shit.

Haldeman: I don't think he knew the details, [cross talk] but I think he knew.

President: He didn't know how it was going to be handled though, with Dahlberg and the Texans and so forth, did he? Well who was the asshole that did this thing? Is it Liddy? Is that the fellow? He must be a little nuts.

Haldeman: He is.

President: I mean he just isn't well screwed on, is he? Isn't that the problem?

Haldeman: No, but he was under pressure, apparently, to get more information, and as he got more pressure, he pushed the people harder to move harder on—

President: Pressure from Mitchell?

Haldeman: Apparently.

President: Oh, Mitchell, Mitchell was at the point that you made on this, that exactly what I need from you is on the—

Haldeman: [Unintelligible]

President: All right, fine, I understand it all. We won't second-guess Mitchell and the rest. Thank God it wasn't Colson.

Haldeman: The FBI interviewed Colson yesterday. They determined that would be a good thing to do.

President: Um hum.

Haldeman: Ah, to have him take a—

President: Um hum.

Haldeman: An interrogation, which he did, and that, the FBI guys working the case had concluded that there were one or two possibilities, one, that this was a White House, they don't think that there is anything at the Election Committee, they think it was either a White House operation and they had some obscure reasons for it, nonpolitical—

President: Uh huh.

Haldeman: —or it was a—

President: Cuban thing—

Haldeman: Cubans and the CIA. And after their interrogation of, of—

President: Colson.

Haldeman: —Colson, yesterday, they concluded it was not the White House, but are now convinced it is a CIA thing, so the CIA turnoff would—

President: Well, not sure of their analysis, I must say that. I'm not going to get that involved.

Haldeman: No, sir. We don't want you to.

President: You call them in.

Haldeman: Good.

President: Good deal. Play it tough. That's the way they play it and that's the way we are going to play it.

Haldeman: O.K. We'll do it.

President: Yeah, when I saw that News Summary item, I, of course, knew it was a bunch of crap, but I thought, ah, well it's good to have them off on this wild hair thing because when they start bugging us, which they have, we'll know our little boys will not know how to handle it. I hope they will though. You never know. Maybe, you think about it. Good!

[Interruption dealing with unrelated matters]
President: When you get in these people, when you get these people in, say: "Look, the problem is that this will open the whole, the whole Bay of Pigs thing, and the President just feels that," I mean, without going into the details, don't, don't lie to them to the extent to say there is no involvement, but just say this is sort of a comedy of errors, bizarre, without getting into it, "the President believes that it is going to open the whole Bay of Pigs thing up again. And, ah, because these people are playing for, for keeps, and that they should call the FBI in and say that we wish for the country, don't go any further into this case," period! And that destroys the case.
Haldeman: Okay.
President: That's the way to put it, do it straight now. [Pause, sounds like the president took a sip of his coffee, and then he turned to other subjects.]

Second Conversation (No. 741-10), Oval Office, 1:04–1:13 p.m.

President: Okay. Take the God damn thing. And, just, just postpone the [unclear word(s)]. What are you [unclear]?
Haldeman: Just [voice inaudible because of noise on desk; president is clearing it].
President: All that [unclear].
Haldeman: [Unclear]
President: [Unclear, but the president can be heard tapping his finger on his desk, a contemplative gesture, before and as he shared his thoughts.] I'd say the primary reason you've got to cut it the hell off. I just don't think, ah, it would be very bad to have this fellow Hunt, ah, you know, he, he knows too damn much. And he was involved, we happen to know that. And if it gets out, the whole, this is all involved in the Cuban thing, it's a, it's a fiasco, and it's going to make the FBI, the CIA look bad, it's going to make Hunt look bad, and it's likely to blow the whole, ah, Bay of Pigs thing, which we think would be very unfortunate for the CIA, and for the country at this time, and for American foreign policy. And he's just got to [tell him], lay off. That what you—?
Haldeman: Yeah, that's, that is the basis I'm going to do it on. Just leave it at that.
President: I don't want them to get any idea that we're doing it because of our concern about the political, and, ah, they know [the], I wouldn't tell them it is not political—
Haldeman: Right.
President: I'd just say, look, it's because of the Hunt involvement, just say, yeah, Hunt got involved, is involved, ah, in this sort of thing, the whole cover is, ah, basically this. Going to be [unclear word]. That cover, it's a good move. [With that comment, the president changed the topic of the conversation, and his tone, when referring to his earlier meetings with his economic advisers, which had addressed, among other things, the problem of rising beef prices and quotas on some foreign beef.] Well, they've got some pretty good ideas on this meat thing. Schultz did a good paper on. . . .

Third Conversation (No. 343-36), EOB Office, 2:20–2:45 p.m.

Haldeman: Well, it's no problem. Had the two of them in, and—

President: You scare Helms to death, did you?

Haldeman: Well it's kind of interesting. Walters sat there. Made the point, I didn't mention Hunt at the opening of it, I just said that, that, ah, this thing would lead in the directions that were going to create some very major potential problems, that they were exploring leads that lead back into, to ah, areas that would be harmful to the CIA, harmful to the government, there were—

[Telephone rings. President has unrelated call with Charles Colson.]

Haldeman: But, ah, Walters, didn't say much.

President: [Unclear]

Haldeman: Helms did too. Helms, ah, said, well, I've had no contact with this, of course, and, but Gray called and said, yesterday, he said, ah, that he thought—

President: Who's that, Gray?

Haldeman: Gray had called, told us what he knew, and said, ah, ah, I think, I think we've run right into the middle of a CIA covert operation here.

President: Gray said that?

Haldeman: Yeah, and Helms said nothing, nothing we've got, at this point, and ah, ah, which is all true, because, that's what we did, or something. And Gray said, well, yeah, it sure looks to me like we did, and Helms said nothing that we've got going at all and, ah, that was the end of that conversation. [Unclear.] We said, well, the problem is that it tracks back to the Bay of Pigs. It tracks back to some other [things], if their leads run out to people who had no involvement in this except by contacts or connections, but it gets to areas that are going to be raised. The whole problem of this, this fellow Hunt, ah, so at that point Helms kind of got the picture, very clearly. He, he said, he said, we'll be very happy to be helpful to, ah, you know, and we'll handle everything you want. I would like to know the reason for being helpful. And it may have appeared, when he wasn't gonna get it explicitly but was gonna get it through generality, he, he said fine. And, ah, Walters, was ready to do it, Walters said that. [Chuckles.] And Walters is going to make a call to Gray, I think. That, that's the way we put it, that's the way it was left, and, ah, [unclear words].

President: How would that work though? How would, for example, if the judge were brought back, if he asked for somebody from Miami bank to be here, account for assets in the bank?

Haldeman: You might, have the CIA [unclear] have a problem [unclear]. The point that John [Ehrlichman] made is the Bureau doesn't, the Bureau is going all on this, because they don't know what they're uncovering. Because they think they need to pursue it, ah, they don't need to, because they've already got their case as far as the, ah charges against these men, or something, so they don't need anything further on that. And, ah, as they pursue it they're uncovering stuff that's none of their business, in there.

President: [Unclear]

Haldeman: I'm not sure exactly what. We didn't in any way, say we, we had any political interest, or concern, or anything like that. Ah, one thing Helms did raise is he said that, that Gray, he asked Gray why he felt they're going into a CIA thing and Gray said because of the characters involved and the amount of money involved. He said there's a lot of dough. [Unclear.] That probably had some suspicion in Helms [unclear].

President: [Unclear] Well, we'll cross that bridge.

Haldeman: Well, I think they will 'cause our, see there isn't any question—

President: If it runs back to the bank so, what the hell, they, who knows, we always [unclear] contributed to the CIA [unclear].

Haldeman: CIA gets money as we know 'cause, I mean their money moves in a lot of different ways, too.

President: Yeah.

APPENDIX E
Jaworski's Letter to Sirica, December 27, 1973

WATERGATE SPECIAL PROSECUTION FORCE
United States Department of Justice
1425 K Street, N.W.
Washington, D.C. 20005
December 27, 1973

PAL:sek

Honorable John J. Sirica
Chief Judge
United States District Court
 for the District of Columbia
Washington, D. C. 20001

Dear Chief Judge Sirica:

When Messrs. Ruth, Lacovara, Ben-Veniste and I met with you and Judge Gesell at your request on Friday, December 14, you suggested that it would be helpful if we could provide you with some sense of the caseload that we would be generating for the Court over the next several months. I have reviewed the status of the investigations currently under way with my task force leaders, and have put together what I believe is a reasonable projection of the scale of indictments that may be returned between the beginning of the new year and the end of April.

In January and February, I foresee the possibility that the grand juries may return three multi-defendant indictments that would take approximately a week each to try. During that time I can calculate approximately three additional indictments that might consume two weeks each of trial. Another case might last for three weeks. I also anticipate that, should an indictment be voted in another area actively under investigation at the present, it would take from four to six weeks to try the case. And finally, I believe that by the end of January or the beginning of February we may have an indictment in a case that could well take three months to try.

Looking ahead to March and April, I have reason to anticipate two or three indictments that may involve one-week trials, one involving a two-week trial, and another possibly leading to a three-week trial. Of course, there are a number of other matters currently at the preliminary stages of investigation which might be ready for indictment during March and April as well. Added to the cases referred to above are a number of relatively straightforward cases that, if not terminated by an agreed upon plea of guilty, should take no more than a day or two to try.

I am sure you can appreciate that the estimates I have given are extremely rough. It is, of course, possible that the grand jury will elect not to return indictments in some of these areas. In addition, willingness by potential defendants to agree to plead guilty before or after indictment may substantially reduce the number or length of the trials. It is my opinion, however, that the estimates I have given, while perhaps erring on the side of being overly inclusive, will provide you with information that you may find helpful in planning for the assignment of cases during the early part of the new year.

No doubt in making your own assessment of caseload you will consider the time that will be consumed between indictments and trials in these cases by pre-trial motions, particularly motions for continuances or transfers based on pre-trial publicity, including the report of the Ervin Committee which is scheduled to be released in the Spring.

If further information or detail would be helpful, I would be happy to respond to any questions you may have. Let me take this opportunity to express again my deepest appreciation for the extremely careful and responsible way you have been handling these matters and for the courtesies you have extended to me and to my staff.

Sincerely,

/s/

LEON JAWORSKI
Special Prosecutor

cc: Mr. Jaworski
    Mr. Ruth
    Mr. Lacovara
    Task Force Leaders
    Files

APPENDIX F

Jaworski's Memorandum to Confidential Watergate File Regarding Meeting with Sirica, February 12, 1974

February 12/1974

For my conf. Watergate file

<u>CONFIDENTIAL</u>

On Monday, February 11, I met with the Judge at which time several matters were covered as we sat alone in the jury room. He again indicated that provided the indictments came down in time he would take the Watergate Case, stating that he had been urged to do so by any number of Judges from across the nation the most recent of them being those who were in attendance with him at a meeting in Atlanta. He expressed the opinion that these indictments should be returned as soon as possible. He also stated that henceforth all guilty pleas would be taken by him. We talked about the Vesco case and he merely expressed the thought that perhaps a sealed indictment might be of some help. He mentioned one or two personal matters such as an effort to smear him because of a completely fabricated tale relating to him and his son, of which he wanted me to be aware. Actually the discussion began with his unburdening himself to me on that particular matter. He also mentioned that he had been urged to speak at the State Bar of Texas in San Antonio and indicated that he would accept this invitation.

He sought my reaction and I urged him to do so.

The Judge commented upon the status of matters before the grand jury which led into further comments on the possibility of the grand jury considering some type of special report or presentment. He considered this a very touchy problem and cautioned as to what the public's reaction would be to a grand jury stepping out with something that was beyond its normal bounds. He cautioned that the whole effort could be tainted by something irresponsibly being done by the grand jury. He stated that the public would rightfully conclude that the entire proceeding had not been judicious but simply one of wanting to hurt the President. He further said that it was not the function of the grand jury but that of the House Impeachment Committee to express itself on that point. He then told me that in the event I observed anything along that line being considered by the grand jury that he thought it would be appropriate for him to meet with the grand jury in camera. I expressed the belief that it was appropriate for the grand jury to refer to having in its possession evidence that it believed to be material and relevant to the impeachment proceedings and to suggest to the Court that it be referred to the House Committee for that purpose. He countered by stating that he believed he should be informed of the discretion that he could exercise in matters of that kind and further requested that I have a memorandum prepared for him that covers this subject. I agreed to have this done.

APPENDIX G
Jaworski's Memorandum to Confidential Watergate File Regarding Events on or about March 1, 1974

On the eve of Thursday, February 28, with the Mitchell-Stans jury selected in New York and sequestered, it became apparent that we would move to bring in the Watergate cover-up indictments on Friday morning. After checking with Judge Sirica, the hour of 11:00 a.m. was decided upon. ~~I had previously talked to Judge Sirica about the bringing in of a sealed report by the grand jury, in addition to the indictment, and this had his approval.~~ I made known to him in advance that such a report was forthcoming. ~~so as not to have him startled by this matter.~~

On Thursday evening, February 28, just as I was preparing to leave the office around 6:45, Alexander Haig called saying that there were so many rumors afloat that he was concerned - that he feared unexpected developments, etc. and he wondered if there was anything I could properly disclose. I told him that there was nothing I could disclose as to the contents of the indictment or the report he had heard would be made. I did tell him that if the grand jury made a report, in addition to returning to an indictment, he should expect Judge Sirica, as would I, to accept it and act on it. He stated that he and the White House generally were fully expecting the grand jury evidence to be made available to the House Judiciary Committee - that they realized it belonged there. I suggested to him that the evidence may well have serious repercussions and he stated that he was aware of that. I suggested that he and the President's counsel take a close look at the March 21 meeting and the actions that followed, even though the President took no personal part in the events that followed the March 21 meeting.

Finally, he asked whether there was any indictment contemplated involving present White House aides, inasmuch as he needed to make arrangements to meet the situation. I told him none was contemplated at this time

Twice during the conversation, he said that he really called to tell me that I was a "great American." The second time he mentioned it, I said "Al, I haven't done anything other than what is my duty and I hope to continue to follow that course."

We parted with my again expressing my concern that the President's counsel had not sufficiently and accurately assessed the facts pertaining to the March 21 conference and the events that took place that night. He said it would be again reviewed.

On the morning of March 1, I met with Judge Sirica in chambers at 10:30. We reviewed the agenda consisting of (1) presentation of indictments and sealed special report of the grand jury; (2) unsealing of the special report and reading by Judge Sirica, and the acceptance of the report and its resealing. I told Judge Sirica that I would ask the Court to specially assign the case in view of its length and protracted nature and that I was estimating the case would take three to four months to try. I asked him to tell the grand jury to return in two weeks for further consideration of other matters that had not been disposed of. I had in mind the possibility of perjury indictments. I also asked the Judge for a gag order under Rule 1-27 restraining extra-judicial statements.

Shortly before 11:00, I left Judge Sirica's chambers and went into the courtroom. As I left Judge Sirica's chambers, I heard the Judge tell his marshal not to be nervous. But the Judge showed some signs of nervousness too. He told me that he had not slept since 3:00 that morning. When court opened, Judge Sirica's marshall was so nervous he could hardly speak the ritual followed in opening a court.

After opening, Judge Sirica looked at me, asked if I had anything to take up with the court. I then rose, went to the lectern, and said: "May it please Your Honor, the grand jury has an indictment to return. It also has a sealed report to deliver to the Court." The rest of the agenda was then followed including delivery of a briefcase of material, along with the special report to the Court - also a key to the briefcase. The Judge indicated that he would have an order on the special report by Monday (he told me he would transmit to the counsel for the House Judiciary Committee under rules that would not interfere with the trial of the accused). The Judge in open court asked if I had any further comments, and I stated: "Due to the length of the trial, conceivably three to four months, it is the Prosecution's view that under Rule 3-3(c), this case should be specially assigned, and we so recommend." This meant that Judge Sirica could assign the case to himself, which he did do by order later entered that day.

The Judge then announced his gag rule and then adjourned court.

We met in the Judge's chambers. I told him I thought all went smoothly. He in turn thanked me for my help. The Judge was leaving today to speak at the University of Virginia tomorrow, to be back on Sunday. I told him I was going to Texas and that I would be back on Tuesday. We both agreed we would call each other in the interim, if necessary.

APPENDIX H

Jaworski's Letter to Rodino, June 28, 1974

HSR:bas

WATERGATE SPECIAL PROSECUTION FORCE
United States Department of Justice
1425 K Street, N.W.
Washington, D.C. 20005

5.3.3

June 28, 1974

Honorable Peter W. Rodino, Jr.
Chairman
Committee on the Judiciary
House of Representatives
Washington, D.C. 20515

Dear Mr. Chairman:

I received your letter, and that of Mr. Doar, requesting access for Mr. Doar to any memorandum which this office has prepared as a summary of evidence pertaining to President Nixon's conduct in the Watergate matter.

Inasmuch as your exercise of subpoena power would be appropriate in this regard, we will make available to Mr. Doar, at his convenience and for his examination, a summary memorandum prepared here in connection with our duty under the Special Prosecutor's mandate to investigate "allegations involving the President."

I suggest that Mr. Doar telephone Mr. Ruth here at the office to make the necessary arrangements.

Sincerely,

/s/

LEON JAWORSKI
Special Prosecutor

cc: File
    Chron
    Mr. Jaworski
    Mr. Ruth
    Mr. Lacovara

NOTES

Introduction
1. Haldeman and Ehrlichman were sometimes called the "Berlin Wall" for their role in insulating Nixon from others.
2. Trump v. U.S., 603 U.S. 593 (2024). This book cites the initial slip sheet of the opinion, which is widely available online.

1. Before the Scandal
1. Senate Select Committee Hearings on Presidential Campaign Activities, 3:915–919 (hereafter, SSC Hearings).
2. SSC Hearings, 3:919–922.
3. Interview of John Dean, July 30, 2007, 16, Nixon Presidential Library, https://www.nixonlibrary.gov/oral-histories. The library is at 18001 Yorba Linda Blvd., Yorba Linda, CA 93886. Nixon aide Bryce Harlow once described Watergate as follows: "Some damn fool got into the Oval Office and did as he was told." Henry Kissinger, *Leadership: Six Studies in World Strategy* (New York: Penguin Press, 2022), 132.
4. The building was renamed the Eisenhower Executive Office Building in 1999. The earlier title is used here.
5. Two of the three Cuban Americans participated in both the Fielding and the Watergate break-ins.
6. U.S. v. Ehrlichman, 546 F.2d 910 (D.C. Cir. 1977), 916, n.7.
7. SSC Hearings, 6:2544. In a tape recording of a September 8, 1971, conversation between Nixon and Ehrlichman, the latter says, "We had one little operation. It's been aborted out in Los Angeles, which, I think, is better that you know about." Stanley Kutler, *Abuse of Power: The New Nixon Tapes* (New York: Free Press, 1997), 28.
8. Dean insulated Fielding from Watergate. Fielding became White House counsel under President Ronald Reagan.
9. Dean interview, 19. Dean's objection to Liddy was not based on that burglary, which he did not learn about until the five burglars were arrested on June 17, 1972.
10. Dean interview, 1:07–1:12 hours.
11. SSC Hearings, 3:930–931.
12. SSC Hearings, 2:794–795.

2. Burglars Arrested, Cover-up Starts
1. Two accounts, read together, provide a reliable description of events between June 18 and 22. One is John Dean's testimony before the Senate Watergate Committee (SSC Hearings, 3:931–940), all of which he personally prepared. Because

this testimony was closer to the events and given under oath, it is more reliable than his book *Blind Ambition* (New York: Simon & Schuster, 1976). The other account is historian Fred Emery's *Watergate: The Corruption of American Politics and the Fall of Richard Nixon* (New York: Times Books, 1994). Narrower firsthand accounts appear in G. Gordon Liddy, *Will: The Autobiography of G. Gordon Liddy* (New York: St. Martin's Press, 1980); E. Howard Hunt, *Undercover: Memoirs of a American Secret Agent* (Berkeley, CA: Berkley Publishing, 1974); and James W. McCord Jr., *A Piece of Tape* (Rockville, MD: Washington Media Services, 1974). Carl Bernstein and Bob Woodward tell the story from the perspective of the *Washington Post* in *All the President's Men* (New York: Simon & Schuster, 1974). A neglected account is *Final Report of the Senate Watergate Committee*, which cites sworn testimony at the Senate hearings. Nixon, Haldeman, Ehrlichman, and Mitchell, whether in testimony or in books, provided highly sanitized versions of the events.

2. Ronald Kessler, "Experts Heap Scorn on Bungled 'Bug' Caper," *Washington Post*, June 19, 1972, A-7. Carl Stern of NBC News, who had excellent sources in the FBI, reported on June 21, 1972, that the bills were sent to banks in Florida and Mexico. Because it did not have sufficient cash on hand, the Miami bank obtained the money from the Federal Reserve Bank, which provided consecutively numbered $100 bills.

3. The *New York Times* assigned coverage of the burglary to Ted Szulk, who ordinarily wrote about Fidel Castro and Latin American issues. One of the most perceptive reporters in Washington, John Osborne, did not mention the break-in in his column in the *New Republic* when it occurred. In a later column he wryly wrote: "Put it down to my reluctance to believe the possible worst about Richard Nixon." John Osborne, *The Fourth Year of the Nixon Watch* (New York: Liveright, 1974), 109 (this is a collection of *New Republic* columns with later comments added). Thereafter, he mentioned the event and subsequent developments skeptically in his weekly column.

4. According to his reporters, Ben Bradlee, editor of the *Washington Post*, took the scoop by the *Los Angeles Times* in stride. Bernstein and Woodward, *All the President's Men*, 110. However, a book on Woodward and Bernstein claims that Bradlee was "enraged." Adrian Havill, *Deep Truth: The Lives of Bob Woodward and Carl Bernstein* (New York: Birch Lane Press, 1993), 110. Bradlee did not mention the incident in his book *A Good Life: Newspapering and Other Adventures* (New York: Simon & Schuster, 1995).

5. O'Brien was a thorn in Nixon's side, and one of the goals of the intelligence operation was to find negative information about him.

6. Richard Reeves, *President Nixon: Alone in the White House* (New York: Simon & Schuster, 2001), 507.

7. L. Patrick Gray III with Ed Gray, *In Nixon's Web: A Year in the Crosshairs of Watergate* (New York: Times Books, 2008), 98, 123–124, 158. The heading "What the FBI

Almost Found" is from McCord's book *A Piece of Tape*, which was published in 1974 and has all but disappeared. My April 2024 search on the website of a major seller of used books showed two copies offered for sale, one in California and one in Texas. The book is not profound, but it is interesting. And although it is rare, it is available.
8. McCord, *Piece of Tape*, 38.
9. McCord's book also states: "There is evidence that senior supervisory personnel in the FBI tried to get to me, seeking confession in July 1972, but were turned down at the highest levels." However, he does not say what that evidence was, offering nothing to support his claims. A book by Acting FBI Director L. Patrick Gray mentions none of this. A book by Assistant FBI Director and later Acting Associate FBI Director Mark Felt does not mention *any* investigation of McCord. The agent in charge of the case from start to finish was Angelo J. Lano. I am aware of no evidence that he did not pursue the investigation wholeheartedly or that he tried to obtain a search warrant for McCord's home and vehicle. Staff at the Nixon Presidential Library interviewed Lano long after McCord's book came out but did not ask him any questions about pursuing McCord. At this late date, I made no attempt to verify or repudiate McCord's statement as to why his vehicle and home were not searched and why he was not contacted promptly.
10. Jeb Stuart Magruder, *An American Life* (New York: Atheneum, 1974), 214, 217.
11. Magruder, 260.
12. Liddy, *Will*, 248–249.
13. Liddy, 218.
14. SSC Hearings, 3:933–934; Liddy, *Will*, 255–258.
15. SSC Hearings, 9:3614.
16. The FBI was attempting to interview Dahlberg and Ogarrio, and evidence of Barker's financial transactions was in the hands of the press. Barry Sussman, *The Great Cover-up: Nixon and the Scandal of Watergate* (New York: Thomas Y. Crowell, 1974), 47.
17. See Richard M. Nixon, *RN: The Memoirs of Richard Nixon* (New York: Grosset, 1978), 595–599. Neither Nixon nor his top aides wrote about why they chose Gray.
18. The tapes of early 1972 conversations were not made public until well after Nixon resigned and were not transcribed until after 2000, when John Dean personally arranged for the transcription of all the remaining Nixon tapes related to Watergate. Dean cited some of these tapes in his book *The Nixon Defense: What He Knew and When He Knew It* (New York: Viking, 2014), 53–63. He did not use or disclose most of the tapes but made many of them available to me.
19. Alexander M. Haig Jr. with Charles McCarry, *Inner Circles: How America Changed the World* (New York: Warner Books, 1992), 456.
20. Haldeman's notes, June 20, 1972, Watergate Collection, Record Groups 460.4–460.5, National Archives and Records Administration (NARA).

21. Letter from Nixon to District Judge Gerhardt Gesell, April 29, 1974, Papers of Alexander Haig, box 28, folder 1, Library of Congress (LOC).
22. Nixon, *RN*, 785.
23. Nixon Recorded Conversation No. 344-14, June 22, 1972, Executive Office Building (EOB) Office, 9:40–11:25 a.m., President and Haldeman, Record Groups 460.4–460.5, NARA.
24. According to Assistant U.S. Attorney Earl Silbert's records, investigators learned about the checks in Barker's account on June 22, 1972, and interviewed Kenneth Dahlberg about his check on July 6, 1972. Dahlberg made it clear that these were campaign contributions.
25. This must have meant tracing the money back to Dahlberg and Andreas. The money had been laundered through the Miami bank account of Bernard Barker, one of the arrested burglars.
26. Nixon, *RN*, 515; see also *RN*, 473, 513–514. For an elaborate analysis of Nixon's relationship with the CIA, see Jefferson Morley, *The Scorpions' Dance: The President, the Spymaster, and Watergate* (New York: St. Martin's Press, 2022).

3. The "Smoking Gun" Conversations

1. In reconstructing the conversation (see appendix B), Dean relied on Haldeman's notes (see appendix C).
2. See appendix C.
3. The last sentence is not part of Dean's reconstruction of the telephone call with Haldeman. However, it is part of other descriptions of this call.
4. According to Gray, Felt had been identified to him as the leaker, "but Mark had vehemently denied it in our face-to-face meetings. I believed Mark, and that was that." L. Patrick Gray III with Ed Gray, *In Nixon's Web: A Year in the Cross Hairs of Watergate* (New York: Times Books, 2008), 169–170.
5. The best analysis is in Max Holland, *Leak: Why Mark Felt Became Deep Throat* (Lawrence: University Press of Kansas, 2012). For a more charitable (and self-serving) account, see Mark Felt and John A. O'Connor, *G-Man's Life: The FBI, Being "Deep Throat," and the Struggle for Honor in Washington* (New York: Public Affairs, 2006).
6. See the transcript in appendix D. The public first learned of the existence of a recording system in the White House a year later. It took another year for the June 23 conversations between Nixon and Haldeman to become public.
7. The words "productive areas" can be construed in various ways, but it is unwise to attribute too much meaning to a single word or phrase. It could refer to areas that were productive or potentially productive to the campaign.
8. Haldeman apparently forgot Henry Petersen's assurance that the DOJ investigation was limited and did not include campaign financing.
9. Apparently, the first page of the news summary for June 23, 1972, is missing. Page 2 deals with Cuba, which implicates the CIA. The specific content is not important to an understanding of the conversation.

10. Helms stated to the Senate Watergate Committee: "the Bay of Pigs is the rubric for a very unhappy event in the life of the CIA." SSC Hearings, 8:3275. The damage done to President Kennedy and the CIA was still on the minds of leaders in Washington. In addition, Nixon had a tendency to inject some of his favorite episodes, such as the Alger Hiss case, into discussions.
11. Richard M. Nixon, *RN: The Memoirs of Richard Nixon* (New York: Grosset, 1978), 641.
12. Interview of H. R. Haldeman, April 17, 1988 (third interview), 23, Nixon Presidential Library, https://www.nixonlibrary.gov/oral-histories. An assistant to Buzhardt called the reference to the Bay of Pigs "irrelevant." Interview of Geoff Shepard, 37-Shepard-oh-4-part 2-mp4, at 26:30 min., Nixon Presidential Library. It is unclear how the Bay of Pigs and Watergate intersect, other than that Hunt and the Cubans were involved in both.
13. Nixon, *RN*, 642.
14. Nixon, 641. This suggests that Nixon was unaware of the Plumbers' break-in at Fielding's office until well after the Watergate arrests.
15. SSC Hearings, 7:3048–3049, 8:3228.
16. SSC Hearings, 8:3063–3064.
17. SSC Hearings, 8:3238, 3275. Haldeman may have invented this exchange to show Nixon that he had needled the CIA.
18. SSC Hearings, 9:3405. Haldeman's insistence on protecting some unidentified CIA project probably seemed strange to Helms.
19. SSC Hearings, 8:3246. Helms's account was even stronger and more specific in his earlier interview with committee staff: "Haldeman in no uncertain terms instructed Walters to see Pat Gray of the FBI and instruct him not to pursue his investigation concerning Kenneth M. Dahlberg since it might involve the CIA."
20. SSC Hearings, 7:2783. Ehrlichman added that the meeting included a discussion of the funds sent to Mexico, although Haldeman testified that Mexico was not discussed. SSC Hearings, 9:3488. Ehrlichman said he had no special knowledge of those funds but had read about them in the newspaper. SSC Hearings, 7:2799.
21. SSC Hearings, 7:2884.
22. SSC Hearings, 7:2948 (Walters's memorandum of the June 23 meeting).
23. SSC Hearings, 9:3422.
24. SSC Hearings, 9:3422–3423.
25. Nixon seems to be speaking as if Haldeman and Ehrlichman had not met with the CIA yet.
26. Holland, *Leak*, 3. A popular anecdote is instructive on the power of Hoover: A guard at the Department of Justice stopped a man from entering because he had no identification. "But I am the attorney general," the man said. "I don't care if you're J. Edgar Hoover," the guard replied, "without identification you are not entering."
27. Interview of Angelo J. Lano, May 28, 2009, Nixon Presidential Library, http://www.youtube.com/watch?v=EYqV-85uosw&t=327s, at 19, 30, 38, 54 min.

28. On June 20, 1972, Petersen told Dean: "Once an FBI investigation has started, and this evidence comes through the U.S. Attorney's office, and up into my office, and up to the attorney general, the track record, you just don't turn off a prosecution at that point. You can't put a fix in. It just won't happen." Interview of John Dean, July 30, 2007, 23, Nixon Presidential Library, https://www.nixonlibrary.gov/oral-histories.
29. SSC Hearings, 9:3815.
30. Gray, *In Nixon's Web*, 248–252.

4. Simmering Below the Surface
1. SSC Hearings, 7:2948 (Walters's memorandum of the June 23 meeting).
2. SSC Hearings, 9:3455.
3. L. Patrick Gray III with Ed Gray, *In Nixon's Web: A Year in the Cross Hairs of Watergate* (New York: Times Books, 2008), 23, 32, 90–91.
4. SSC Hearings, 2:650.
5. Interview of John W. Dean, July 30, 2007, 16, Nixon Presidential Library, https://www.nixonlibrary.gov/oral-histories.
6. Petersen placed Assistant U.S. Attorney Earl Silbert, the second-highest official in the U.S. attorney's office, in charge of the day-to-day investigation and prosecution.
7. Petersen had supplied Dean with the grand jury testimony of other witnesses. SSC Hearings, 3:953–954; interview I of John Dean, July 30, 2007, 32 min., Nixon Presidential Library.
8. Jeb Stuart Magruder, *An American Life: One Man's Road to Watergate* (New York: Atheneum, 1974), 263–264.
9. Attorney General Richard Kleindienst and the Justice Department praised the investigation and the result. Kleindienst announced, "We have absolutely no evidence to indicate any others should be charged." John W. Dean, *Blind Ambition: The White House Years* (New York: Simon & Schuster, 1976), 133.
10. Dean, 135–139.
11. After the 1972 election, the *Post*'s ownership of two television stations in Florida was challenged, and the value of its stock dropped by 50 percent. Several persons connected to Nixon were among the challengers. Carl Bernstein and Bob Woodward, *All the President's Men* (New York: Simon & Schuster, 1974), 220.
12. Dwight Chapin, *The President's Man: The Memoirs of a Trusted Nixon Aide* (Oklahoma City: Oklahoma Heritage Association, 2022), 322–323. The *Washington Post* had tied Chapin, who was extremely loyal to Nixon, to Donald Segretti, and he had become a liability. Barry Sussman, *The Great Cover-up: Nixon and the Scandal of Watergate* (New York: Thomas Y. Crowell, 1974), 112–118; Dean, *Blind Ambition*, 147–150. Obviously, Dean's position was secure. Chapin was later convicted of lying to a grand jury about his knowledge of Segretti's activities. Chapin had claimed he did not recall certain events. See U.S. v. Chapin, 515 F.2d 1274 (1975).

13. Bryce Harlow, a Nixon aide who was not tarnished by Watergate, commented many years after the Nixon landslide that the firings gave too much power to the administration. Harlow mused, "If it hadn't been Watergate, it would have been something much worse." Bob Burke and Ralph G. Thompson, *Bryce Harlow: Mr. Integrity* (Oklahoma City: Oklahoma Heritage Foundation, 2000), 224.
14. SSC Hearings, 1:132–141.
15. SSC Hearings, 1:138.
16. SSC Hearings, 1:257, 260, 268.

5. Watergate Burglars Convicted, Judge Sirica Stirs the Pot

1. "Contrary to his reputation as a hero, Sirica was in fact a corrupt, incompetent, and a dishonest figure with a close connection to Joseph McCarthy and clear ties to organized crime." Renata Adler, *Gone: The Last Days of the* New Yorker (New York: Simon & Schuster, 1999), 125. Adler, a journalist, discussed the aftermath of writing that sentence in *Canaries in the Mineshaft* (New York: St. Martin's Griffin, 2001), 345–377. She served on the staff of the House Impeachment Committee in 1974 and wrote her book before the *ex parte* meetings between Sirica and Jaworski (discussed in a later chapter) were made known. *Time* magazine chose Sirica "Man of the Year" in 1974, and he was lauded extravagantly at the time. John Dean's second book, *Lost Honor: The Rest of the Story* (Los Angeles: Stratford Press, 1982), 255–257, like numerous others, was very critical of Sirica's performance as a judge, including how he pummeled people who were telling the truth and bludgeoned some to testify against others.
2. G. Gordon Liddy, *Will: The Autobiography of G. Gordon Liddy* (New York: St. Martin's Press, 1980), 268, 272, 276.
3. Sirica made no secret of the fact that he did not believe Sloan. Sirica's statements, which caused unwarranted damage to Sloan, are examples of why trial judges should be cautious when expressing their views.
4. The Senate committee included Democrats Herman Talmadge of Georgia, Joseph Montoya of Arizona, and Daniel Inouye of Hawaii and Republicans Lowell Weicker of Connecticut and Joseph Gurney of Florida (both serving their first terms). Gurney became one of Nixon's strongest defenders, while Weicker was one of his strongest critics. Ervin, a former judge, was an elderly, crusty southerner who favored states' rights (e.g., racial discrimination) but was often on the liberal side of issues. Baker said of Ervin that no one would have guessed that he went to Harvard Law School.
5. Richard M. Nixon, *RN: The Memoirs of Richard Nixon* (New York: Grosset, 1978), 777–779.
6. H. R. Haldeman, *The Haldeman Diaries: Inside the Nixon White House* (New York: G. P. Putnam's Sons, 1994), 578.
7. John Ehrlichman, *Witness to Power: The Nixon Years* (New York: Simon & Schuster, 1982), 368, 372. It seemed that Ehrlichman wanted to say as little as possible.

When Ehrlichman asked Gray a rather elementary question, Gray noted, "it wasn't surprising to me that Nixon knew more about the investigation than Ehrlichman." L. Patrick Gray III with Ed Gray, *In Nixon's Web: A Year in the Cross Hairs of Watergate* (New York: Times Books, 2008), 158.

8. John Dean had an explanation for Gray's nomination: "I kicked myself for not having protested his resignation more vigorously. It was an idle regret; we had no choice. We couldn't afford an angry Pat Gray loose on the streets. It was just one more example of the Watergate tar baby; the only thing worse than nominating Gray would have been not nominating him." John Dean, *Blind Ambition* (New York: Simon & Schuster, 1976), 184.
9. Conversation 858-003, NARA.
10. Gray later sought to rebut the *Washington Post*'s allegation that he had blackmailed Nixon into choosing him to head the FBI. Gray, *In Nixon's Web*, 153–176, 178–179. If Gray did blackmail Nixon, Gray did not keep his end of the bargain. More likely, there was no blackmail involved; rather, it was a bad and poorly thought out decision and follow-up by Ehrlichman, who may have been trying to conceal his past activities involving Gray and Dr. Fielding from Nixon. Ehrlichman harmed Nixon in a number of ways.
11. Barry Sussman, *The Great Cover-up: Nixon and the Scandal of Watergate* (New York: Thomas Y. Crowell, 1974), 163. Also brewing was the convicted burglars' demands for support of their families.
12. Gray, *In Nixon's Web*, 213. Nixon's memoirs praised Gray and the investigation. He claimed to be anxious to have Gray tell the story of the FBI's investigation publicly—a rather strange position. Nixon, *RN*, 778. Books by Haldeman and Ehrlichman did not mention the circumstances of Gray's nomination.
13. Contrary to his instructions, Liddy employed McCord, who was quickly tied to the Nixon campaign. Liddy did not take proper precautions to ensure that the burglars had no incriminating information on their persons or in their hotels rooms, such as address books that contained Hunt's name and telephone number.
14. John Sirica, *To Set the Record Straight* (New York: W. W. Norton, 1979), 89–109, 119–124. Shortly after Sirica read McCord's letter in open court and imposed provisional sentences on the defendants, Attorney General Kleindienst sent Sirica a letter defending the Department of Justice. At the same time, Kleindienst was telling Ehrlichman that "Sirica is really lousing this thing up." Sirica, 109–115.
15. After several meetings in late March, Haldeman and Nixon sent Dean to Camp David, where he was supposed to write a report on Watergate. He realized that such a report would incriminate himself and that anyone he named would just deny the allegations.
16. Dean, *Blind Ambition* , 227.
17. Dean, 278, 293.
18. Interview of Alexander M. Haig Jr., November 30, 2006, 32, Nixon Presidential Library, https://www.nixonlibrary.gov/oral-histories.

19. Interview of Alexander M. Haig Jr., February 5, 1998, 1, box 72.7, Bob Woodward and Carl Bernstein papers (including notes of interviews they conducted for their book *The Final Days*), Harry Ransom Center, University of Texas at Austin (hereafter, HRC-W&B). Haldeman wrote, "General Alexander Haig, whom I recommended as my replacement as White House Chief of Staff was, fortunately for him, ignorant of most Watergate matters." H. R. Haldeman with Joseph DiMona, *The Ends of Power* (New York: Times Books, 1978), 299. Haldeman left the White House before Haig was appointed, and there is no evidence that Haig ever asked Haldeman or anyone else to brief him on the events of Watergate.
20. Alexander M. Haig Jr. with Charles McCarry, *Inner Circles: How America Changed the World* (New York: Warner Books, 1992), 386–387. See Myers v. U.S., 272 U.S. 52 (1926), which states: "the Tenure of Office Act of 1867, insofar as it attempted to prevent the president from removing an executive officer who had been appointed by him with the advice and consent of the Senate, is invalid."
21. Cox relied on fellow Harvard Law School Professor James Vorenberg to select his staff and later to act as an adviser to him.
22. Nixon, *RN*, 911.
23. SSC Hearings, 6:2555. Nixon's announcement was the first public revelation of his June 23, 1972, conversations with Haldeman, but his discussion of the contents of those conversations was limited, and the importance of the meetings did not resonate at the time.

6. Senate Watergate Committee Hearings
1. Originally, the committee intended to hold hearings on campaign financing first, but the cascade of revelations about the break-in changed that.
2. Rotating court reporters recorded the testimony, and transcripts were available within hours. It was not common knowledge that the committee had documents and testimony stored in computers by a staff of researchers using punch cards and that these records were retrievable by a word search. It is my understanding that neither the special prosecutor nor the House Impeachment Committee employed computers but relied on paper copies.
3. Senator Lowell Weicker distributed witness summaries to the press. He believed that everything should be made public.
4. Petersen's most serious legal problem was his provision of copies of grand jury minutes to Dean.
5. SSC Hearings, 2:794, 6:2282–2283. LaRue corroborated Magruder's testimony that Mitchell approved Liddy's Gemstone plan. SSC Hearings, 6:2339.
6. SSC Hearings, 2:915–924, 4:1521.
7. SSC Hearings, 3:957.
8. SSC Hearings, 3:1078. According to Dean, the conversation took place on March 13 rather than March 21, 1973, as part of his "cancer on the presidency" remarks. These were later cited by those seeking to discredit Dean.

9. SSC Hearings, 3:1017; John Dean, *Blind Ambition* (New York: Simon & Schuster, 1976), 262–263. There is no recording of this conversation; the White House claimed the recorder had run out of tape earlier.
10. SSC Hearings, 4:1556. By then, Dean's defection from the official White House position was known.
11. SSC Hearings, 4:1608–1616, 5:1855–1857.
12. SSC Hearings, 5:1890–1891.
13. Leonard Garment, *Crazy Rhythm: My Journey from Brooklyn, Jazz, and Wall Street to Nixon's White House, Watergate, and Beyond* (New York: Times Books, 1997), 275–277.
14. H. R. Haldeman with Joseph DiMona, *The Ends of Power* (New York: Times Books, 1978), 305–306.
15. Bob Burke and Ralph G. Thompson, *Bryce Harlow: Mr. Integrity* (Oklahoma City: Oklahoma Heritage Foundation, 2000), 232.
16. Richard M. Nixon, *RN: The Memoirs of Richard Nixon* (New York: Grosset, 1978), 899–900.
17. Alexander M. Haig Jr. with Charles McCarry, *Inner Circles: How America Changed the World* (New York: Warner Books, 1992), 373.
18. Haig, 379.
19. Interviews of Leonard Garment, April 6, 2007, 33–35, and November 3, 2007, 14–15, Nixon Presidential Library, https://www.nixonlibrary.gov/oral-histories.
20. Nixon, *RN*, 901.
21. Haig, *Inner Circles*, 382.
22. Interview II of John J. Wilson, 4–5, box 8.11, HRC-W&B.
23. There was some concern among Senate committee staff that the White House was setting a major trap. That is, the committee would fight to obtain the tapes, only to find that there was nothing incriminating on them; the incriminating conversations had not been recorded.
24. John Sirica, *To Set the Record Straight* (New York: W. W. Norton, 1979), 137.
25. Ken Gormley, *Archibald Cox: Conscience of a Nation* (Reading, MA: Addison, Wesley, 1997), 290, 291. Scholars often care more about issues being properly decided than about winning cases.
26. SSC Hearings, 8:3045.
27. SSC Hearings, 9:3546–3547.
28. SSC Hearings, 8:3044–3045.
29. SSC Hearings, 9:3577.
30. SSC Hearings, 8:3062–3063.
31. SSC Hearings, 6:2884.
32. SSC Hearings, 8:3249.
33. SSC Hearings, 6:2611.
34. SSC Hearings, 6:2570. The White House could have relied on the Cubans' patriotism during the Bay of Pigs invasion to justify supporting them.

35. SSC Hearings, 7:2888–2897.
36. SSC Hearings, 7:2849. According to Haldeman, he listened to the March 21 tape on April 25, 1973. Haldeman, *Ends of Power*, 271.
37. SSC Hearings, 8:3225. There were no follow-up questions. Even though Haldeman was expressing two concerns—the anonymous donors and interference with CIA operations in Mexico—Thompson reduced it to a single concern. This is reminiscent of questions prosecutor Richard Ben-Veniste asked Haldeman at the cover-up trial (discussed in a later chapter), which Haldeman rejected on the grounds that it was mixing apples and oranges.
38. SSC Hearings, 8:3163.
39. SSC Hearings, 8:3166.
40. SSC Hearings, 8:3184–3187.
41. SSC Hearings, 8:3252–3253, 3276.
42. SSC Hearings, 9:3420. The exchange also appears to contradict Walters's memorandum of the meeting (discussed in chapter 3), to the effect that the White House said it wanted the investigation to go no further than the five burglars who were initially arrested. SSC Hearings, 7:2948. According to Walters's memorandum of his meeting that same afternoon with Gray, he told Gray, "if the investigation were pushed 'south of the border' it could trespass upon some of our covert operations." SSC Hearings, 9:3815.
43. John W. Dean, *Lost Honor: The Rest of the Story* (Los Angeles: Stratford Press, 1982), 229.
44. Howard Hunt did not testify until September 1973. By then, he had distanced himself from the White House and Liddy and his earlier lies and gave damaging testimony about the White House Plumbers, money received by the Watergate burglars, and other matters.

7. The Watergate Special Prosecutor and the Fight for Nixon's Tapes

1. In re Grand Jury Subpoena Duces Tecum, 360 F. Supp. 1 (D.D.C 1973).
2. An admitted leaker was Republican Senator Lowell Weicker, who said he did so because the public deserved to be fully informed. His leaks frustrated many committee staff members, who did not want the White House to know what they knew.
3. Nixon v. Sirica, 487 F.2d 700 (D.C. Cir. 1973).
4. *Nixon v. Sirica*, 700. Meanwhile, on October 10, 1973, Vice President Spiro Agnew, who was not close to Nixon and was not involved in the Watergate scandal, resigned and pleaded no contest to tax charges connected with an unrelated bribery scheme. Most (but not all) of the illegal activity had taken place while Agnew was an official in the Maryland government, including when he was governor.
5. *Nixon v. Sirica*, 711, 722.
6. See Richard M. Nixon, *RN: The Memoirs of Richard Nixon* (New York: Grosset, 1978), 929.

7. The president's team was hampered by a lack of knowledge of Watergate in general and the tapes in particular. Only Nixon was present earlier, and his knowledge and memory were limited.
8. Interview of Buzhardt, pt. 1, 4, box 4.16, HRC-W&B.
9. Alexander M. Haig Jr. with Charles McCarry, *Inner Circles: How America Changed the World* (New York: Warner Books, 1992), 399–404.
10. Interview of Alexander Haig, November 30, 2006, 49, Nixon Presidential Library, https://www.nixonlibrary.gov/oral-histories.
11. Nixon, *RN*, 920–935; Haig, *Inner Circles*, 393–404.
12. Bork remained solicitor general and was later nominated to the Supreme Court.
13. H. R. Haldeman with Joseph DiMona, *The Ends of Power* (New York: Times Books, 1978), 37.
14. Nixon, *RN*, 937.
15. James Breslin, *How the Good Guys Finally Won: Notes from an Impeachment Summer* (New York: Viking Press, 1975), 93–94. Celler also maintained a private law practice, which many condemned.
16. Haig, *Inner Circles*, 128–132. The WSPF, which investigated the gap extensively, called Haig before the grand jury three times. Haig, 449.
17. Howard Fields, *High Crimes and Misdemeanors: The Dramatic Story of the Rodino Committee* (New York: W. W. Norton, 1978), 96–98. Although Zeifman had supporters, many believed he was far too partisan. After he was passed over, he was considered "resentful" and "obstructive." Interview of Richard Gill, September 30, 2011, 30; interview of Francis O'Brien, September 29, 2011, 6, Nixon Presidential Library, https://www.nixonlibrary.gov/oral-histories. Doar spent the first decade of his professional life working in his family's law firm in New Richmond, Wisconsin, and then had an illustrious career in the Civil Rights Division of the Department of Justice opposing discrimination in the South. After that, he worked for a minority regional project in New York City before becoming president of the New York City Board of Education. His later career seemed directed toward accommodation and compromise, not designed to hone the skills of someone destined to lead a heated and confrontational impeachment inquiry.
18. Haig's memoirs mentioned Jenner only twice in connection with Watergate: first, when the House Impeachment Committee announced his appointment in January 1974 (described as "more than bizarre" because he was close to Democrats, had predicted Nixon's political demise, and had been considered for the post that eventually went to Doar), and second, when he was replaced in July 1974. Haig, *Inner Circles*, 445, 469. Nixon did not mention Jenner in his memoirs. This situation can be contrasted with the Senate Watergate Committee. See SSC Hearings, 8:3204.
19. Haig, *Inner Circles*, 445.
20. See appendix E; Geoff Shepard, *The Real Watergate Scandal: Collusion, Conspiracy, and the Plot that Brought Nixon Down* (Washington, DC: Regency History,

2015, 2019), 254–255. Interviewers at the Nixon Presidential Library did not ask Ruth about *ex parte* meetings with Sirica. Jaworski's letter is not included in the John J. Sirica Collection at the Library of Congress. Other letters written by the special prosecutor in the same period are in box 24, folders 5 and 6, and box 43, folder 1.
21. For example, in U.S. v. Haldeman, 559 F.2d 31, 107–109 (D.C. Cir. 1976) (*en banc*), the court of appeals affirmed Sirica's ruling to admit all the Nixon tapes on the grounds that it was not an abuse of discretion.

8. The House Impeachment Committee Gears Up

1. Bob Woodward and Carl Bernstein, *The Final Days* (New York: Simon & Schuster, 1976), 110. Nixon confidant Charles Colson recommended St. Clair.
2. Interview I of St. Clair, 1, box 7.21, HRC-W&B.
3. Haig wrote, "At long last, the President appointed a seasoned trial lawyer, James St. Clair, as head of his legal team." Haig, *Inner Circles*, 449.
4. Alexander M. Haig Jr. with Charles McCarry, *Inner Circles: How America Changed the World* (New York: Warner Books, 1992), 448–449; interview of James Lichtenstein, October 2, 1974, 9, box 6.11, HRC-W&B; interview of Geoff Shepard, 37-Geoff Shepard-oh-3-mp4, 10–12 min., Nixon Presidential Library, https://www.nixonlibrary.gov/oral-histories.
5. White House Tape 42-33, March 22, 1973.
6. John Dean, *Blind Ambition: The White House Years* (New York: Simon & Schuster, 1976), 121; interview of Henry Ruth Jr., November 12, 2011, session 1, 1:08 hours, session 4, 13 min., Nixon Presidential Library. There is no transcript of the Ruth interview; the tape is available at the library in Yorba Linda, California, or on YouTube.
7. For example, Jaworski and Ruth had arranged to meet with Haig in the White House during a snowstorm. Ruth later recalled that they were kept waiting twenty minutes, and Jaworski was outraged. One lawyer working on the Nixon defense later criticized the political skills of many at the White House. Interview of John J. Chester, July 30, 2002, Nixon Presidential Library, https://www.nixonlibrary.gov/oral-histories.
8. Nussbaum later became White House counsel under President Bill Clinton.
9. Howard Fields, *High Crimes and Misdemeanors: The Dramatic Story of the Rodino Committee* (New York: W. W. Norton, 1978), 107.
10. See Renata Adler, *Gone: The Last Days of the* New Yorker (New York: Simon & Schuster, 1999), 120–121. Some referred to Doar's associates as the "kitchen cabinet." Interview of Robert Sack, September 27, 2011, 2, 33, Nixon Presidential Library, https://www.nixonlibrary.gov/oral-histories.
11. Fields, *High Crimes and Misdemeanors*, 119, 205.
12. Haig, *Inner Circles*, 460.
13. Dean's statement to me.

14. When Haldeman informed Nixon that Senator Howard Baker had appointed Fred Thompson minority counsel, Nixon responded, "Oh, shit. That kid. Well, we seem to lose them all don't we?" John W. Dean, *The Nixon Defense: What He Knew and When He Knew It* (New York: Penguin, 2014), 230.
15. Haig, *Inner Circles*, 450. For comparison, consider that the first impeachment and trial of President Donald J. Trump started on September 24, 2019, and ended with Trump's acquittal in the Senate on February 5, 2020, four and a half months later.
16. Richard M. Nixon, *RN: The Memoirs of Richard Nixon* (New York: Grosset, 1978), 928.
17. Richard Ben-Veniste and George Frampton Jr., *Stonewall: The Real Story of the Watergate Prosecution* (New York: Simon & Schuster, 1977), 241, 243–244.
18. Ruth interview, session 1, 1:23–1:25 hours.
19. Ruth interview, session 1, 1:21–1:23, 1:29 hours. Ruth did not explain what he believed the source of this duty was.
20. Watergate Road Map, National Archives, folder 5, https://archives.gov/files/research/investigations/watergate/roadmap/docid-70105884.pdf.
21. References to the often strained relations between Jaworski and his staff appear in Ben-Veniste and Frampton, *Stonewall*, 241; Jill Wine-Banks, *The Watergate Girl: My Fight for Truth and Justice against a Criminal President* (New York: Henry Holt, 2020); and William H. Merrill, *Watergate Prosecutor* (East Lansing: Michigan State University Press, 2008), 47–48. The authors of these three books were all assistant Watergate prosecutors.
22. Grand Jury Material, Leon Jaworski Papers, box 20307, box 3, papers of Leon Jaworski from Baylor University, NARA.
23. Nixon, *RN*, 990.
24. Shepard, *Real Watergate Scandal*; Geoff Shepard, *The Nixon Conspiracy: Watergate and the Plot to Remove the President* (New York: Bombardier Press, 2021). I do not accept at least two positions taken by Shepard: that Nixon did not commit any crimes and that Dean willfully lied before the Senate Watergate Committee and at the cover-up trial. These are important facets of Shepard's books, but both positions are readily severable from allegations of improper *ex parte* communications, for which there is independent documentary corroboration. December 14 was also the date of the initial meeting between staff members of the House Impeachment Committee, led by Doar, and attorneys for the White House, led by St. Clair. Fields, *High Crimes and Misdemeanors*, 117.
25. See appendix F. Jaworski memorandum, February 12, 1974, Papers of Leon Jaworski from Baylor University, box 1, folder: Memos (2 of 3), Watergate Collection, NARA. The memorandum suggests that Sirica had communicated this concern to Jaworski previously.
26. Jaworski memorandum, 2.
27. John J. Sirica, *To Set the Record Straight: The Break-in, the Tapes, the Conspirators, the Pardon* (New York: W. W. Norton, 1979), 217.
28. Ben-Veniste and Frampton, *Stonewall*, 242.

29. Watergate Road Map, National Archives, folder 5, 40, 45. https://archives.gov/files/research/investigations/watergate/roadmap/docid-70105884.pdf.
30. Sirica, *To Set the Record Straight*, 360.
31. Telephone call with Geoff Shepard, August 5, 2023. Shepard had successfully filed a Freedom of Information request to obtain documents that Jaworski removed from the WSPF files.
32. Interview of St. Clair, December 4, 1974, 1, box 7.21, HRC-W&B.
33. Leon Jaworski, *The Right and the Power* (New York: Reader's Digest Press, 1976), 103.
34. Sirica, *To Set the Record Straight*, 211.
35. There were discussions about the propriety of the contacts, including several articles in the *Atlantic* in 2013. Judgments by experts and journalists were mixed, and many believed that the meetings did not raise a serious issue of judicial misconduct. See, e.g., Andrew Cohen, "What Sirica Did Right and Wrong in the Watergate Cover-up Trial," *Atlantic*, August 14, 2013. In my opinion, many of the commentators and their sources understated the seriousness of the *ex parte* contacts.
36. The DC Circuit declined to reverse on that ground. *U.S. v. Haldeman*, 559 F.2d at 88–91.
37. Ben-Veniste and Frampton, *Stonewall*, 253.
38. Ruth interview, session 1, 1:26–1:28 hours.
39. Fields, *High Crimes and Misdemeanors*, 107. The WSPF conducted no independent investigation, although one or two of its task forces conducted private interviews, including of Charles Colson and Donald Segretti, but they apparently played no role in the impeachment process. Interview of Richard Gill, September 30, 2011, 12–13, Nixon Presidential Library, https://www.nixonlibrary.gov/oral-histories.
40. Fields, *High Crimes and Misdemeanors*, 122 (emphasis added).
41. Jaworski, *Right and the Power*, 97–98.
42. Barry Sussman, *The Great Cover-up: Nixon and the Scandal of Watergate* (New York: Thomas Y. Crowell, 1974), 290.
43. Sussman, 290. Sussman retained the same text in subsequent editions; see, e.g., *Great Cover-up* (3rd ed., 1992), 279. The cover of the 1992 edition quotes John Dean: "The best book on Watergate." Its strength is its discussion of events in 1972 and the first half of 1973.
44. Interview of John Doar, January 24, 2014, 46–50, 56; interview of Bernard Nussbaum, October 21, 2014, 39; interview of Robert Sack, September 27, 2011, 6, Nixon Presidential Library, https://www.nixonlibrary.gov/oral-histories.
45. Fields, *High Crimes and Misdemeanors*, 125. The staff of the Impeachment Committee made no effort to slow matters down. See, e.g., interview of Evan Davis, January 14, 2014, 20, 27, Nixon Presidential Library, https://www.nixonlibrary.gov/oral-histories.
46. Fields, *High Crimes and Misdemeanors*, 175; Haig, *Inner Circles*, 455–456.

47. Stanley Kutler, *The Wars of Watergate: The Last Crisis of Richard Nixon* (New York: Alfred A. Knopf, 1990), 464.

9. Cover-up Indictment and Transmission of a "Road Map"

1. The prosecution in Watergate was rivaled only by the 1920s Teapot Dome scandal, when Albert Bacon Fall, President Warren G. Harding's interior secretary, was convicted of bribery in a case that involved the sale of petroleum reserves on federal land. He was the first former cabinet member to go to prison. Mitchell was the second.
2. "Final Decisions" memorandum, February 20, 1974; memorandum from Lacovara to Jaworski, "Status of Charles Colson in Watergate Case," February 22, 1974. One reason Bittman escaped prosecution was that he concealed damaging evidence against himself until after the trial started. Bittman's extensive activities on Hunt's behalf are described in E. Howard Hunt, *Undercover: Memoirs of an American Secret Agent* (New York: Berkley Publishing, 1974), 268–296. Some of the people involved—Dean, Magruder, LaRue, and Porter—had already pleaded guilty and would not go to trial; they would be prosecution witnesses.
3. Leon Jaworski, *The Right and the Power: The Prosecution of Watergate* (New York: Reader's Digest Press, 1976), 104.
4. Members of the WSPF acknowledged that the press and the public "learned nothing" on March 1. Richard Ben-Veniste and George Frampton Jr., *Stonewall: The Real Story of the Watergate Prosecution* (New York: Simon & Schuster, 1977), 264.
5. Edward Mezvinsky with Kevin McCormally and John Greenya, *A Term to Remember* (New York: Coward, McCann & Geoghegan, 1977), 123.
6. Elizabeth Drew, *Washington Journal: The Events of 1973–1974* (New York: Random House, 1975), 157.
7. Timothy Neftali, "Richard Nixon," in *Impeachment: An American History*, ed. Jon Meacham et al. (New York: Random House, 2018), 107. Some of the mystery surrounding the report was removed by James Doyle, press officer of the WSPF: "This is how the road map worked: One page might say, 'On March 16, 1973, E. Howard Hunt demanded $120,000.' Then it would list page references to grand jury testimony from witnesses who saw Hunt's blackmail note and references to the tapes where Hunt's demand was discussed. The grand jury transcripts and the tape transcripts would be included." James Doyle, *Not above the Law: The Battles of Watergate Prosecutors Cox and Jaworski* (New York: William Morrow, 1977), 290–291. The WSPF gave a one-side account but was not argumentative.
8. Ben-Veniste and Frampton, *Stonewall*, 264.
9. That action made it difficult for any other person to object later.
10. At a hearing before Sirica on March 4, St. Clair complained about prejudicial publicity appearing in the *Washington Post* but disclaimed any interest in seeing the contents of the report: "I have not seen nor request to see the contents of the

bulging briefcase." Hearing transcript, March 4, 1974, 15; see also hearing transcript, 11. Three days later, St. Clair changed his mind and requested access to it. He never received it.

11. Geoff Shepard, *The Real Watergate Scandal: Collusion, Conspiracy, and the Plot that Brought Nixon Down* (Washington, DC: Regency History, 2015, 2019), 264.

12. In re Report and Recommendations of June 5, 1972 Grand Jury Concerning Transmission of Evidence to House of Representatives, 370 F. Supp. 1219 (D.D.C. 1974). Sirica said that Haldeman and Strachan lacked "standing." That was untrue; they had every right to complain that publicity about the grand jury's work could prejudice their forthcoming trial. Their arguments, however, concerned prejudice at trial, which courts have traditionally addressed only after conviction. Their right to claim that the grand jury exceeded its powers was only tangentially related to their complaint.

13. See Trump v. U.S., Slip Op. 37 (U.S. Supreme Court, 2024).

14. One question is whether the "judicial proceeding" required by Rule 6(e) of the Federal Rules of Criminal Procedure is intended to ensure that defendants or subjects are afforded their full constitutional rights, including the Fifth and Sixth Amendments, which are not respected in grand jury proceedings.

15. Haldeman v. Sirica, 501 F.2d 714, 715 (D.C. Cir. 1974). Both sides filed detailed briefs in the court of appeals. Rule 35 of the Federal Rules of Appellate Procedure governs *en banc* hearings. Rule 35(a) reads in part: "An en banc hearing or rehearing is not favored and will not be ordered unless: (1) en banc consideration is necessary to insure or maintain uniformity in the court's decisions; or (2) the proceeding involves a question of exceptional importance." There is no mention of the importance of the case.

16. *Haldeman v. Sirica*, 501 F.2d at 715.

17. Jaworski, *Right and the Power*, 104–108. Sirica's decision did not mention that the Nixon tapes were part of the grand jury's report.

18. *Haldeman v. Sirica*, 501 F.2d at 715–716. Nothing prevents a convicted defendant from rearguing the issue on direct appeal. But obviously, the judges would know that they had denied the petition earlier and would be reluctant to start a trial all over again.

19. Recently, the Supreme Court reaffirmed that conclusion: "As for the Government's assurances that prosecutors and grand juries will not permit political or baseless prosecutions from advancing in the first place, . . . [w]e do not ordinarily decline significant constitutional questions based on the Government's promise of good faith. . . . Nor do we do so today." *Trump v. U.S.*, Slip Op. 37.

20. MacKinnon served briefly as a Republican member of the House of Representatives from Minnesota and was an unsuccessful Republican candidate for governor of that state.

21. *Haldeman v. Sirica*, 501 F.2d at 716.

22. *Haldeman v. Sirica*, 501 F.2d at 717 (footnote omitted). What the prosecution

referred to is not clear. MacKinnon also rejected the WSPF's argument that Rule 6(e) does not limit disclosure of grand jury minutes by a judge, a position supported by the rule's language.

23. It would have been like a court deciding the Pentagon Papers case without knowing their content.
24. Interview of Jaworski, I at 1, II at 1, box 6.2, HRC-W&B.
25. Interview of Bernard Nussbaum, October 21, 2014, 19, Nixon Presidential Library, https://www.nixonlibrary.gov/oral-histories.
26. Richard M. Nixon, *RN: The Memoirs of Richard Nixon* (New York: Grosset, 1978), 948, 992.
27. Bob Woodward and Carl Bernstein, *The Final Days* (New York: Simon & Schuster, 1976), 122–123.
28. See Alexander M. Haig Jr. with Charles McCarry, *Inner Circles: How America Changed the World* (New York: Warner Books, 1992), 448–452.
29. Interview of Henry Ruth Jr., November 12, 2011, session 1, 1:27 hours, Nixon Presidential Library.
30. Woodward and Bernstein, *Final Days*, 122–123.
31. Haig, *Inner Circles*, 453. Haig and Jaworski met multiple times.
32. "Jaworski conducted his White House negotiations exclusively with Haig." Stanley Kutler, *The Wars of Watergate: The Last Crisis of Richard Nixon* (New York: Alfred A. Knopf, 1990), 448.
33. Interview of St. Clair, November 11, 1974, box 7.21, HRC-W&B; John W. Dean, *Blind Ambition: The White House Years* (New York: Simon & Schuster, 1976), 346.
34. St. Clair interview.
35. Jaworski memorandum, January 15, 1974, Papers of Leon Jaworski from Baylor University, box 2, Memos, Watergate Collection, NARA.
36. St. Clair interview.
37. Woodward and Bernstein, *Final Days*, 253.
38. Suppose the WSPF had acquired evidence illegally and transmitted it to the House Impeachment Committee. Could Haldeman and Strachan claim that the prosecutor was attempting to benefit collaterally from the use of tainted evidence that it could not use itself? Was this case weaker or stronger than the one presented by the facts in Watergate? There was little law on these questions.
39. John J. Sirica, *To Set the Record Straight: The Break-in, the Tapes, the Conspirators, the Pardon* (New York: W. W. Norton, 1979), 217–219. Sirica knew that the law was unclear and that the report was of great value to the Impeachment Committee.
40. Jaworski, *Right and the Power*, 104.
41. Jaworski, 104; interview of Jaworski, December 5, 1974, box 6.2, HRC-W&B.
42. Ben-Veniste and Frampton, *Stonewall*, 264.
43. Nixon v. Sirica, 487 F.2d 700, 711 (D.C. Cir. 1973).
44. Haig, *Inner Circles*, 451.

45. Fred Emery, *Watergate: The Corruption of American Politics and the Fall of Richard Nixon* (New York: Simon & Schuster, 1994), 427.
46. Kutler, *Wars of Watergate*, 462–465. Kutler, whose lawsuit resulted in the public release of the Nixon Watergate tapes, prepared important transcripts of many of the tapes. Stanley I. Kutler, *Abuse of Power: The New Nixon Tapes* (New York: Free Press, 1997). Some of the Watergate tapes were disclosed in 1974 by Nixon and at the cover-up trial.
47. See Stephen E. Ambrose, *Nixon: Ruin and Recovery 1973–1990* (New York: Simon & Schuster, 1991), 305–306.
48. Importantly, the product of the Senate Watergate Committee was on computer, albeit in a primitive program, and was searchable by word. This was particularly useful in preparing questions for committee members and staff to ask witnesses.

10. Impeachment Proceedings Begin
1. The White House repeatedly put itself in a vulnerable position. In late March Nixon told an audience, "Farmers never had it so good." Iowa Democrat Edward Mezvinsky called it "one of the most politically irresponsible statements in [Nixon's] long career." Edward Mezvinsky with Kevin McCormally and John Greenya, *A Term to Remember* (New York: Coward, McCann & Geoghegan, 1977), 108.
2. Mezvinsky, 102.
3. Jimmy Breslin, *How the Good Guys Finally Won: Notes from an Impeachment Summer* (New York: Viking Press, 1975), 154–155.
4. Interview of Francis O'Brien, September 29, 2011, 19–20, Nixon Presidential Library, https://www.nixonlibrary.gov/oral-histories.
5. Mezvinsky, *Term to Remember*, 133; Jerry Zeifman, *Without Honor: The Impeachment of President Nixon and the Crimes of Camelot* (New York: Thunder's Mouth Press, 1995), 242–246.
6. Barry Sussman, *The Great Cover-up: Nixon and the Watergate Scandal*, 3rd ed. (Arlington, VA: Seven Locks Press, 1992), 285.
7. Interview of Bernard Nussbaum, October 21, 2014, 39, Nixon Presidential Library, https://www.nixonlibrary.gov/oral-histories.
8. Zeifman, *Without Honor*, 133–134, 144–155, 164. See generally Howard Fields, *High Crimes and Misdemeanors: The Dramatic Story of the Rodino Committee* (New York: W. W. Norton, 1978); Mezvinsky, *Term to Remember*; Timothy Neftali, "Richard Nixon," in *Impeachment: An American History*, ed. Jon Meacham et al. (New York: Random House, 2018), 111.
9. Mezvinsky, *Term to Remember*, 98–99.
10. Mezvinsky, 130.
11. Fields, *High Crimes and Misdemeanors*, 194; Neftali, "Richard Nixon," 122–123.
12. See, e.g., interview of Hillary Rodham (Clinton), August 9, 2018, 10; interview of Robin Johansen, October 28, 2011, Nixon Presidential Library, https://www.nixonlibrary.gov/oral-histories.

13. Interview of Fred Altshuler, October 28, 2011, 4, Nixon Presidential Library, https://www.nixonlibrary.gov/oral-histories.
14. Several individuals, including the permanent counsel to the House Judiciary Committee (Doar was special counsel), claimed that Democratic members of the committee were slowing down the process because they thought a delay would be advantageous to Democrats in the 1974 elections. Zeifman, *Without Honor*. That position lacks significant evidentiary support.
15. Zeifman, 95–96, 138–144. Nixon was granted the right to counsel on April 9.
16. Zeifman, 39. By and large, the committee staff confined itself to preparing for a hearing, while the committee members discussed and decided policy issues.
17. For example, on May 9, 1974, the traditionally conservative *Chicago Tribune* editorialized that Nixon should resign as president.
18. Mezvinsky, *Term to Remember*, 126–127.
19. Interviews with Geoffrey Shepard.
20. See Bob Woodward and Carl Bernstein, *The Final Days* (New York: Simon & Schuster, 1976), 123–143. One source credits aide Bryce Harlow for delaying the release of the tapes. He said, "We can not have the President of the United States talking like that." Bob Burke and Ralph G. Thompson, *Bryce Harlow: Mr. Integrity* (Oklahoma City: Oklahoma Heritage Association, 2000), 237.
21. Richard M. Nixon, *RN: The Memoirs of Richard Nixon* (New York: Grosset, 1978), 968.
22. Interview II of Jaworski, December 5, 1974, box 6.2, HRC-W&B.
23. Interview II of Shepard, May 26, 2009, 18:30 min., Nixon Presidential Library, https://www.nixonlibrary.gov/oral-histories; interview I of St. Clair, box 7.21, HRC-W&B.
24. Nixon, *RN*, 994.
25. Fields, *High Crimes and Misdemeanors*, 156.
26. Nixon, *RN*, 994–995. The transcripts released on April 29, 1974, were created by Shepard under the supervision of Fred Buzhardt. Interview II of Shepard, 17–23 min.
27. Alexander M. Haig Jr. with Charles McCarry, *Inner Circles: How America Changed the World* (New York: Warner Books, 1992), 452.
28. Shepard has acknowledged that he was responsible for the phrase "expletive deleted." Interview II of Shepard, 22–25 min.
29. One Republican senator sympathetic to Nixon called the tapes "deplorable, disgusting, shabby, [and] immoral." John Osborne, *The Last Nixon Watch* (New York: Liveright, 1975), 127, 136 (reprinting a March 18, 1974, column from the *New Republic*).
30. Neftali, "Richard Nixon," 116.
31. Submission of Recorded Presidential Conversations to the Committee of the House of Representatives by President Richard Nixon, April 30, 1974, 193–194.
32. The case may have been too important to be based on Nixon's previous delivery

of tapes to the WSPF and his public release of tapes on April 29, which eliminated his presidential privileges. Also, each tape was unique and arguably involved different considerations.
33. Interview of St. Clair, November 21, 1974, box 7.21, HRC-W&B. See also Woodward and Bernstein, *Final Days*, 130–131.
34. St. Clair interview.
35. Jaworski does not mention the matter in *The Right and the Power*. It is not clear whether he had any input into the response.
36. U.S. v. Mitchell, 377 F. Supp. 1312 (D.D.C. 1974). Instead of the facts, Sirica discussed the timing of the cover-up trial and his assignment to preside over the case.
37. U.S. v. Mitchell, 397 F. Supp. 166 (D.D.C. 1974).
38. Mitchell v. Sirica, 502 F.2d 375, 376 (D.C. Cir. 1974) (MacKinnon, J., concurring and dissenting).
39. Brady v. Maryland, 373 U.S. 83 (1963).
40. Memorandum from Lacovara to Jaworski, Ruth, and two other assistant prosecutors, July 23, 1974, Watergate File, NARA.
41. What went on in the committee out of the public eye has been the subject of some controversy. See, e.g., Zeifman, *Without Honor* (accusing Doar of incompetence and failing to proceed with the impeachment as required). Zeifman alleged that Doar, Bernard Nussbaum, Burke Marshall, and Hillary Rodham had unusual views and were dragging their feet. The evidence indicates that the staff was acting conscientiously to bring along southern Democrats and moderate Republicans. Mezvinsky, *Term to Remember*, 133. There is no doubt, however, that Doar was methodical, cautious, and slow.
42. Sirica, *To Set the Record Straight*, 220.
43. Professor Charles Alan Wright of the University of Texas Law School returned to Washington to work on the White House's case before the Supreme Court.
44. After Colson pleaded guilty in the Ellsberg case, the prosecutors dismissed the cover-up indictment against him.
45. Colson claimed his guilty plea was part of his conversion to Christianity and his devotion to a life of penitence. His attorneys had advised him that he had a good chance of being acquitted. Charles W. Colson, *Born Again* (Tappan, NJ: Chosen Books, 1976), 208–224. Another Nixon aide who had a similar experience was Harry Dent, who was concerned primarily with activities in the South. See Harry S. Dent, *Cover-up: The Watergate in All of Us* (San Bernardino, CA: Here's Life Publishers, 1986).
46. Interview of Jack McCahill, November 5, 1974, box 10, HRC-W&B. Normally, the prosecutor identifies unindicted coconspirators. I know of no investigation into the leak of secret grand jury action to the *Los Angeles Times*.
47. Richard Ben-Veniste and George Frampton Jr., *Stonewall: The Real Story of the Watergate Prosecution* (New York: Simon & Schuster, 1977), 286–287.

48. See appendix H.
49. Nixon, *RN*, 1018–1020. Nixon devoted thirty pages of his memoirs to his overseas trips in the summer of 1974. Nixon, 1009–1039. It was a last-gasp effort to get the public behind him.
50. For example, problems with SALT and the Soviet Union and the Syrian-Israeli disengagement took place in June–July 1974. See Henry Kissinger, *Years of Upheaval* (New York: Little Brown, 1982), 1111–1178. Negotiations frequently consume more of statesmen's time than wars do.
51. Kissinger, 6. According to Woodward and Bernstein's notes, from which this quotation is taken, St. Clair was referring to the Senate.
52. St. Clair interview I.
53. "Dean's memory was stunningly corroborated by the Nixon tapes." Anthony Summers, *The Arrogance of Power: The Secret World of Richard Nixon* (New York: Viking, 2000), 534. The White House tended to exaggerate the significance of relatively minor lapses by Dean.
54. Comparison of White House and Judiciary Committee Transcripts of Eight Recorded Presidential Conversations, Hearing of the Committee on the Judiciary, House of Representatives, 63rd Cong., 2nd sess., pursuant to H. Res. 803, serial no. 34 (May–June 1974), 27.
55. Interview of Buzhardt, pt. I, box 4.16, HRC-W&B.
56. Geoff Shepard, *The Nixon Conspiracy: Watergate and the Plot to Remove the President* (New York: Post Hill Press, 2021), 231, 234. See also Neftali, "Richard Nixon," 115–116.
57. Fields, *High Crimes and Misdemeanors*, 176–178.
58. A summary of Doar's reading of the Statements of Information to the House Impeachment Committee appears in Fields, 164–178.
59. Fields, 188.
60. Fields, 181, 185.
61. Neftali, "Richard Nixon," 132–133; Fields, *High Crimes and Misdemeanors*, 209–212. St. Clair also spent June 27 and 28 arguing against the evidence presented by the committee. Fields, 183.
62. Elizabeth Drew, *Washington Journal: The Events of 1973–1974* (New York: Random House, 1975), 319.
63. Nixon, *RN*, 1050.
64. Fields, *High Crimes and Misdemeanors*, 216.

11. The Supreme Court Rules and Nixon Resigns
1. U.S. v. Nixon, 418 U.S. 683, 712 (1974); Timothy Neftali, "Richard Nixon," in *Impeachment: An American History*, ed. Jon Meacham et al. (New York: Random House, 2018), 83–153. The court did not discuss other situations, including presidential impeachment. Some White House lawyers had been optimistic about their chances in the Supreme Court, including St. Clair. Interview I of St. Clair,

6, box 7.21, HRC-W&B; interview of McCahill, September 14, 1974, 1, box 76.10, HRC-W&B. On July 24 the *Atlanta Constitution* ran a story under a banner headline across the front page reporting that Nixon had been urged to destroy the tapes immediately after they were revealed to the public. The story was based on a leaked Buchanan memorandum. Patrick J. Buchanan, *Nixon's White House Wars: The Battles that Made and Broke a President and Divided America Forever* (New York: Crown Forum, 2017), 378–379.
2. The WSPF also had a strong argument based on the waiver of executive privilege, which the Supreme Court did not discuss. The White House delivered the first batch of tapes to the WSPF pursuant to a court order, but it did not object to the WSPF giving them to the House Impeachment Committee. The White House voluntarily gave the committee all the tapes it had given to the WSPF and then released transcripts of dozens of additional tapes to the public on April 29, 1974. In addition, it had allowed witnesses to testify to those same conversations. After that, it was a stretch to claim that the tapes were privileged and confidential.
3. Buzhardt told Woodward and Bernstein that he had not talked to Nixon for some time before July 24. Interview of Buzhardt, pt. I, box 4.16, HRC-W&B.
4. Alexander M. Haig Jr. with Charles McCarry, *Inner Circles: How America Changed the World* (New York: Warner Books, 1992), 173.
5. Haig, 173. Secondary sources are similar but not identical. See, e.g., Roger Morris, *Haig: The General's Progress* (New York: Playboy Press, 1982), 290; Anthony J. Lukas, *The Underside of the Nixon Years* (Athens: Ohio University Press, 1999), 290–293.
6. Buzhardt interview.
7. Haig, *Inner Circles*, 471–472.
8. Raymond A. Price, *With Nixon* (New York: Viking Press, 1977), 324.
9. Haig, *Inner Circles*, 473.
10. Bob Woodward and Carl Bernstein, *The Final Days* (New York: Simon & Schuster, 1976), 274–275.
11. Interview of St. Clair, November 21, 1974, box 7.21, HRC-W&B. St. Clair was not challenging the conventional interpretation of the tape and seemed oblivious of his role in the events.
12. "When the June 23 tape emerged, I thought it was not so different from, or more harmful than other evidence we had seen." Leonard Garment, *Crazy Rhythm: My Journey from Brooklyn, Jazz, and Wall Street to Nixon's White House, Watergate, and Beyond* (New York: Times Books, 1997), 294–295.
13. Evan Thomas, *Being Nixon: A Man Divided* (New York: Random House, 2015), 490. Haig tried to avoid reading the transcripts of the March 1973 Nixon-Dean conversations but finally read them on December 21, 1973. Woodward and Bernstein, *Final Days*, 108.
14. Fred J. Maroon and Tom Wicker, *Nixon Years 1969–1974: White House to Watergate* (New York: Abbeville Press, 1999), 170.

15. The Impeachment Committee soon released the material to the public. It took seven and a half months from the time the impeachment investigation was authorized until the committee heard witnesses and nearly another month before it voted on articles of impeachment. In contrast, it took just over three months for the Senate Watergate Committee to commence public hearings, and it was starting from scratch. Presidential impeachment proceedings in the twenty-first century have been much faster. On September 24, 2019, House Speaker Nancy Pelosi announced the commencement of an impeachment investigation of President Donald J. Trump; on October 31, the House of Representatives voted to hold proceedings; and on December 13, the committee approved articles of impeachment. One book on Watergate observed, "As time passed, the House Judiciary Committee, which had begun its work in October, 1973, fell far behind. . . . Hoping at first that its work would be completed by April, [the] Chairman kept pushing the date back." Barry Sussman, *The Great Cover-up: Nixon and the Watergate Scandal*, 3rd ed. (Alexandria, VA: Seven Locks Press, 1992), 285.
16. Ironically, although the proposed bill of impeachment included obstruction of justice, the committee deliberately excluded the crime of conspiracy from the impeachable charges. Jerry Zeifman, chief counsel of the House Judiciary Committee, explained that Special Counsel Doar had "a theory that the President could not be charged with participating in a conspiracy," so the bill of impeachment was drafted without that charge. Jerry Zeifman, *Without Honor: The Impeachment of President Nixon and the Crimes of Camelot* (New York: Thunder's Mouth Press, 1995), 198.
17. The Senate Watergate Committee supplied the House Impeachment Committee with evidence of the milk fund scandal.
18. Elizabeth Drew, *Washington Journal: The Events of 1973–1974* (New York: Random House, 1975), 365–366, 379.
19. John J. Sirica, *To Set the Record Straight* (New York: W. W. Norton, 1979), 227.
20. Sirica, 227.
21. Buzhardt interview.
22. Information about the probable votes of members of the House Impeachment Committee was frequently wrong. Interview of James Lichtenstein, October 2, 1974, 6, 8, box 6.11, HRC-W&B. Before July 24, 1974, the White House tended to be optimistic about Nixon's future. Bob Burke and Ralph G. Thompson, *Bryce Harlow: Mr. Integrity* (Oklahoma City: Oklahoma Heritage Foundation, 2000), 246 (assessments of Ford and Harlow).
23. Haig, *Inner Circles*, 479–481.
24. Lichtenstein interview.
25. Haig, *Inner Circles*, 436–437.
26. Interview of Haig, November 30, 2006, 49, Nixon Presidential Library, https://www.nixonlibrary.gov/oral-histories.
27. Haig, *Inner Circles*, 475.

28. Buzhardt interview.
29. Gerald R. Ford, *A Time to Heal: The Autobiography of Gerald Ford* (New York: Harper & Row, 1979), 2. See also Morris, *Haig*, 318; Haig, *Inner Circles*, 489–491.
30. Haig, *Inner Circles*, 482, 484. Haig may have counseled Nixon to resign before he read a transcript of the June 23 tapes; he never listened to them.
31. Haig, 391.
32. Haig, 479.
33. Henry Kissinger, *Years of Upheaval* (New York: Little, Brown, 1982), 1199.
34. Richard L. Lyons and William Chapman, "GOP Leaders Seen Voting to Impeach; Bottom Falls out of Save-Nixon Effort," *Washington Post*, August 6, 1974, A-1; Woodward and Bernstein, *Final Days*, 379.
35. Buzhardt interview.
36. St. Clair interview.
37. St. Clair interview.
38. Buchanan, *Nixon's White House Wars*, 380–381; Morris, *Haig*, 295; Haig, *Inner Circles*, 359–366; Price, *With Nixon*, 332–333. A reading of the documents and accounts, including the notes of Woodward and Bernstein and the tapes at the Nixon Presidential Library, indicates that Ziegler did not play a substantial role in the decision-making process.
39. Haig, *Inner Circles*, 490–491; Price, *With Nixon*, 334–336.
40. Geoff Shepard, *The Nixon Conspiracy: Watergate and the Plot to Remove the President* (New York: Bombardier Press, 2021), 274.
41. Patrick J. Buchanan, *Nixon's White House Wars* (New York: Crown Forum, 2017), 382.
42. Richard M. Nixon, *RN: The Memoirs of Richard Nixon* (New York: Grosset, 1978), 1064; Buzhardt interview; Woodward and Bernstein, *Final Days*, 381. Some newscasts later on the evening of August 5 were negative. Price, *With Nixon*, 336.
43. Interview of Geoff Shepard, 7-Shepard-oh-4, part 2-mp4, 7–9 min., Nixon Presidential Library, https://www.nixonlibrary.gov/oral-histories. There is some evidence that Buzhardt consistently took a harsher view of the June 23 conversations than others did. Garment, who took a milder view but did not speak to Nixon, wrote in his memoirs, "after talking with Fred Buzhardt and getting a sense of how fast Nixon's support was ebbing, I decided to hold my peace." Garment, *Crazy Rhythm*, 295.
44. Geoff Shepard, email to author, April 9, 2024. See Ford, *Time to Heal*, 178–181.
45. The headline is misleading in several respects. In addition to claiming that Nixon was concerned about the investigation of "Watergate," it says that his efforts to stop it were successful.
46. The story continued: "The President disclosed that he had tried to keep the Federal Bureau of Investigation from pursuing an investigation of the source of the money that financed the Watergate break-in." In this context, it is difficult to read "the source of the money" as a reference to donors rather than the finance arm of

the Nixon reelection committee. The statement that Nixon ordered a halt to the investigation of the Watergate break-in was typical of news stories at the time.
47. For example, the *Philadelphia Inquirer* stated: "President Nixon released Monday three taped conversations that showed that just six days after the Watergate burglary he and his chief aides were plotting to use the CIA and the FBI to cover up involvement by his election committee in the break-in." Peter S. Kumper's report in the *Baltimore Sun* stated: "President Nixon admitted yesterday that he ordered the FBI to limit the scope of the Watergate investigation six days after the burglary—allegedly for 'national security' reasons—knowing it would help him politically." Harry Kelly wrote in the *Chicago Tribune*: "A transcript Nixon released today of a June 23, 1972 conversation reveals his chief aide, H. R. Haldeman, warned him the FBI investigation 'goes in some directions we don't want it to go' and that Nixon authorized an effort to use the CIA to sidetrack the FBI."
48. *Impeachment of Richard Nixon President of the United States*, Report of the Committee on the Judiciary, House of Representatives, Report No. 93-1305, 360, 394.
49. See Nixon, *RN*, 1065–1066. Buzhardt said that Nixon's statement was a reaction to a call by Rep. Robert Griffin (R-MI) to resign. Buzhardt interview.
50. Haig, *Inner Circles*, 394–395.
51. Woodward and Bernstein, *Final Days*, 401–403.
52. Haig mentioned that some former senior aides were seeking pardons, an idea Goldwater and almost everyone else opposed. There was no discussion about the events of June 23, 1972, at the time. See Nixon, *RN*, 1071.
53. Nixon decided to resign exactly one year after the first phase of the Senate Watergate Committee hearings concluded. According to Haig, Goldwater did not tell Nixon he had to resign. Haig interviews, February 5, 1998, 8, and November 6, 1997, 16, box 72.7, HRC-W&B. Haig apparently was not interviewed for *Final Days*; these interviews occurred after its publication.

12. A Missed Opportunity: Representing Nixon

1. Nixon's memoirs do not mention Buchanan in entries for 1975. See Patrick J. Buchanan, *Nixon's White House Wars* (New York: Crown Forum, 2017).
2. Leonard Garment, *Crazy Rhythm: My Journey from Brooklyn, Jazz, and Wall Street to Nixon's White House, Watergate, and Beyond* (New York: Times Books, 1997), 267. Theodore White put it more broadly: "For months, for over a year actually, the President's defense had been a clearly uncoordinated one—fragmented, compartmentalized, at cross-purposes, secrets within secrets." Theodore H. White, *Breach of Faith: The Fall of Richard Nixon* (New York: Atheneum, 1975), 20. White did not focus on Nixon's legal representation.
3. Interview of Buzhardt, pt. 1, box 4.16, HRC-W&B.
4. Haig, *Inner Circles*, 476.
5. Haig, 445–446, 477, 486. Price, who was less involved in these events than some of the others, thought Nixon should resign, although it seems he did not share his

opinion with anyone. Raymond A. Price, *With Nixon* (New York: Viking Press, 1977), 329–330.
6. Bob Woodward and Carl Bernstein, *The Final Days* (New York: Simon & Schuster 1976), 314, 317.
7. Geoff Shepard prepared a transcript of the "smoking gun" tape, but he did not say when he did so. Interview of Shepard, May 9, 2009, Nixon Presidential Library, https://www.nixonlibrary.gov/oral-histories. It seems the transcript prepared by Shepard was the one Buzhardt referred to.
8. Haig, *Inner Circles*, 476.
9. Buzhardt spoke to Nixon on July 30 about the second and third June 23 conversations. Buzhardt interview, 7, 12. See also Haig, *Inner Circles*, 348.
10. Haig, *Inner Circles*, 313–314.
11. Buzhardt interview, 12. According to Buzhardt, Haig said, "Good God." Haig never listened to a single tape. Timothy Neftali, "Richard Nixon," in *Impeachment: An American History*, ed. Jon Meacham et al. (New York: Random House, 2018), 144.
12. Interview of Haig, November 30, 2006, 41–42, Nixon Presidential Library, https://www.nixonlibrary.gov/oral-histories.
13. St. Clair "spoke and acted only when the President ordered him to do so." Leon Jaworski, *The Right and the Power* (New York: Reader's Digest Press, 1976), 136.
14. Deborah Hart Strober and Gerald S. Strober, *The Nixon Presidency: An Oral History of the Era* (Washington, DC: Brassey's, 2003), 467.
15. Strober and Strober, 467–468.
16. Woodward and Bernstein, *Final Days*, 246; interview of St. Clair, November 21, 1974, box 7.21, HRC-W&B. St. Clair was never told he could not listen to the tapes, and it is highly unusual for a lawyer to refuse to examine crucial evidence about to be given to the opposition.
17. Buzhardt interview; St. Clair interview 1, 6 ("I was anxious to leave Friday, had to come and play in golf-tournament, member-guest tournament on the Cape ... won the lowest prize possible"). It is not clear what St. Clair needed to recuperate from. The Woodward-Bernstein interview notes indicate that St. Clair was very nervous, so they did not press him, evidently concerned that he would terminate the interview.
18. Buzhardt interview, 20; interview of Haig, November 6, 1997, 4, box 72.7, HRC-W&B. Woodward and Bernstein, *Final Days*, 308; White, *Breach of Faith*, 10.
19. A popular misconception was that expressed by Theodore White, who wrote that St. Clair was "overworked for months" and "exhausted." White, *Breach of Faith*, 10. Surprisingly, he also called St. Clair "hapless" and said St. Clair believed the eighteen-and-a-half-minute gap in the June 20, 1972, tape was accidental—at least until a group of experts concluded otherwise (293). White, whose book had no footnotes or endnotes, was not a reliable raconteur of the key events of Watergate. He devoted only one sentence to the events of March 1, 1974 (292).

20. Neftali called St. Clair "hapless" but provided few details: "The president's hapless personal lawyer, James St. Clair, remained blissfully ignorant of the content of the tapes and just asked to be able to give the House something, anything." Neftali, "Richard Nixon," 112. There was other criticism of St. Clair's legal performance, including his brief in the case heard by the Supreme Court on July 8, 1974. See, e.g., interview III of Jaworski, box 6.2, HRC-W&B. Yet Jaworski wrote: "I would wince when I read a description of James St. Clair, as I did in one widely read Washington column, as 'Nixon's inept lawyer.'" Leon Jaworski with Mickey Herskovitz, *Confession and Avoidance: A Memoir by Leon Jaworski* (New York: Anchor/Doubleday, 1979), 233. Jaworski condemned Nixon's practice of being his own lawyer. So did Haig. Haig interview, November 30, 2006, 68.
21. Interview of John J. Chester, July 30, 2006, 18, Nixon Presidential Library, https://www.nixonlibrary.gov/oral-histories.
22. Woodward and Bernstein, *Final Days*, 354. As noted, St. Clair was on vacation between July 26 and 30. He apparently did not discuss the content of the June 23 tapes with his deputy in July, and perhaps he never did so prior to Nixon's resignation.
23. Buzhardt interview, pt. II, 16; interview of McCahill, December 7, 1974, box 75.10, HRC-W&B.
24. Chester and McCahill, both deceased, were interviewed by the Nixon Presidential Library or by Woodward and Bernstein, and I have transcripts or notes of those interviews. Most of St. Clair's staff came from the Department of Justice. Interview of Geoff Shepard, 37-Shepard-oh-4, part 2-mp4, 14:50 min., Nixon Presidential Library. It is unclear whether any lawyers other than McCahill came from the firm Hale and Dorr; efforts to find out were unsuccessful. Communications with junior lawyers were consistent with the conclusion about the lack of discussion of Nixon's defense. Theodore J. Garrish, James Prochnow, and Loren A. Smith (now a senior judge on the Federal Court of Claims) were not involved in substantive discussions regarding Nixon's situation. Telephone interview of Garrish, October 2, 2024; telephone interviews of Prochnow; interview of Smith, January 22, 2025.
25. A short passage in the Woodward-Bernstein notes of their interview of Buzhardt suggests that there also might have been disorganization in Buzhardt's operation. About Hauser, their interview notes state: "Hauser resigned on Aug. 5 and Fred [Buzhardt] says that he didn't have time to try to talk him out of it. Fred [was] a little upset that Hauser would lose his cool and jump out. Hauser was having domestic problems and had to take care of his two children, girls. Once [he] had to give Hauser two weeks off to take care of them." Buzhardt interview, pt. II, 10, 12.
26. Haig, *Inner Circles*, 490.
27. Woodward and Bernstein, *Final Days*, 323. The entry for August 1: "They'd all be hung—St. Clair, Buzhardt and Haig—if they withheld the evidence any longer" (323).

28. Buzhardt's status was different from St. Clair's. He was a government employee assigned to the White House and was not in charge of the defense. Haig, who was not a lawyer, had spent almost all his adult life in the military.
29. Woodward and Bernstein, *Final Days*, 272–273.
30. Haig, *Inner Circles*, 476.
31. Haig, 490–491.
32. Haig, 491. Nixon gave a similar account. Richard M. Nixon, *RN: The Memoirs of Richard Nixon* (New York: Grosset, 1978), 1062–1063. In *With Nixon*, Price indicates he did not communicate directly with Nixon on this issue or in any significant way with Nixon's lawyers.
33. Richard Ben-Veniste and George Frampton Jr., *Stonewall: The Real Story of the Watergate Prosecution* (New York: Simon & Schuster, 1977), 293.
34. Haig wrote, "It was not my role to be his conscience and whisper to him in private he must resign." Haig, *Inner Circles*, 488–489. Compare this with: "'Mr. President,' I said, 'I just don't see how you can survive this one. We have to face the facts, and the facts are that this tape will deal a fatal blow to public opinion, to your supports on the Hill, and to the party. The Cabinet won't hold, the Republican Party won't hold, your own staff won't hold. Once this tape get out. It's over.'" Haig, 476–477.
35. Buzhardt interview, pts. I and II.
36. Woodward and Bernstein, *Final Days*, 332.
37. Nixon, *RN*, 1063.
38. Stephen E. Ambrose, *Nixon: Ruin and Recovery 1973–1990* (New York: Simon & Schuster, 1991), 414.
39. Woodward and Bernstein, *Final Days*, 336.
40. Ben-Veniste and Frampton, *Stonewall*, 292.
41. Haig, *Inner Circles*, 472–473.
42. Haig, 484.
43. Haig, 484. See also Woodward and Bernstein, *Final Days*, which makes no mention of meetings with Republican committee members.
44. Interview of John Wilson, February 13, 1975, conversation II, 4–5, box 8.11, HRC-W&B.
45. Referring to Nixon's statement in his memoirs that "I still believe it is a tragedy of circumstance that Bud Krogh and John Ehrlichman went to jail and Daniel Ellsberg went free," Ehrlichman wrote, "I find this passage notable, too, as the only known expression of regret by Richard Nixon on the subject of my going to jail. At no time before, during or since have I heard from him directly." John Ehrlichman, *Witness to Power: The Nixon Years* (New York: Simon & Schuster, 1982), 402 fn.
46. Haig, *Inner Circles*, 452. Other accounts say no more. Stans's book does not mention Haig, St. Clair, or Buzhardt.
47. Haig, 287–289. One possible exception is Charles Alan Wright.

48. Exploring why Haig acted as he did is beyond the scope of this book. One book that takes a conventional view of the June 23 tapes also suggests that Haig tried to undermine Nixon for his personal aggrandizement and self-protection in connection with a totally different matter, which is unlikely. Ray Locker, *Haig's Coup: How Nixon's Closest Aide Forced Him from Office* (Washington, DC: Potomac Books, 2019).
49. See, e.g., Nixon, *RN*, 1051–1087; Woodward and Bernstein, *Final Days*; Haig, *Inner Circles*, 466–505.
50. Although the trial was scheduled to begin on September 9, the WSPF needed a monthlong continuance to process the tapes and for the defense to examine them. It took only seven months—from March 1 to October 8—for the case to come to trial.

13. The Cover-up Trial

1. Alexander M. Haig Jr. with Charles McCarry, *Inner Circles: How America Changed the World* (New York: Warner Books, 1992), 509–516.
2. Haig, 511–515.
3. WSPF counsel Philip Lacovara resigned in protest over Ford's pardon of Nixon.
4. Some, such as Leon Jaworski, were against prosecuting Nixon and made their position known. Most of the assistant prosecutors favored prosecution. Interview of John Dean, July 30, 2007, 49, Nixon Presidential Library, https://www.nixonlibrary.gov/oral-histories. Ford's pardon of Nixon created problems for the prosecution of the former president's aides. A separate scandal threatened to erupt when Haig was accused of offering Ford the presidency in return for pardoning Nixon. That issue was quickly defused when both Ford and Haig denied the rumor. Haig, *Inner Circles*, 514–519; interview of Haig, November 6, 1997, 10, box 72.7, HRC-W&B.
5. Also indicted were Charles Colson and Gordon Strachan. The prosecution dismissed the charges against Strachan (represented by Jack Bray with the assistance of Strachan's wife, who was an accomplished appellate lawyer), and Colson pleaded guilty to a separate indictment that charged him with obstruction of justice in the Daniel Ellsberg case. The Senate Watergate Committee had given Strachan testimonial immunity, which would have made his prosecution difficult. If he were tried and convicted, Strachan could have argued, with a respectable chance of success, that his protected testimony was improperly used against him, if not directly then indirectly. See U.S. v. North, 910 F.2d 843 (D.C. Cir. 1990); Richard Ben-Veniste and George Frampton Jr., *Stonewall: The Real Story of the Watergate Prosecution* (New York: Simon & Schuster, 1977), 316.
6. The transcript is not available online. The case is *U.S. v. John Mitchell et al.*, Crim. No. 74-110, U.S. District Court for the District of Columbia.
7. See Ben-Veniste and Frampton, *Stonewall*, 256.

8. *U.S. v. Mitchell*, October 14, 1974, 2698–2699. The summations by the prosecutor and by Haldeman's lawyer took about the same amount of time. *U.S. v. Mitchell*, December 20, 1974, 11,735; December 23, 1974, 11,847.
9. *U.S. v. Mitchell*, October 16, 1974, 2727. Later, Dean testified that Walters said "this" was not a CIA operation. *U.S. v. Mitchell*, 2737.
10. *U.S. v. Mitchell*, October 23, 1974, 3395.
11. Author's conversations with Dean.
12. Department of Justice, Watergate Special Prosecution Force, memorandum for Richard Ben-Veniste by Peter F. Rient, "White House Interference with FBI Investigation," January 14, 1974, Watergate Collection, Record Groups 460.4–460.5, NARA.
13. *U.S. v. Mitchell*, November 9, 1974, 6204–6205.
14. U.S. v. Haldeman, 559 F.2d 31 (D.C. Cir. 1976). Without a doubt, Sirica's rulings generally favored the WSPF, but that does not necessarily mean they were wrong.
15. John J. Sirica, *To Set the Record Straight: The Break-in, the Tapes, the Conspirators, the Pardon* (New York: W. W. Norton, 1979), 246, 272. Sirica ruled that the transcripts were substantially accurate, and the jury was told to rely on the tapes. The jurors were not allowed to keep the transcripts.
16. Another Richard said, "And whatsoe'er you will employ me in . . . / I will perform it to enfranchise you. / Meanwhile this deep disgrace in brotherhood / Touches me deeper than you can imagine. . . . / Well, your imprisonment shall not be long / I will deliver you or else lie for you / Meanwhile, have patience." William Shakespeare, *Richard III*, act 1, scene 1.
17. Customarily, after the prosecution completes its presentation, the several defendants proceed in the order in which they are listed in the indictment.
18. It was entirely possible for Nixon's senior aides to be involved in a conspiracy to obstruct justice that Nixon had not yet joined. If Nixon was not part of the conspiracy on June 23, 1972, the recorded conversations, which were used effectively and extensively during the cover-up trial, would have been inadmissible as hearsay against Mitchell and Ehrlichman, who were not parties to the conversation. But with Nixon as a coconspirator, this was not inadmissible hearsay but a statement by a conspirator in furtherance of the conspiracy.
19. *U.S. v. Mitchell*, November 29, 1974, 8479.
20. *U.S. v. Mitchell*, November 29, 1974, 8480–8481.
21. *U.S. v. Mitchell*, November 29, 1974, 8818. Ben-Veniste's statement was incorrect in another respect. James McCord, one of the five people arrested on June 17, 1972, was CRP's security chief, so that was not the first time the CRP and the burglars were linked.
22. *U.S. v. Mitchell*, November 29, 1974, 8479–8480; see also 8806–8807, 8809–8817.
23. *U.S. v. Mitchell*, December 3, 1974, 8817–8818. Haldeman's statement that "Mr. Liddy . . . turned them over to Mr. Barker to have the checks cleared through his

bank account so the sources would not be uncovered" is incorrect. It was anticipated that receipt of the checks would never be disclosed; the cash derived from them was going to be placed in the FCRP safe. There would be no record of the contributions anywhere. Since the contributors could not deduct the contributions on their income tax returns, disclosure was unlikely.

24. *U.S. v. Mitchell*, December 3, 1974, 8817–8818. Gray testified that the Bay of Pigs did not come up in his conversation with Walters. *U.S. v. Mitchell*, November 11, 1974, 6238.
25. *U.S. v. Mitchell*, December 3, 1974, 8820. Haldeman was not thoroughly prepared to testify before the Senate Watergate Committee in part because the White House refused to let him see his records. That refusal is difficult to justify, at least in retrospect.
26. *U.S. v. Mitchell*, December 3, 1974, 8823.
27. *U.S. v. Mitchell*, December 3, 1974, 8849.
28. This was a major point for the prosecution.
29. *U.S. v. Mitchell*, December 3, 1974, 8856. Haldeman was admitting to a crime, which was relevant to his credibility. Moreover, he had testified on direct examination about the anonymous donors, so he "opened the door" to such questioning. In any event, there is no rule that cross-examination—as opposed to direct examination—must be confined to the allegations in the indictment.
30. *U.S. v. Mitchell*, December 3, 1974, 8857.
31. *U.S. v. Mitchell*, December 3, 1974, 8859–8860.
32. *U.S. v. Mitchell*, December 3, 1974, 8877. Because the Bay of Pigs was part of the same conversation, it was not an afterthought. But references to the Bay of Pigs by Nixon and Haldeman could reasonably be characterized as a smoke screen.
33. *U.S. v. Mitchell*, December 3, 1974, 8873. Here, the question was more important than the answer. Everyone expected Haldeman to answer in the negative.
34. *U.S. v. Mitchell*, December 3, 1974, 8877.
35. *U.S. v. Mitchell*, December 3, 1974, 8878–8879.
36. See Nixon's grand jury testimony, June 23, 1975, 123–126, 156–158, https://www.documentcloud.org/documents/265875-transcript-of-nixon-grand-jury.
37. Interview of Henry Ruth, November 12, 2011, session 4, 14 min., Nixon Presidential Library, https://www.nixonlibrary.gov/oral-histories.
38. Parkinson and his lawyer Jacob Stein placed their table as far as possible from the other defendants and did not speak to them or their counsel in the presence of the jury to emphasize how divorced Parkinson was from them.
39. Dean agrees. John Dean, *Blind Ambition: The White House Years* (New York: Simon & Schuster, 1976), 377–378.
40. *Washington Post*, November 30, 1974, A4.
41. *Washington Post*, December 4, 1974, A14.
42. *U.S. v. Mitchell*, 551 F.2d 1252 (D.C. Cir. 1976).

14. Thoughts on Prosecuting Nixon

1. This chapter makes extensive use of an unpublished memorandum by John W. Dean.
2. *Final Report of the Judiciary Committee of the House of Representatives*, 93d Cong., 2d sess., pursuant to H.Res. 803, October 1975, 488.
3. *Final Report of the Judiciary Committee*, 717.
4. See, e.g., U.S. v. Mohney, 949 F.2d 899, 904 (6th Cir. 1991). See generally Christian Davis and Eric Waters, "Federal Criminal Conspiracy," *American Criminal Law Review* (2007): 523–553; U.S. Department of Justice, Criminal Tax Manual, http://www.justice.gov/tax/readingroom/2001ctm/23ctax.htm.
5. U.S. v. Fasilimo, 586 F.2d 938, 942 (2d Cir. 1978).
6. Virtually any method can be employed to defraud—the relevant statute is read more broadly than common-law fraud—and the courts are not clear whether dishonesty must be involved. It should be noted that absent a conspiracy, there is no offense called "defrauding the government."
7. Osborn v. U.S., 385 U.S. 323 (1966).
8. U.S. v. Lazzerini, 611 F.2d 940 (1st Cir. 1979).
9. U.S. v. Shoup, 608 F.2d 950 (3d Cir. 1979).
10. Perhaps an argument could be made that an unauthorized FBI investigation does not constitute an FBI investigation under the statute.
11. U.S. v. Fayer, 573 F.2d 741 (2d Cir. 1978) ("conduct under U.S.C. § 1503 must relate to an investigation by the grand jury, not the F.B.I."); U.S. v. Scoratow, 137 F. Supp. 620 (W.D. Pa. 1956) ("The Federal Bureau of Investigation is an investigating rather than a judicial arm of the government. It does not 'administer justice' within the meaning of Section 1503."); U.S. v. Ryan, 455 F.2d 728 (9th Cir. 1971) (concerning the IRS). Since then, the law has been amended to include FBI investigations, among others.
12. U.S. v. Simmons, 591 F.2d 206 (3d Cir. 1979).
13. A district court judge wrote an opinion in 1977 that a court of appeals affirmed in 1978: "A person who knows that a Grand Jury is investigating certain possible violations of federal law, and who has reason to believe that a certain incriminating document is likely to come to the Grand Jury's attention, and who intentionally causes the destruction of that document in order to prevent it from falling into the hands of the Grand Jury, may, in my opinion, properly be convicted of obstruction of justice under 18 U.S.C. § 1503." U.S. v. Fineman, 434 F. Supp. 797 (E.D. Pa. 1977), *aff'd sub nom.*, U.S. v. Adams, 571 F.2d 572 (3d Cir. 1978). Twenty-five years earlier, the same U.S. Court of Appeals for the Third Circuit stated: "We can see no reason why persons who conspire together to obstruct justice in a proceeding before a United States Commissioner or in a district court which they expect or fear will be instituted should not incur the penalties prescribed by Section [1503] of the Criminal Code even if it be assumed that they could not be

guilty of the substantive crime [of obstructing justice]." U.S. v. Perlstein, 126 F.2d 789, 794 (3d Cir. 1942).
14. See, e.g., Pettibone v. U.S. 148 U.S. 197 (1893); U.S. v. Haas, 583 F.2d 216 (5th Cir. 1978); U.S. v. Neiswender, 590 F.2d 1269 (4th Cir. 1979).
15. The tapes from before June 23, 1972, contain only one mention of a grand jury proceeding. On June 21, 1972, Colson told the president: "I think when the grand jury convenes that there'll be stories about it."
16. No source is given for the statement about Mrs. McCord. The news summary for June 20 states: "U.S. Atty [Harold] Titus announced a Federal Grand Jury will be empaneled to take evidence."
17. Richard M. Nixon, *RN: The Memoirs of Richard Nixon* (New York: Grosset, 1978), 639; emphasis added.
18. Both Nixon and Haldeman ordinarily read the daily news summaries. They sometimes wrote comments or underlined passages, although they customarily used different types of pens. No marks of any kind appeared on this page of the news summary.
19. Former Assistant U.S. Attorney Earl Silbert's Watergate Case Diary Excerpts re Ogarrio and Dahlberg, Appendix H, Watergate Collection, NARA. Because any reference to grand jury subpoenas to banks in Miami and Mexico City would have been deleted, the material available at the National Archives is not protected by grand jury secrecy.
20. Cole v. U.S., 329 F.2d 437, 441–442 (9th Cir. 1964) ("We hold the constitutional privilege against self-incrimination is an integral part of the due administration of justice, and to which there is an absolute right in every witness. A witness violates no duty to claim it, but one who bribes, coerces, or forces or threatens a witness to claim it, or advises with corrupt motive the witness to take it, can and does himself obstruct or influence the due administration of justice."); U.S. v. Cioffi, 493 F.2d 1111, 1119 (2d Cir. 1974) (citing *Cole* with approval and upholding a charge to the jury that closely paralleled portions of the opinion in that case); U.S. v. Baker, 611 F.2d 964 (4th Cir. 1979) ("Even before subpoenas were served upon the two witnesses, [Baker] had repeatedly evidenced a desire that the two witnesses not cooperate with law officials for obvious reasons. The jury could readily infer that, when [they] were subpoenaed to appear before the grand jury, it was in his interest that they not testify, because if they testified truthfully, they were bound to incriminate him. Thus, the jury could find beyond a reasonable doubt that Baker's motive and intent in advising them to interpose their right not to incriminate themselves, and in supplying [one of the witnesses] with a powerful sedative which adversely affected her ability to testify, was to further his interest and conceal his crime not to protect them against self-incrimination; hence his endeavor to impede was corrupt and one proscribed by the statute.").

15. Fifty Years of Misunderstanding

1. I made no effort to analyze books on Watergate with respect to their treatment of the material prepared by the WSPF for the benefit of the House Impeachment Committee. Many books did not even mention that important development, which was instrumental in the impeachment investigation. Alexander M. Haig Jr. with Charles McCarry, *Inner Circles: How America Changed the World* (New York: Warner Books, 1992), 447–450; Stephen E. Ambrose, *Nixon, Ruin and Recovery, 1973–1990* (New York: Simon & Schuster, 1991), 305–306; Evan Thomas, *Being Nixon: A Man Divided* (New York: Random House, 2015), 480–481; Jonathan Aitken, *Nixon: A Life* (Washington, DC: Regency, 1993), 514–516; Melvin Small, *The Presidency of Richard Nixon* (Lawrence: University Press of Kansas, 1999), 291–292.
2. Bob Woodward and Carl Bernstein, *The Final Days* (New York: Simon & Schuster, 1976), 268. The book also reported that on August 5, 1974, "the President [was] saying the transcript didn't mean what it said." Woodward and Bernstein, 368. It is unclear what Nixon meant.
3. Woodward and Bernstein, 457.
4. Ben Bradlee, *A Good Life: Newspapering and Other Adventures* (New York: Simon & Schuster, 1995), 376–377.
5. Theodore H. White, *Breach of Faith: The Fall of Richard Nixon* (New York: Atheneum, 1975), 11. Although neither of John Dean's first two books, *Blind Ambition* (1976) and *Lost Honor* (1982), discussed the meaning of the "smoking gun" tape, his wife Maureen ("Mo" to her friends) wrote a book with Hays Gorey that states: "President Richard Nixon had been forced to release the tape of June 23, 1972, on which he and Bob Haldeman were agreeing to get the CIA to halt the FBI's investigation of the Watergate break-in and bugging." Maureen Dean with Hays Gorey, *"Mo": A Woman's View of Watergate* (New York: Simon & Schuster, 1976), 208.
6. Clark R. Mollenhoff, *Game Plan for Disaster* (New York: W. W. Norton, 1976), 353. There were six days of obstruction before June 23.
7. Samuel Dash, *Chief Counsel, Inside the Ervin Committee: The Untold Story of Watergate* (New York: Random House, 1976), 259–260.
8. Edward Mezvinsky with Kevin McCormally and John Greeenya, *A Term to Remember* (New York: Coward, McCann & Geoghegan, 1977), 227.
9. Lawrence Spinelli, *Watergate's Unexpected Hero: The Life of Peter W. Rodino, Jr.* (Herndon, VA: Amplify Publishing, 2024), 204.
10. Richard Ben-Veniste and George Frampton Jr., *Stonewall: The Real Story of the Watergate Prosecution* (New York: Simon & Schuster, 1977), 291.
11. Leon Jaworski, *The Right and the Power: The Prosecution of Watergate* (1976; reprint, New York: Reader's Digest Press, 1986), 206–207.
12. John J. Sirica, *To Set the Record Straight: The Break-in, the Tapes, the Conspirators, the Pardon* (New York: W. W. Norton, 1979), 229–230.

13. Richard Nixon, *RN: The Memoirs of Richard Nixon* (New York: Grosset, 1978), 640.
14. H. R. Haldeman with Joseph DiMona, *The Ends of Power* (New York: Times Books, 1978), 133, 218. That formulation suggests they were trying to conceal the criminal activities of the Plumbers, which had a factual basis. Haldeman later sought to distance himself from a number of assertions in the book. John Dean spoke to coauthor DiMona, who told him that Haldeman approved of every word in the book. Even more cryptic than Haldeman was Leonard Garment: "When the June 23 tape emerged, I thought it was not so different from, or more harmful than, other evidence we had seen." Leonard Garment, *Crazy Rhythm: My Journey from Brooklyn, Jazz, and Wall Street to Nixon's White House and Beyond* (New York: Times Books, 1997), 294–295.
15. See, e.g., Haig, *Inner Circles*, 456 (Nixon was "author of Watergate cover-up"). As discussed, Haig was essentially ignorant of the details of Watergate, including some important ones.
16. Haig, 475–476.
17. Thomas Powers, *The Man Who Kept the Secrets: Richard Helms and the CIA* (New York: Alfred A. Knopf, 1979), 248.
18. J. Lee Annis Jr., *Howard Baker: Conciliator in an Age of Crisis* (New York: Madison Books, 1995), 81.
19. Tom Brokaw, *The Fall of Richard Nixon: A Reporter Remembers Watergate* (New York: Random House, 2019), 103.
20. Stanley I. Kutler, *The Wars of Watergate: The Last Crisis of Richard Nixon* (New York: Alfred A. Knopf, 1990), 535. It was a rare miss by Kutler. Historian Timothy Neftali referred to the tape "in which Nixon ordered the CIA to obstruct the FBI Watergate investigation." Timothy Neftali, "Richard Nixon," in *Impeachment: An American History*, ed. Jon Meacham et al. (New York: Random House, 2018), 150. As noted elsewhere, the identity of the person who gave the money to the FCRP was not relevant to the Watergate break-in, although it certainly could have been related to a campaign finance violation. Obviously, the fact that money given to the burglars had been donated to the Nixon reelection campaign was politically embarrassing.
21. Ambrose, *Nixon, Ruin and Recovery*, 404, 413.
22. Maurice H. Stans, *The Terrors of Justice: The Untold Side of Watergate* (New York: Everest House, 1978), 152–154, 202–206.
23. Stanley I. Kutler, *Abuse of Power: The New Nixon Tapes* (New York: Free Press, 1997).
24. John W. Dean, *The Nixon Defense: What He Knew and When He Knew It* (New York: Penguin, 2014), 53–63.
25. In two books, Shepard accepts Dean's argument about the meaning of the June 23, 1972, conversations and discusses the conduct of John Sirica, Leon Jaworski, and John Doar, including engaging in *ex parte* communications, arranging for Sirica

to preside at the cover-up trial, arranging for the transfer of secret grand jury minutes from the WSPF to the House Impeachment Committee (under penalty of federal criminal prosecution), and the WSPF's preparation of a meticulous guide for Congress to follow in the effort to impeach Nixon. See Geoff Shepard, *The Real Watergate Scandal: Collusion, Conspiracy, and the Plot that Brought Nixon Down* (Washington, DC: Regency History, 2015, 2019); Geoff Shepard, *The Nixon Conspiracy: Watergate and the Plot to Remove the President* (New York: Post Hill Press, 2021), 231, 234. As noted earlier, I do not accept a number of Shepard's conclusions. Roger Stone, a conservative politician who later became associated with Donald Trump, endorsed Dean's 2014 interpretation of the conversations of June 23, 1972, in an otherwise seriously flawed book. Roger Stone, *Nixon's Secrets: The Rise, Fall, and Untold Truth about the President, Watergate, and the Pardon* (New York: Skyhorse Publishing, 2014).

26. Several books focus on bogus conspiracy theories, such as that the FBI was responsible for the Watergate break-in or that John Dean highjacked the Watergate burglars for his personal benefit. The supposed reason for the latter was that Dean's fiancée at the time (later his wife) was allegedly part of a prostitution ring being run out of the Democratic National Committee and that Dean wanted to ascertain her role. These false allegations provoked lawsuits by Dean and his wife and by a DNC secretary that G. Gordon Liddy claimed was running the prostitution ring. By and large, I have not referenced these books, which are not based on fact.

27. Jill Wine-Banks, *The Watergate Girl: My Fight for Truth and Justice against a Criminal President* (New York: Henry Holt, 2020), 177–178.

28. Garrett M. Graff, *Watergate: A New History* (New York: Avid Reader Press, 2022), 209, 633.

29. Graff, 586–587, 748.

Conclusion

1. L. Patrick Gray III with Ed Gray, *In Nixon's Web: A Year in the Cross Hairs of Watergate* (New York: Times Books, 2008), 124.

Acknowledgments

1. In the interest of full disclosure, I represented John and Maureen Dean in a defamation suit against St. Martin's Press, G. Gordon Liddy, author Len Colodny, and others. That case was settled. I also represented a secretary who worked at the DNC in 1972 in a defamation suit against Liddy. The first trial in that case ended in a deadlocked jury and a mistrial. At the second trial, the defendant prevailed on the grounds that the libel did not refer to the plaintiff. I believe that Judge Frederick Motz prematurely accepted the first jury's statement that it was deadlocked—a result that satisfied both defendant Liddy and plaintiff Wells. If the jury had been ordered to deliberate further, the likely result would have been

a compromise verdict in which the jury found that although Liddy's defamatory remarks about Wells were false, she failed to prove that Liddy was at fault. That result would have satisfied neither party. Liddy did not want his defamatory statements about Wells to be labeled false, in large part because he was making similar allegations against John Dean, who had turned against President Nixon. Wells did not want that result because it would have meant losing her suit for damages against Liddy.

INDEX

Adler, Renata, 231n1
Agnew, Spiro, 76, 235n4
Allen, Robert, 21, 31, 160, 172, 187
All the President's Men, 29
Ambrose, Stephen E., 111, 187
American Bar Association, 77
American Civil Liberties Union (ACLU), 120
Andreas, Dwayne, 20, 31, 160, 172, 187
anonymous campaign contributions, 12–13, 24–25, 141–142
April 7, 1972, 12–13
April 30, 1973, 3, 58
archives. *See* National Archives
August 5, 1974, 1, 29, 133–138
August 9, 1974, 1, 141–142

Baker, Howard H., Jr., 53, 70, 72, 186, 186–187
Baldwin, Alfred, 15–17, 99, 172
Barker, Bernard, 15, 20–21, 31–32, 42, 52, 161–163, 177, 179, 251n23
Bay of Pigs
    invasion, 19, 26, 228n10
    relation to Watergate, 34–40, 162–165
Ben-Veniste, Richard, 79, 86–87, 88
Berlin Wall, 68, 98, 166
Bernstein, Carl, 2, 23, 52, 66, 76, 82, 92, 105, 106, 109, 116, 118, 128–133, 138, 140, 152, 183–184, 197
Beverly Hills Hotel, 18
Bittman, William O., 48, 87
Boggs, Hale, 177
Bork, Robert H., 77, 236
Boston, 83, 124, 149
Bradlee, Ben, 184
Brady v. Maryland, 121
break-in. *See* Watergate break-in
break-in trial. See *U.S. v. Liddy*
Breslin, Jimmy, 78
Brokaw, Tom, 187
Brookings Institution, 9
Buchanan, Patrick J., 66, 135, 144, 242n1

Bull, Stephen, 65, 78
Burch, Dean, 133, 141
Burning Tree Country Club, 18
Butler, Caldwell, 114, 126
Butterfield, Alexander, 64–66, 78, 177
Buzhardt, J. Fred, 75–76
    accepting service of subpoena, 67–68
    appointment, 3, 59, 143
    August 5, 1974, 135–138
    background, 59
    Camp David, 133
    Cox and, 76
    destruction of tapes, 66
    Haig and, 59, 128–129, 133
    heart attack, 14, 128
    July 24, 1974, 128–129
    June 23, 1972, 147
    Nixon and, 59, 116, 146, 150–151
    Nixon resignation, 132
    pessimism, 130, 131, 140
    press contacts, 137–138
    release of tapes, 137–142
    release of tapes (April 1974), 116
    release of transcripts, 118
    responsibilities for tapes, 59, 74, 115, 147
    staff, 2, 24
    St. Clair and, 107
    Stennis and, 78
    transcribing tapes, 59, 74, 115, 116, 124, 133–135, 147
    Woodward and Bernstein and, 76
    work habits, 74

campaign finance laws, 12–13
Camp David, 48, 64, 135, 144, 149
Cape Cod, 147
Castro, Fidel, 14–15, 19, 158, 178
Caulfield, John J. (Jack), 48
CCRP (Finance Committee to Re-elect the President), 13, 21 29–31, 40. *See also* Sloan, Hugh W., Jr.; Stans, Maurice H.

[259]

Celler, Emanuel, 78
Chapin, Dwight, 47, 143, 226n12
Chester, John J., 148–149
Chicago Tribune, 246n47
CIA (Central Intelligence Agency)
  Dean and, 44
  Ehrlichman and, 37–39
  Haldeman and, 37–39
  involvement in Watergate break-in, 15, 19, 26, 31, 38, 41
  June 23, 1972, 1, 37–39
  Mexican operation, 26, 38, 41, 69, 72, 158, 181
  Nixon and, 26, 31–41
  Senate Watergate Committee minority and, 72–73
  White House requests for money, 44
  works with administration, 45–46
  See also Helms, Richard; Hunt, E. Howard; Mexico; Walters, Vernon
clemency, 47–48, 63
Cohen, William (Bill), 126, 153
Colson, Charles W., 83
  break-in, 22
  Brookings Institution, 15
  Dean and, 21
  FBI, 21, 127
  Gemstone, 12
  guilty plea, 122, 241n45
  Hunt and, 14
  indictment, 98, 250n5
  Nixon and, 22, 39, 143
  resignation, 122, 143
  St. Clair and, 83
  taping system, 65
Connally, John, 4
cover story, 40, 46, 60, 167
cover-up trial. See *U.S. v. Mitchell*
Cox, Archibald
  appointment as Watergate Prosecutor, 59
  approach, 74
  background, 59–60
  rejection of compromise, 75–77
  Saturday Night Massacre, 3, 76–77
  staff, 60

  subpoenas, 67–68
  See also Saturday Night Massacre
Cox, Edward, 140
Crewdson, John M., 29
CRP (Committee to Re-elect the President)
  dirty tricks, 47
  Segretti, 10, 54, 86
  See also Magruder, Jeb Stuart; McCord, James; Mitchell, John N.
Cuba, 15, 30
Cuban burglars
  arrest, 14–15
  background, 14
  burglary of Dr. Fielding, 10, 29
  commitments to, 19
  guilty pleas, 48
  hush money, 19
  indictment, 46–47
  U.S. v. Liddy, 46, 51–52
  See also Barker, Bernard; Hunt, E. Howards; hush money

Dahlberg, Kenneth H., 20, 31–33, 43, 45, 145, 158–162, 168, 178–179
Dash, Samuel, 10, 56, 62, 72, 184
Dean, John W.
  anonymous contributions, 12–13
  appointment as White House Counsel, 9, 62
  books, 188
  Brookings Institution, 9
  "cancer on the presidency," 74
  Colson and, 21
  cooperation with authorities, 56–57
  Dash and, 56
  Dr. Fielding and, 19
  Ehrlichman and, 9, 18, 21, 44
  entry into cover-up, 18–19
  firing of, 3, 58, 143
  Glanzer and, 56
  Gray and, 21, 46, 54–55, 228n8
  Haldeman and, 9, 12, 27–29, 47, 68, 85
  House Impeachment Committee, 125
  Hunt safe, 21
  Huston and, 57

immunity, 56–57, 76
June 23, 1972, 27–29
Liddy and, 11–12, 19
Magruder and, 11, 19, 62
meetings with Mitchell and Liddy, 11, 62
Mitchell and, 11, 26
Nixon and, 47, 62–63, 159
Nixon Defense, The, 15, 188
Petersen and, 20
Reisner and, 46
safe deposit box, 57
selection as White House Counsel, 9, 62
Senate Judiciary Committee, 54–55
Senate Watergate Committee, 62–63
September 15, 1972, 47
Shaffer and, 56
Sloan and, 19
Silbert and, 56
Sirica and, 57–58
Smoking Gun tape interpretation, 2, 187–188
Strachan and, 19
transcription of White House tapes, 23
U.S. v. Mitchell, 157–160
Walters and, 94
Deep Throat, 29
Democratic National Committee (DNC), 11, 13–15
demonstrations, 9
Dent, Harry, 241n45
Department of Justice, 11, 54
destruction of CRP records, 15–19, 47, 54
Diem, Ngo Dinh, 21
dirty tricks, 10, 47, 54
District of Columbia Metropolitan Police, 25
Doar, John, 2
  appointment, 21, 79
  articles of impeachment, 125–127, 130–131, 244n16
  background, 84, 232n17
  positions, 2, 79
  presentation at hearings, 95, 121–122
  receipt of grand jury material, 94–95
  Ruth and, 85, 94–95, 123
  slow pace of, 113–115
  staff, 84
  See also House Impeachment Committee
Donaldson, Sam, 95
Dorsen, David M., 57, 58, 156
Doyle, James, 240n7
Drew, Elizabeth, 99

Ehrlichman, John D.
  anonymous contributions, 42, 142
  Brookings Institution, 8
  CIA, 32, 37–39, 68, 71–73
  conviction, 2, 166
  Dean and, 9, 18, 21–22, 62
  Dr. Lewis Fielding and, 30, 68, 93
  Ellsberg and, 68
  Gray and, 21, 53–54, 193
  Haldeman and, 24, 32, 37–39
  Helms and, 37–39
  Hunt safe, 21
  hush money, 41, 70, 91
  indictment, 98
  June 17, 1972, 18
  June 23, 1972, 37–42, 71–73
  knowledge of taping system, 65
  Nixon and, 22, 24, 49, 69, 249n45
  positions held, 2
  resignation, 3, 58, 145
  Senate Watergate Committee testimony, 68–69
  U.S. v. Mitchell, 157, 166, 183
  Walters and, 37–39
  Watergate scandal and, 62, 196
eighteen-and-a-half-minute gap, 3
Ellsberg, Daniel
  Dr. Lewis Fielding, 30
  Pentagon Papers, 10
  U.S. v. Ellsberg, 58
Emery, Fred, 110–111
Ends of Power, The, 186
Enemies List, 4
Ervin, Sam, 53, 56, 61, 70–71
executive privilege, 79. *See also U.S. v. Nixon* (1974)
expletive deleted, 115, 117, 125

Falk, Carl H., 138
FBI (Federal Bureau of Investigation)
  break-in investigation, 1, 15–17
  CIA, 15, 26, 31–32, 35–43
  CIA approach, 43–45
  Colson and, 21, 33
  Dean and, 21, 46, 158–150
  Dr. Fielding and, 30
  Ellsberg and, 10, 68
  Gray nomination, 53–55, 193
  leaks by, 28, 32
  Mexico, 10, 26, 31, 38
  McCord and, 15–17
  scope of investigation, 15–17, 28–32, 37–42, 45, 137, 142. 158–159, 164–165, 192–194
  tracing money, 29, 30, 160–161
  views of, 14, 26, 28, 34
  White House, 37, 41
  See also Felt, Mark; Gray, L. Patrick, III; Hoover, J. Edgar
Felt, Mark, 29, 31, 41, 53, 64, 228n4
Fielding, Fred, 11
Fielding, Dr. Lewis, 10, 11, 19, 23–26, 42, 58, 68, 79, 93, 171, 177–178, 189, 191, 193
Fifth Amendment, 110, 117, 189
Final Days, The, 105–106, 183–184
Fish, Hamilton, 126
Ford, Gerald R., Jr.
  Haig and, 133–134, 250n4
  Nixon and, 177
  pardon of Nixon, 121, 156, 157, 171, 163
  pardon of conscientious objectors, 156
  president, 141, 158
  removes self from impeachment inquiry, 134
Frampton, George, Jr., 86–90, 94, 114, 123, 185
fundraising (see also hush money), 12–13

Garment, Leonard, 58–59, 64–66, 74, 77, 130, 143, 144, 243n12, 245n42
Garrish, Theodore J., 248n24
Gemstone, 11–12, 18, 33
Gesell, Gerhardt, 79

Glanzer, Seymour, 56
Goldwater, Barry, 132, 141
Graff, Garrett M., 188–189
grand jury (*U.S. v. Liddy*), 47, 66
grand jury (*U.S. v. Mitchell*)
  independence, 93–94
  Jaworski and, 89–90
  Lacovara and, 87
  Nixon and, 53, 122
  presentment, 100–101
  road map, 88, 107–108
  Sirica and, 89–90
Gray, L. Patrick, III
  appointment, 29
  book, 16, 45
  CIA, 142
  confirmation hearings, 53–55
  control of FBI, 28–31
  Dahlberg and, 45
  Dean and, 21–22, 45–46, 54–55
  destruction of records, 54
  Ehrlichman and, 21–22, 53–54
  Haldeman and, 38–39
  Hunt records, 21, 54
  Nixon and, 45, 53–54
  nomination, 53, 228n8
  Ogarrio and, 45
  resignation, 55
  Senate Judiciary Committee, 54–55
  Watergate investigation, 16
Griffin, Robert P., 132
Gurney, Joseph, 227n4

Haig, Alexander M., Jr.
  access to tapes, 96–97
  appointment as chief of staff, 3, 58–59, 144
  August 5, 1974, 135–136
  background, 58
  Buzhardt and, 133
  Camp David, 135
  destruction of tapes, 66
  errors, 23, 59, 110, 148, 151
  Ford and, 133–134, 156, 250n4
  Goldwater and, 141
  Haldeman and, 152

Inner Circles, 63, 65, 109, 145, 146–147, 189
Jaworski and, 107
July 24, 1974, 128–130
June 23, 1972, transcript, 107, 133–135
knowledge of taping system, 59, 83
listening to tapes, 133, 195, 243n13
Nixon and, 129, 133, 144, 150
Nixon resignation, 142–144, 249n34
Nixon statement, 135, 149–150
pessimism, 107, 126, 129, 130, 133, 134, 135, 140, 144, 145
prior knowledge of Watergate, 59, 83 145, 146
responsibilities, 83, 107, 129
Richardson and, 76
resignation, 134
road map, 105–106
St. Clair and, 107, 129
Saturday Night Massacre, 75
self-interest, 149, 149–151
Smoking Gun tape, 129–130, 133–137
tapes, 64, 66, 77, 116
taping system knowledge, 65
transfer of road map, 105–106, 109
transcripts of tapes, 116, 117, 133–135
Wiggins and, 134
Haldeman, H. R. (Bob)
  anonymous contributors, 30, 31, 42, 160–163
  Bay of Pigs, 38–40, 163–165
  book, 53, 186
  campaign finance law, 13
  CIA, 37–38, 43, 60
  conviction, 166
  cover-up, scope, 18, 70–71
  Dean and, 27–29, 68
  Dr. Fielding break-in, 68
  FBI investigation, risk of, 43–44
  Gemstone, 11, 12, 18, 33, 64
  Gray and, 53
  Haig and, 144, 152
  Helms and, 37–41
  Higby and, 64, 70
  hush money, 70
  indictment, 48

  installation of taping system, 64–65
  June 23, 1972, 27–43, 69–70, 152–153, 160–165
  Kalmbach and, 44, 70
  Liddy and, 68
  March 21, 1973, 70, 117–118
  Nixon and, 21, 24, 38–41, 103
  perjury, 70, 117
  Plumbers, 11
  resignation, 58, 143
  road map, 91, 100, 104–110
  Senate Watergate Committee, 68–72, 252n25
  Sept. 15, 1972, 46–47
  slush fund, 47
  taping system, 64–66
  tapes listened to, 70
  U.S. v. Mitchell, 160–166
  verdict, 166
  Walters and, 37–41
  See also *U.S. v. Mitchell*
Hamilton, James, 57
Harlow, Bryce, 227n13, 240n20
Harry Ransom Collection, 2, 199
Hart, George L., Jr., 181
Harvard Law School, 59–60
Hauser, Richard, 125, 148
Hays, Wayne B., 113
Helms, Richard, 26–28, 32, 35, 36–40, 44–45, 71–73, 137, 159, 164–165, 186–187
Herbers, John, 138
Higby, Lawrence, 9, 53–54, 69
Hogan, Lawrence, 126
Holtzman, Elizabeth, 78
Hoover, J. Edgar, 10, 21, 29, 41, 64, 229n26
House Impeachment Committee
  access to tapes, 94, 106
  advisors, 84
  articles of impeachment, 125, 130–131
  creation, 77–78
  Dean and, 84
  debate, 130
  final report, 140
  Jenner and, 78–80, 84, 96
  Judiciary Committee, 77

[264] INDEX

House Impeachment Committee (cont.)
   June 23, 1974, tape, 139–140
   hearings, 121, 125–126, 130–131
   legal issues, 115
   members, 94–96
   public hearings, 130–131
   receipt of road map, 100–110
   Ruth and, 85, 94, 123
   schedule, 85
   slow pace of, 113–115, 244n15
   staffing, 79, 84, 239n39
   timetable, 85
   transcripts of White House tapes, 124
   votes, 114, 126, 130–131, 139–130
   White House, 152
   witnesses, 125
   WSPF, 94–96
   See also Doar, John; Rodino, Peter W., Jr.
House of Representatives, 77, 88, 104, 131, 140
Howard Johnson Motel, 15–16
Hunt, Dorothy, 48
Hunt, E. Howard
   arrest of, 38, 45
   Bay of Pigs, 19, 35, 164
   burglary of Dr. Lewis Fielding, 30, 58
   CIA, 15, 16, 33. 37, 40, 45
   clemency, 47–48, 63
   Colson and, 12, 14
   Cuban connection, 10, 14, 19
   FBI, 16–17
   guilty plea, 48, 51
   hush money, 19, 46, 48, 55, 118, 181, 193
   indictment, 3, 46–47
   ITT, 37
   June 23, 1972, 30–40
   Nixon and, 32, 36
   office, 21, 54–55
   Plumbers, 10, 30
   Senate Watergate Committee, 69, 235n44
   sentence, 52
   Watergate burglary, 12, 16
   White House payroll, 21, 164–165
Hutchinson, Edward, 95, 111, 151
Humphrey, Hubert and, 13, 20, 162
hush money, 3, 91, 98, 125, 160, 168, 181, 193
Hutchinson, Edward, 95, 111, 116, 151

impeachment petitions, 77
indictments. *See individual names*
Inouye, Daniel, 227n4
IRS (Internal Revenue Service), 113
ITT (International Telephone and Telegraph Company), 19, 37

Jackson, Robert L., 139
January 1, 1975, 2, 66
Jaworski, Leon
   appointment as Watergate Special Prosecutor, 3, 77
   book, 165
   background, 77
   Buzhardt and, 107
   ex parte meetings, 79–80, 87–92, 157, 193
   files, 91
   grand jury, 93–94, 105
   Haig and, 107, 122, 144, 185
   House Impeachment Committee, 123
   memorandum of meeting with Sirica, 79–80
   public statements, 95
   relationship with staff, 77, 87
   resignation, 91
   retention of records, 91
   return of indictments, 88–90, 92–93
   Sirica and, 79–82, 87–90, 92, 98
   staff, 77, 87
   White House and, 237n7
   Woodward and Bernstein, 92
Jenner, Albert, Jr., 79–80, 84, 96, 232n17
Johnson, Lyndon B., 54
Jordan, Barbara, 131
July 24, 1974, 128–129
June 17, 1972. *See* Watergate break-in
June 23, 1972, conversations, 1, 29–41
   Allen, 31
   Andreas, 31
   Bay of Pigs, 34, 35, 36, 38, 40
   CIA, 30–41
   CIA operations, 37, 39
   Colson, 33
   CRP, 37
   Cubans, 30, 32, 39
   Dahlberg, 31, 32, 33
   Dean, 30, 32, 35, 39

INDEX [265]

Ehrlichman, 30, 32, 39, 40
FBI, 29–41
FCRP, 31
Felt, 31
Fielding, Dr., 30
Gemstone, 33
Gray, 30, 31, 32, 38, 39, 40
Haldeman, 29–35, 69
Helms, 32, 35, 37, 38, 39
Hunt, 30, 32, 35–41
Kennedy, John F., 35
Liddy, 33, 38
Mexican bank, 30, 31
Mexico, 38
Miami bank, 30, 40
Mitchell, 30, 32, 33
Nixon, 30–41
perjury, 32
Petersen, 32
Plumbers, 30
Presidential News Summaries, 34
Walters, 31, 32, 35, 37, 38, 39
Walters memoranda, 38
Watergate break-in, 27
Justice Department. *See* Department of Justice

Kalb, Barry, 130
Kalmbach, Herbert, 20, 44–45, 47, 70, 84, 91, 122, 143
Kennedy, Edward, 54
Kennedy, John F., 21, 35
Key Biscayne, Florida, 12, 62, 122
Kissinger, Henry A., 58, 133–134, 144, 187
Kleindienst, Richard G., 18, 20, 58, 181, 247n13
Kreindler, Peter, 86, 88
Krogh, Egil (Bud), Jr., 10, 11, 84
Kutler, Stanley I., 111, 187–188, 239n46, 256n20

Lacovara, Philip A.
  MacKinnon and, 121
  memoranda, 87–88
  position, 57, 87, 95
  resignation, 121
  Sirica and, 79–80, 87–88

Lano, Angelo J., 41
LaRue, Frederick C., 12, 18, 63, 181
Latta, Delbert L., 172
leaks, 9, 10, 29, 54, 61, 114, 116, 122
Library of Congress, 92
Lichtenstein, James, 133
Liddy, G. Gordon
  arrest of, 38, 45
  cover story, 51
  Dean and, 11–12, 19
  destruction of records, 18
  Dr. Fielding and, 10–11, 19, 58
  failures of, 55
  Gemstone, 10–12, 19, 62–63
  Hunt and, 12, 45
  Kleindienst and, 18
  Magruder and, 11–12, 62–63
  McCord and, 55
  Mitchell and, 11, 62–63
  money received, 20–21
  Nixon and, 33
  Plumbers, 10
  positions, 11
  silence, 41, 51, 55–56
  Sloan and, 20–21, 41, 46, 52
  Stans and, 161
  U.S. v. Liddy, 51–52
  verdict, 52
Los Angeles Times, 15, 122, 139

MacKinnon, George E., 103–104, 120–121, 168, 194
Magruder, Jeb Stuart
  Book, 78
  Dean and, 11–12, 20
  destruction of records, 10
  FBI, 46
  Haldeman and, 18, 22
  Liddy and, 11–12, 18
  McCord and, 16–17
  Mitchell and, 11–12, 19, 46
  perjury, 45–46
  Porter and, 46, 66, 84
  resignation, 143
  Senate Watergate Committee, 62
  Sloan and, 46
  Slush fund, 47

Magruder, Jeb Stuart (*cont.*)
  U.S. v. Liddy, 50, 52
  Watergate break-in, 19, 192
Mandamus, 101–102, 120
March 1, 1974, 98–101
March 18, 1974, 100
March 21, 1973, 98, 117, 124
Mardian, Robert, 18, 157, 166, 167
Marshall, Burke, 84
McCahill, John (Jack), 148
McCarthy, Joseph, 83
McCord, James
  arrest, 14, 16, 18, 19
  background, 14
  book, 15–17, 225n7
  Caulfield and, 48
  clemency, 47–48
  CIA, 14, 15, 17, 55
  cover-up, 192
  CRP, 14
  Dean and, 48
  destruction of records, 15–18, 192
  FBI investigation, 15–17
  going public, 18, 19, 41
  indictment, 46–47
  letter to Sirica, 55–56
  Mitchell and, 48
  Piece of Tape, A, 226n7
  Sirica and, 55–56
  verdict, 52
  U.S. v. Liddy, 46, 47, 51–52
McGovern, George, 13, 15, 47, 178
Mexican bank, 30–31
Mexico, 15, 25, 38, 41, 72, 142, 158, 162, 173, 185
Mexico City, 21
Mezvinsky, Edward, 99
Middle East, 76, 124
Milk Fund, 4
Mitchell, John N.
  anonymous contributions, 12–13, 24–25, 142
  approval of Watergate break-in, 11–12, 16–18. 63
  Attorney General, 2, 11
  CIA, 26, 28, 30–31, 184
  conviction, 166
  Dean and, 26, 58, 172
  FBI, 32
  Fundraising, 12–13
  Gemstone, 12
  hush money, 44
  indictment, 98
  Kalmbach and, 44–45
  Liddy and, 11–12, 15, 18–20, 46, 52, 65
  Magruder and, 11, 18
  Nixon and, 18, 25–26, 45, 66
  resignation, 45, 143
  sacrificial lamb, 160
  Senate Watergate Committee testimony, 63–64, 166
  slush fund, 47
  U.S. v. Mitchell, 158–160, 165–166
  Vesco, 115
Mitchell, Martha, 54, 89
Mollenhoff, Clark R., 184
Montoya, Joseph, 227n4
Muskie, Edmund, 10, 13

National Archives, 2, 4, 91, 179
NATO, 156
NBC, 30
Neal, James F., 86, 157
New York Times, 13, 138, 161
Ngo Dinh Diem, 211
Nixon, Julie, 135, 141
Nixon, Pat, 48, 135
Nixon, Richard M.
  Agnew and, 73
  anonymous contributions, 25, 30, 31, 142, 194
  April 30, 1973, 58
  August 5, 1974, 135–136
  August 9, 1974, 141–142
  Bay of Pigs, 26, 34–35
  book, 185–186
  Bork and, 66
  Buchanan and, 66, 135, 144
  Butterfield and, 64–65
  Buzhardt and, 129, 146
  campaign financing, 12–13, 24–25, 27–30
  Camp David (1974), 135

categorical responses, 60
CIA, 26, 28, 29, 32–40
clemency, 47, 48, 63
Colson and, 22. 39, 122
Cox and, 59–60, 76
Dean and, 47, 62–63
defenses, 2, 173–183
departure, 142
destruction of tapes, 242n1
editing transcripts, 115–117
Ehrlichman and, 21, 43–44, 249n45
eighteen-and-a-half-minute gap, 78–79
Ellsberg and, 191
erasing tape, 78, 79
executive privilege, 70
expletive deleted, 115, 117, 125
Fielding, Dr. Lewis break-in and, 23, 24, 25, 191
firing staff, 43
Ford and, 134
Garment and, 58–59
grand jury, 87, 88
Gray and, 45, 53–54
Griffin and, 132
Haig and, 58, 106, 123, 129, 123, 130–131, 140, 144, 150
Haldeman and, 23, 24, 28–41
House Impeachment Committee, 85–86, 130–131, 140
Hunt and, 31, 32, 33, 36, 41
hush money, 62–63, 70
illnesses, 66, 166
impeachment vote, 130–131
installation of taping system, 64
IRS, 113
June 23, 1972, conversations, 29–41, 42, 119
July 24, 1974, 128–130
Kennedy (John F.) and, 35
Kissinger and, 133
knowledge of break-in, 23, 24, 29
legal representation, 144–151, 153, 154–155
listening to June 23, 1972, tapes, 119
Liddy and, 33
March 21, 1973, 57

Memoirs. See *RN*
mental state, 132, 140
Middle East, 76
Mitchell and, 25, 26, 33
national security, 42
Quaker religion, 117
pardon, 156, 171
phlebitis, 166
press conferences, 25, 115
prosecution of, 171–182, 250n4
release of tapes, 115–117, 135
resignation, 1, 3, 134, 141–142
restrictions on aides, 96–97
Rhodes and, 141
Richardson and, 58, 59, 76
RN, 53, 65, 66, 104–105
road map, 108–109
Ruckelshaus and, 76
Saturday Night Massacre, 76–78
Senate Watergate Committee, 57
September 15, 1972, 46–47
Soviet Union, 76, 123
statement, August 5, 1972, 135–137, 149–150
State of the Union address (1974), 85
St. Clair and, 83, 106–107, 109, 129, 135
"stonewall," 84, 117
support in Congress, 132
U.S. v. Liddy, 93–94
U.S. v. Mitchell, 166
Woods and, 78
Zeigler and, 22, 25, 135
Nixon, Trish, 135
Nixon Defense, The, 168
Nussbaum, Bernard, 84

O'Brien, Lawrence F., 13, 15, 19
O'Brien, Paul, 99, 166
Obstruction of justice, 144, 173–182, 253n13
Odle, Robert C., 18
Ogarrio, Manuel, 21, 43, 45, 145, 158–159, 167, 178–179
Old Executive Office Building, 10, 21, 22, 37, 64, 125
one-hundred-dollar bills, 15, 20–21

Oval Office, 22, 25, 27, 28, 37, 46, 58, 64, 70, 141, 177

pardons, 141, 156–157
Parkinson, Kenneth W., 98, 166
Petersen, Henry E., 20, 28, 32, 41, 62
Philadelphia Enquirer, 246n47
Plumbers, 10–12, 19, 23, 30, 42, 68, 73, 136, 175
Political intelligence, 11
Polk, James R., 139
Porter, Herbert L. (Bart), 46, 66, 84
Presidential News Summaries, 34, 171–172, 254n18
Presidential polls, 48, 63, 130
Pregelj, Vladamir, 111
Price, Raymond K., 129, 135, 144, 246n6
Prochnow, James, 248n23

Railsback, Thomas F., 126, 182
Rehnquist, William H., 128
Reisner, Robert, 118
Republican National Convention, 16
Responsiveness Program, 4, 84
Rhodes, John J., 141
Richard M. Nixon Presidential Library, 2, 91, 92, 137, 197
Richardson, Elliot L.
  appointment of Special Prosecutor, 59
  Attorney General, 58
  background, 59
  confirmation hearings, 59
  negotiations over tapes, 75–76
  resignation, 76–77
  "Saturday Night Massacre," 77
road map
  briefcase, 99
  content, 99, 104, 240n7
  creation, 87–88, 92–93
  Doar and, 94–95
  Haig and, 105–110
  motion to bar transmission, 100
  Nixon and, 91, 104–106
  preparation, 87–91
  revisions to, 90–91
  Ruth and, 87, 94
  significance of, 108–109, 111
  Sirica and, 88–90, 189–192
  St. Clair and, 105–119
  transmission to House Impeachment Committee, 100
  White House and, 105–110
Rockefeller, Nelson A., 156
Rodham, Hillary (Clinton), 84
Rodino, Peter W., Jr., 2, 77, 79, 84, 92, 94, 97, 108, 114, 116, 131, 185
Ruckelshaus, William, 77
Rule 6(e), 101, 103, 107–108, 179, 241n14
Ruth, Henry S., Jr., 2, 79, 87
  deputy special prosecutor, 2
  Doar and, 85, 94–95, 106–107, 123
  Sirica and, 79, 106
  transfer of grand jury material, 94, 106, 193
  WSPF documents, 91

St. Clair, James D.
  appointment, 3, 83, 143
  attendance at hearings, 147–148
  Buzhardt and, 107
  Camp David, 133
  Chester and, 148
  Colson and, 83
  Congress and, 115
  deficiencies, 83, 86, 106, 110, 126, 132, 145, 146, 149, 153, 154, 195, 240n10
  Haig and, 106–107, 129
  interview by Woodward, 83, 92, 130
  June 23, 1972, tape, 107
  March 1, 1974, 105–110
  McCahill and, 148
  Nixon and, 106–107
  Nixon statement, 150
  optimism, 124, 125, 127, 129
  performance, 107–109, 115, 130, 248n20
  release of tapes, 116–119, 240n10
  road map, 88, 105–110
  self-interest, 147, 148
  Sirica and, 131–132, 147
  Smoking Gun tapes, 129–130
  staff and, 143, 148
  vacation in July 1974, 143, 247n18

Woodward and Bernstein, 83, 130
  work habits, 119, 148, 247n19
San Clemente, California, 1, 113
Saturday Night Massacre, 2, 3, 52, 76–77, 104, 115, 116
Saxbe, William, 148
Scott, Hugh, 142
Secret Service, 64, 65, 78
Segretti, Donald, 10, 54, 86
Senate
  impeachment trial, 131
  support for Nixon, 131, 132, 139–140, 141
  See also Senate Watergate Committee
Senate Judiciary Committee, 54, 76
Senate Select Committee on Presidential Campaign Activities. *See* Senate Watergate Committee
Senate Watergate Committee
  computer, 239n48
  creation, 52–53
  court activities, 57–58, 67–68, 74–75
  Dean and, 62–63
  final report, 112
  format and schedule, 61–72
  hearings, 61–73
  investigations, 4
  leaks to media, 61
  Milk Fund, 4
  Responsiveness Program, 4
  timetable, 73, 85, 114, 244n15
  White House tapes, 73, 85, 114
  See also Baker, Howard H., Jr.; Ervin, Sam
separation of powers, 85, 109
September 15, 1972, 46–47, 115, 118
Shaffer, Charles N., 56, 76
Shakespeare, William, 251n16
Shepard, Geoffrey (Geoff)
  books, 2, 186, 234n24, 256n25
  Buzhardt and, 116, 137, 188
  Dean and, 234n24, 256n25
  "expletive deleted," 117
  Nixon and, 1, 116, 117, 234n24, 256n25
  Nixon lawyer, 2, 116
  retrieving records, 2
  transcribing tapes, 116, 117, 128, 247n8

Shoumacher, David, 95
Silbert, Earl, 56, 178–179
Sirica, John J.
  admission of tapes, 159
  assignment of cases, 88–89, 92–93, 99, 119–121
  Barker and, 8, 52
  bias, 119, 120
  birthday, 80
  book, 90, 92, 108, 131–132, 185
  Chief Judge, 2, 67, 80, 99, 100, 181
  Dean and, 57–58
  ex parte meetings, 79–80, 87–90, 92, 107–108, 119, 239n35
  gaffes, 166–167
  granting House Impeachment Committee access to tapes, 74
  Jaworski and, 79–80, 87–90, 92, 107–108, 119
  March 1, 1974, 98–101
  McCord and, 55
  media coverage, 166–168
  motion to recuse, 119–121
  reputation, 51, 93, 227n1
  retirement as chief judge, 80, 93
  road map, 89, 99–100, 102
  sentencing of burglars, 55–56
  Sloan and, 52
  To Set the Record Straight, 90
  U.S. v. Liddy, 52–53, 55
  U.S. v. Mitchell, 92–93, 98–101, 157–166
  White House tapes, 74, 251n15
  Wilson and, 100
Sloan, Hugh W., Jr.
  April 7, 1972, 12–13, 20
  cash to Liddy, 19–21, 46
  CRP concern over, 46
  Dahlberg and, 20
  Dean and, 20
  FBI interview, 46
  FCRP, 12, 13, 20, 163
  Liddy and, 20
  Nixon and, 41
  resignation, 143
  Sirica and, 52
  U.S. v. Liddy, 46, 52
slush fund, 46, 47, 62

[270] INDEX

Smoking Gun tapes
  access to, 121–122
  books on, 183–189
  Buchanan and, 135
  Buzhardt and, 129, 137–138, 146
  Haig and, 129, 135
  naming, 129
  Nixon and, 129, 135
  Price and, 135
  St. Clair and, 129, 130
  transcription of, 133–135
  U.S. v. Mitchell, 159–155, 159
  Wiggins and, 144
  Ziegler and, 135
Smoking Gun tapes release
  Buzhardt and, 135–138
  Congress, 134–143
  Haig and, 129, 135
  Nixon statement, 135–137
  Shepard and, 137–138
Smoking Gun transcript, 133–135
Soviet Union, 76, 123
Stans, Maurice H.
  anonymous contributors, 12–13, 24–25, 142, 154, 161–162, 172
  April 7, 12–13
  book, 187, 236n36
  FCRP, 31, 37, 42–43
  finance chairman, 13
  Liddy and, 46, 52
  Nixon and, 24–26
  Vesco, 89, 115
Stennis, John C., 75–76
Stevenson, Adlai E., III, 79
Stone, Roger, 188, 256n25
"Stonewall," 84, 87, 96–97, 117, 119, 198
Stonewall: The Real Story of the Watergate Prosecution, 121, 151, 181, 185
Strachan, Gordon C.
  Dean and, 19
  immunity, 250n5
  Senate Watergate Committee, 250n5
  U.S. v. Mitchell, 98, 100–101, 111
  Watergate scandal and, 18, 47, 53, 192
subpoenas, 67, 122
Sullivan, William C., 53

Supreme Court
  impeachment, 87, 90
  Nixon and, 129, 141, 195
  U.S. v. Mitchell, 128
  U.S. v. Nixon, 122, 124, 126, 128, 195
Sussman, Barry, 54, 95–96

Talmage, Herman, 227n4
tape recording system
  Butterfield testimony, 64–65
  Dean and, 63
  disclosure of, 64–65
  installation of, 64
  knowledge of, 65
  purpose of recording, 65
  quality of recordings, 65
  Secret Service, 54–65
tapes
  authentication, 159
  availability of, 227n178
    Butterfield disclosure, 64–65
  Buzhardt listening to, 129
  Congress, 74–75
  custody of, 64, 65, 68
  destruction of, 66
  experts and, 78
  Haig and, 129, 133–135
  Haldeman listening to, 70
  Nixon listening to, 96–97
  release of (October 1972), 77
  release of (April 29, 1974), 115–117
  release of (August 5, 1974), 135
  Secret Service, 64, 65, 68
  Sirica and, 93, 159–160
  St. Clair and, 146–147
  U.S. v. Mitchell, 135–137
  U.S. v. Nixon (1973), 74–75
  See also Smoking Gun tape
tape transcripts
  availability of, 227n18
  editing, 117
  expletive deleted, 115, 117, 125
  Haig and, 133–135
Teapot Dome scandal, 240n1
Texas, 4, 21, 30–31, 77, 87, 89
Thompson, Fred D., 39, 62, 70–71, 234n14

Time Magazine, 15, 25
Title 18, U.S.C.
  sec 371, 173–174
  sec 1503, 173–174, 178
Trump v. U.S., 5, 241n19
Tunny, John, 54

University of Texas, 2, 57, 77, 83
U.S. Attorney, District of Columbia, 56, 60
U.S. Attorney, Southern District of New York, 60, 84
U.S. Court of Appeals for the District of Columbia Circuit, 75, 76, 101–104, 168, 194, 241n16
U.S. District Court, District of Columbia, 2, 79, 119, 147, 176
U.S. v. Ellsberg, 58
U.S. v. Liddy
  Barker and, 52
  grand jury, 46–47
  indictments, 46–47
  Liddy and, 46–47
  Magruder and, 46
  McCord and, 52
  Porter and, 46
  Sirica and, 53–54
  Sloan and, 46, 52
  trial, 3, 51–52
  verdict, 52
U.S. v. Mitchell
  appeal, 168
  assignment to judge, 88, 93, 119
  Ben-Veniste and, 157–164
  Dean and, 158–159
  Ehrlichman and, 98, 166
  grand jury, 87
  Haldeman and, 98, 158–166
  indictments, 98
  Jaworski and, 88
  jury selection, 87
  media coverage of, 166–168
  Mitchell and, 98, 166
  motions to bar road map transfer, 100
  motion to recuse Sirica, 119–121
  Neal and, 157
  Nixon and, 160–164

  postponement, 157
  scope of cover-up, 158–165
  Sirica and, 88, 93, 119–121, 157–166
  tapes, 157–160
  trial, 156–166
  Verdict, 166
  Wilson and, 163
U.S. v. Nixon (hypothetical), 135, 171–172
U.S. v. Nixon (1973)
  Court of Appeals, 76
  District Court, 74
  Nixon and, 76
  Senate Watergate Committee, 67–68, 74
  subpoenas, 67–68
  Watergate Special Prosecution Force, 74
  White House compliance, 77
U.S. v. Nixon (1974)
  compromise unsuccessful, 122
  Court of Appeals, 122
  District Court, 122
  subpoenas, 122
  St. Clair and, 122
  Supreme Court (argument), 124
  Supreme Court (decision), 128

Vesco, Robert, 89, 115
Vietnam, 9, 21, 76, 156

Wallace, George C., 13, 126
Wall Street Journal, 138
Walter Reed Hospital, 66
Walters, Vernon
  appointment, 26
  background, 26
  book, 186
  Dean and, 44
  Ehrlichman and, 57–59, 71–72
  FBI, 26, 30–31, 137
  Gray and, 159
  Haldeman and, 35–39, 57–59, 71–72
  June 23, 1972, meeting, 27–29, 30, 35–36
  memoranda, 38, 39, 45
  Mexico, 26, 28, 31, 35, 43, 72, 159, 186
  Nixon and, 26, 28, 38–43, 60, 136–137
  Senate Watergate Committee, 71–72

Washington, DC, Metropolitan Police, 14–15, 25
Washington Post
 August 5, 1974, 138
 early coverage of Watergate scandal, 29, 52
 leaks to, 29
 U.S. v. Mitchell, 167–168
 See also Bernstein, Carl; Woodward, Bob
Washington Star, 15, 139, 176, 177
Watergate break-in
 arrests, 14, 45
 Baldwin and, 16
 Cuban-Americans, 14–15
 Hunt and, 12, 17, 19
 Liddy and, 13
 McCord and, 14–17
 Mitchell and, 16–17
 media coverage of, 3, 14, 15
 U.S. v. Liddy, 51–52
Watergate grand jury, 46, 87–88, 93–94, 98–102, 175–176, 179–180
Watergate Hotel, 14–16, 176, 190
Watergate Office Building, 1, 4, 15, 18, 37, 45, 83, 99, 138, 154, 157, 169, 171, 176, 102, 196
Watergate Special Prosecution Force (WSPF)
 creation, 59
 Dean and, 57
 Doar and, 85, 94–95, 106–107, 123
 guilty pleas, 76, 84
 indictments, 98
 litigation by (1973), 74–75

litigation by (1974), 101–102
March 1, 1974, 98–99
records, 91
road map, 87–91
Saturday Night Massacre, 76–77
Senate Watergate Committee, 4, 57
Sirica and, 79–80, 89–92
staff, 2, 59–60, 86, 87
subpoenas, 67–68, 122
U.S. v. Mitchell, 156–168
Weicker, Lowell, 231n4, 235n2
Welch, Joseph N., 83
White, Theodore H., 184, 246n2, 247n19
"White House Horrors," 63
White House logs, 16, 107
White House tapes. *See* tape recording system; tapes
Wiggins, Charles, 126, 134, 151
Wilson, John J., 66–68, 100, 152, 158, 163
Wine-Banks, Jill, 188
WNBC, 15
Woods, Rose Mary, 78
Woodward, Bob, 2, 23, 52, 66, 76, 82, 92, 105, 106, 109, 116, 118, 128–133, 138, 140, 152, 183–184, 197
Woodward and Bernstein notes, 83, 90, 152, 248n25
Wright, Charles Alan, 68, 75, 77, 82, 83, 160

Young, David P., 10, 11

Zeigler, Ronald L., 22, 25, 45, 65, 128, 135, 144
Ziefman, Jerome, 79, 236n17, 241n41, 245n38